Advance Praise for *Hard Power*

"This is a particularly timely and important contribution by two of the most prolific and insightful commentators on national security in America today. While O'Hanlon and Campbell make no bones about their political affiliation—they are proud members of the Party of Roosevelt, Truman, and Kennedy—their book is anything but a partisan polemic. It is a penetrating, lively read, whose central thesis—that national security is a threshold issue in voters' minds—cannot be ignored."

–Congressman Steny Hoyer (D-MD),
House Democratic Whip

"Kurt Campbell and Michael O'Hanlon, both seasoned scholars and practitioners, have provided a deeply insightful look into the current state of our national security politics. It is on these matters of war and peace that the fate of our country rests. *Hard Power* offers real wisdom that will help enable the United States to achieve a greater security in the years ahead."

–William J. Perry, former Secretary of Defense

"America won the Cold War by combining hard and soft power into smart power. Today's Democrats need to learn more about hard power, Republicans more about soft power, and both need to re-learn how to combine them effectively. This important book tells us how America can again become a smart power."

–Joseph S. Nye, author of *Soft Power:
The Means to Success in World Politics*

"In *Hard Power*, Kurt Campbell and Michael O'Hanlon have provided an extraordinarily readable and provocative look inside the changing politics of national security in the United States. Combining anecdotes with analysis, *Hard Power* should be "top priority" reading for those wishing to understand the hard choices and heavy responsibilities that America faces in the world today. For politicians and practitioners alike, this book can provide the essential framework and important reference points in the critical debate over how best to protect the nation."

–Sam Nunn, Former U.S. Senator,
Co-Chairman, Nuclear Threat Initiative

HARD POWER

ALSO BY KURT M. CAMPBELL

The Nuclear Tipping Point:
Why States Reconsider Their Nuclear Choices, 2004
(with R.J. Einhorn and M.B. Reiss)

To Prevail: An American Strategy for
the Campaign Against Terrorism, 2001
(with M.A. Flournoy)

ALSO BY MICHAEL E. O'HANLON

Crisis on the Korean Peninsula:
How to Deal with a Nuclear North Korea, 2003
(with Mike M. Mochizuki)

Defense Strategy for the Post-Saddam Era, 2005

HARD POWER

THE NEW POLITICS OF NATIONAL SECURITY

Kurt M. Campbell
Michael E. O'Hanlon

A Member of the Perseus Books Group
New York

Designed by BackStory Design
Set in 11 point Caledonia

Library of Congress Cataloging-in-Publication Data
Campbell, Kurt M., 1957-
Hard power : the new politics of national security /
Kurt Campbell and Michael O'Hanlon.
    p.   cm.
Includes index.
ISBN-13: 978-0-465-05166-3 (alk. paper)
ISBN-10: 0-465-05166-9 (alk. paper)
1. United States—Politics and government—2001-
2. National security—United States   3. United States—Military
policy.   4. Democratic Party (U.S.)   5. Presidents—United
States—Election. I. O'Hanlon, Michael E.   II. Title.
JK275.C36 2006
355'.033073—dc22

                                        2006021681

10 9 8 7 6 5 4 3 2 1

Basic Books are available at special discounts for bulk purchases in
the U.S. by corporations, institutions, and other organizations. For
more information, please contact the Special Markets Department:
Special Markets Department
Perseus Books Group
11 Cambridge Center
Cambridge, MA 02142
(800)–255–1514
specialmarkets@perseusbooks.com

to my mother Barbara
who loved politics
K. C.

to my parents Frieda and Ed
M. O'H.

Contents

Preface

The cheering in the Pentagon hallways on that December day in 2000 was something Kurt Campbell would never forget. The Supreme Court had just decided the fate of the contested presidential election after weeks of tense indecision and uncertainty, and many of the military roaming the Pentagon decks that day were thrilled that Republicans would be back in the saddle again. Campbell had been around these people for more than a decade, working first as a Navy officer and later as a politically appointed civilian in the five-sided-puzzle palace, and yet their antipathy to Democrats always surprised him. Under a Democratic president, the United States had seen unprecedented prosperity, military successes in the Balkans, a nation at peace (but only for a few more months . . .), and a growing defense budget—but still most of the uniformed patriots that day could not hide their pleasure at the imminent arrival of the Republicans to power. In just a few days, they would see the backs of these Democratic pretenders, and the true professionals—the so-called A Team—would return to their rightful place as masters of the most mighty military machine on the planet. Campbell wondered, What had gone so terribly wrong for his party when the nation contemplated going to battle stations?

Mike O'Hanlon had an idea just after U.S. military forces swept to a decisive military victory in Afghanistan and chased the Taliban into the distant hills. These were some of the same guys who had helped take down the Soviet empire, and the United States had done much to dispatch them with a combination of precision weapons and Special Forces. After a bitter presidential campaign during which the Republicans had relentlessly criticized the Democratic stewardship of the Pentagon, the United States had just overwhelmingly prevailed with a military recruited, armed, and trained largely by President Clinton's Department of Defense. To be sure, Ronald Reagan began the defense buildup that created this fine force, and the Bush team provided the civilian oversight of the Afghanistan war plan, but Democrats had played a central role too.

O'Hanlon decided to write a piece staking a claim to the Democrats' contribution to this triumph. To his surprise, not a single Democratic strategist or spinner picked up on the idea of taking credit for the successful military venture—while Secretary Rumsfeld and the Bush administration were garnering all the public praise for the victory. O'Hanlon kept at it, hammering home the message that Democrats as well as Republicans had a clear record of competence in preparing the nation for this fight against the Taliban. But most Democrats continued to prefer to fight politically on other, more hospitable terrain such as jobs and health care. O'Hanlon worried that a nation at war was looking at different battlefields. This raised the question as to whether Americans would trust the Democrats to keep them safe? As a new politics of national security emerged in the months and years after 9/11, even some moderate Republicans—many of whom had been closely associated with the first Gulf War—were also worried about being marginalized from power. Their brand of competent pragmatism was not what George W. Bush favored in the defining period that followed the most deadly attack on American soil in the nation's history.

Jump forward just a few years to the winter of 2006, when a group of retired senior military officers gathered in an upstairs room at a private Washington restaurant to talk about the current civilian tenants at the Pentagon. Their anger and frustration were palpable, at times threatening to boil over. Finally, one retired general summed up the harsh words and tough assessments swirling around the table with this blunt gauntlet: "Look, this whole approach is not what I signed up for. Sure, I saluted and did my duty—in Iraq and elsewhere—but not without some serious misgivings. We in the military, and hopefully in the country at large, have got to look much more carefully next time around at what we are buying. White knights on chargers are for fairy tales; we have learned this the painful way. What we want from the next group of folks who come to power is simple: Lead us well, give us the means to do our jobs, respect us for our professional advice, and, most importantly, be accountable for your actions from top to bottom. Is that really so much to ask from politicians on either side of the aisle?"

Clearly it's not, and it is precisely this set of challenges that motivated us—Kurt Campbell and Mike O'Hanlon—to undertake this book. *Hard Power* is an attempt to fully appreciate the sometimes treacherous new politics of national security and to provide some advice about how to negotiate these swirling currents. *Hard Power* is our attempt to bridge the gaps between the legacy of the past and the performance of the present when it comes to securing the nation, and between the theory and practice of national security in all its many dimensions. With this book, we aspire to help prepare U.S. elected officials, public servants, and an informed electorate to meet the challenge posed by the retired general above.

This book grew out of a long friendship and a successful collaboration on an article for *The National Interest* about the Democrats' national-security problem. The article attracted numerous comments (and not a few complaints) from friends and commentators on both sides of the political aisle. We had touched a nerve.

Our agenda goes well beyond the Democratic Party. Moderate and internationalist Republicans, too, find themselves out of favor and struggling to project a vision for how to handle hard foreign-policy matters that complements their well-earned reputation for competence and pragmatism. We hope to catch the attention of all those, irrespective of party, who might be open to new ideas and a better approach to governance on these critical questions of martial competence.

We have both been struck by the polemical and bitterly partisan nature of the debates and commentary on Iraq—and, indeed, on most other national-security issues, including domestic surveillance, the means for waging a larger struggle against radical jihadists, and worries over the spread of nuclear weapons. We wanted to write a book that, rather than simply castigating the Bush administration for the mistakes made over the course of the last several years, would attempt to put national security into a broader and historical political context. We vowed to stay away from partisan, ad hominem critiques and instead sought to explore the strengths and weaknesses of both parties when it comes to decisions for when and how the nation should take up arms. As such, we are critical of some Democratic approaches to national-security issues during recent political campaigns and hard on the Bush administration for its handling of Iraq. On the flip side, we are generally complimentary about how the Republicans have handled homeland security despite serious problems in starting up the new department, as evidenced during Hurricane Katrina, and give equal praise to those Democrats who are beginning to talk the talk and walk the walk on national-security matters.

Finally, *Hard Power* presents a series of coherent, credible approaches to a number of pressing security challenges confronting the nation now and in the immediate future.

This book owes an enormous debt to several friends and colleagues who assisted us along the way with both research and writing. John Hamre and Strobe Talbott have been both mentors and friends; they encouraged us through the entire process of writing this book, from early research to correcting galleys. We are grateful to the institutional support provided by each of our employers, notably the Center for Strategic and International Studies and the Brookings Institution; they have provided each of us with an intellectual home where pursuits like this book are encouraged. The Aspen Strategy Group of the Aspen Institute and Walter Isaacson also provided consistent intellectual stimulation and encouragement to undertake this project. We are deeply indebted to Richard Weitz of the Hudson Institute, Nina Kamp and David Sandalow of the Brookings Institution, Sharon Burke of Third Way, Jennifer Harris of Pembroke College of Oxford University, Vinca LaFleur of the Center for Strategic and International Studies, and Virginia Liberatore of Rappahannock County for their very generous, expert assistance in research and editing. Strobe Talbott, John Hamre, Carlos Pascual, Tom Donilon, Julianne Smith, Richard Danzig, Miles Lackey, Jim Kelly, Kevin Nealer, Clark Murdock, and Dan Benjamin all provided useful critiques and suggestions for revision of earlier versions of this manuscript. Our thanks also go to our external reviewers Aaron Friedberg, David Mosher, and Stephen Biddle for their very strong suggestions for how to make this a better book. Billy Sountornsorn of the International Security Program at the Center for Strategic and International Studies helped enormously with the production and formatting of the tables and drafts. We would like to offer profuse thanks to Ellen Garrison of Basic Books for shepherding this book into print. Additionally, we would like to thank Julie McCarroll, our publicist at Basic Books. We are also both deeply grateful to Anna Stein, our most intrepid agent, for encouraging us in this entire endeavor, finding us a publisher, and helping see this into print.

Finally, we are both profoundly indebted to our loving families, notably Cathy, Grace, Lily, Frieda, Ed, siblings, cousins, and others for Mike, and Lael, Caelan, Ciara, Barbara, Viv, Karen, Craig, and many others for Kurt. You have encouraged us in this endeavor and put up with the occasional late night, early morning, and lost weekend. It is to you, our beloved families, that this book is dedicated.

Kurt M. Campbell
Center for Strategic and International Studies

Michael E. O'Hanlon
The Brookings Institution

THE NEW POLITICS OF NATIONAL SECURITY

"The vast majority of Democrats chose a middle ground: Supportive of a war . . . they voted troops and money for the war effort, but they were increasingly critical of the evolving goals and tactics of the Republican administration. . . . For their criticism of the conduct of the war, they were accused of treason. Defined as lacking national loyalty and identity by Republicans, Democrats struggled to find a role for themselves as a loyal opposition party in a democracy at war.

"The tendency to conflate Republicanism with loyalty and Democracy with treason assumed [various forms] during these war years. For radical Republicans . . . the principles of the Republican Party had become the principles of the nation. Republican victory . . . was the fruition of years of labor for a cause many believed to be a religious as well as national imperative . . . loyalty to the nation could only be expressed through loyalty to the Republican Party."

A POWERFUL DEPICTION of the Democratic Party's recent political predicament vis-à-vis Iraq? Well, not exactly. These words may generally describe the current political context in the United States when it comes to the civil war raging on distant Iraqi battlefields, but they were actually written about the sharp political combat that animated Washington's Republicans and Democrats during the American Civil War a century and a half ago.

In her 2002 book, *Patriot Fires: Forging a New American Nationalism in the Civil War North*, historian Melinda Lawson captured the expertly conceived Republican efforts during the Civil War to conflate Republicanism

2 • HARD POWER

with patriotism and loyalty, and, as importantly, to identify Democrats in the minds of the public with weakness, dishonor, and even treachery.[1] *Patriot Fires* received quiet praise and modest reviews from the community of Civil War scholars, but Melinda Lawson also received something else: a letter of congratulations and sincere appreciation from the acknowledged wizard of modern political strategy, Karl Rove.[2]

As if Rove did not have enough to do in implementing the reelection campaign strategy for President George W. Bush in the midst of an increasingly unpopular war and an uncertain economy, he found the time to send a letter of effusive praise to an obscure university professor. Why? To try to wrap his own man in the cloak of Lincoln, probably. But there was likely something else at work. Perhaps Rove felt duty-bound to acknowledge the recounting of President Lincoln's masterful political strategy for a more direct reason—because it was a game plan that Rove had studied closely and employed effectively on George W. Bush's behalf.[3]

The blending of fear, patriotism, and military power into a potent political weapon has been the Republicans' singular calling card in this age of sacred terror since September 11, 2001. Former president Bill Clinton captured the post–9/11 mindset of the American people—and the existential problem of the Democratic Party—when he suggested that, in choosing leaders to meet national-security challenges, the electorate would choose "strong and wrong" over "timid and right" every time. (Here the analogy to Lincoln clearly loses relevance.) This essential conundrum helps explain repeated Democratic losses in national electoral contests since 2000.

Since then, America's approach toward national security has undergone a dramatic transformation. In less than five years, the Bush administration has launched two major military campaigns, conducted the most significant reorganization of our government's national-security architecture since 1947, and articulated a bold agenda for the exercise of American power in the world.

Former senator Arthur Vandenberg remarked in 1948, at the beginning of the Cold War, that "politics stops at the water's edge." The same would prove true after the 9/11 terrorist attacks—for a time.

On the night of the attacks, Democratic and Republican members of Congress gathered on the steps of the Capitol to sing "God Bless America." Democrats lined up behind the president on the decisions to go to war in Afghanistan and to tighten domestic security through the PATRIOT Act. Indeed, Senator Tom Daschle literally embraced George W.

Bush under the Capitol dome, the emotion of the moment showing clearly on both men's faces, as a suddenly united group of Republicans and Democrats stood nearby. The Russians and Chinese pledged assistance, and NATO invoked its self-defense clause for the first time in the alliance's history. Even the French had a change of heart: An opinion piece in *Le Monde* proclaimed "we are all Americans!"

The comity would not last, of course, for either the Democrats or the French. In fact, a study undertaken by the *Congressional Quarterly* found that 2005 was one of the most partisan years on record when it came to votes in both the House and the Senate.[4] The cohesion and discipline inside each of the parties lends an almost tribal quality to current American politics that is especially noteworthy when the two parties find themselves in positions opposite those traditionally associated with their respective philosophies. One campaign partisan, when questioned about the seeming contradictions of his candidate's approach to a problem during the 2004 campaign, responded with some annoyance that "I may not know what the right position is on some issue or another, but I can assure you I know where my friends are, and that's where you'll find me."

For close observers of American foreign policy and the general public alike, these events—and the debates surrounding them—have often proved disorienting. A president who entered office in 2000 calling for a more "humble" approach to the world and greater emphasis on traditional national interests instead of "nation building" has instead outlined a broad interventionist doctrine of preemption and placed the promotion of democracy in the Middle East and elsewhere at the heart of the foreign-policy agenda.[5]

Meanwhile, many progressives who embraced the Clinton administration's "humanitarian interventions" in Bosnia and Kosovo (and decried the non-intervention in Rwanda) are deeply skeptical of the actions taken in Iraq, even though a deeply repressive regime has been removed. And many Democrats bristle at the Bush administration's focus on democracy promotion—even though such ideas have been articulated by Democratic presidents and strategic thinkers from Woodrow Wilson with his Fourteen Points to Bill Clinton and his policy of "democratic enlargement" (former national security adviser Anthony Lake's slogan for NATO expansion).

This topsy-turvy debate is seen in military affairs as well. The powerful cadre of conservative strategic thinkers in the Bush administration who once warned of "breaking" the military have presided over an era of tremendous strain on the American fighting force. Indeed, the March

2006 outcry from retired flag officers created the greatest rupture of civil-military relations in a generation. In response, many Democrats who are usually thought of as focused on soft foreign-policy issues such as foreign assistance and development (and who, frankly, can be a little uncomfortable around the armed services) are rushing to embrace the military.[6]

These debates within policy circles and Washington's political corridors take place against a political backdrop marked by polarization and a deeply skeptical public. Americans' trust in government has been declining since the 1960s, and this trend has continued in the first half decade of the twenty-first century. If anything, popular mistrust of the government has increased, especially when it comes to national security.

With the September 11 attacks and the U.S. government's failure to find weapons of mass destruction in Iraq, Americans have witnessed two of the greatest intelligence failures in American history. The bloody occupation of Iraq and the inadequate response to the 2005 Hurricane Katrina disaster have cast alarming doubts about the government's competence to plan and implement policies. Add to all this the unrelenting drumbeat of scandal in Washington—from the outing of CIA agent Valerie Plame to the Jack Abramoff lobbying crimes—and it's unsurprising that many people's cynicism about government and its motives has only deepened. While hardly becoming isolationist or defeatist, Americans are losing confidence in their government's ability to be a consistently constructive force in world affairs.

Recent public-opinion polls illustrate these trends. In a November 2005 survey done by the Pew Research Center and the Council on Foreign Relations, 42 percent of respondents said the United States should "mind its own business" internationally, reflecting a climate similar to that of the Vietnam hangover of the mid–1970s and Bill Clinton's post–Cold War foreign-policy difficulties of the early to mid–1990s. Only a quarter of the public favors a strong U.S. role in the world, and just a third thinks that the government has done a good job of protecting the country. Such figures are especially startling when compared to the strong consensus about America's interests and role in the world in the aftermath of 9/11.[7]

Now, with public anxieties and outright disapproval mounting in response to Republican performances from Iraq to North Korea to the Gulf Coast of the United States, there is a glimmering of hope among Democrats that the doors of the political game have finally opened again. Just as much, the door has reopened to internationalist GOP moderates such as George H. W. Bush, Brent Scowcroft, Richard Haass, and Colin

Powell as they compete within their own party for power and influence against conservatives and neoconservatives.

Yet, so far, the shift in public support toward the Democrats, especially on the core Republican issues of national security, is largely due to perceived Republican shortcomings rather than the appeal of a forward-looking Democratic national-security agenda. Without answers of their own to the questions they pose to the Bush administration about how to keep the country safe and secure, Democrats are likely to find current gains in national polls to be fleeting or illusory. Similarly, internationalist Republicans who want to improve their own political fortunes may need to convey more than simple competence to compete with neoconservatives on vision.

Leading Democrats, many independents, and an increasing number of Republicans have expressed anxiety about the Bush administration's success in claiming the political high ground on matters of national security since the terrorist attacks of September 11, 2001. Democrats want the nation to associate their party with Roosevelt's stoic courage during 1942 in the darkest days of the struggle with the Axis powers, Truman's construction of the NATO alliance and strengthening of Western Europe (not to mention his "take no prisoners" pursuit of atomic weapons), Kennedy's defense buildup, and Clinton's resolve in dealing with the Chinese over Taiwan and his ultimately effective use of force in the Balkans. Moderate Republicans, for their part, want the GOP to be associated with Dwight Eisenhower, the soldier-statesman who kept the Cold War from turning hot; Nixon's opening to China; Reagan's call on Mikhail Gorbachev to "tear down this wall"; and George H. W. Bush's skillful management of the dissolution of the Soviet empire.

Of course, neither party has a monopoly on wisdom or success. Democrats belong to the party that split over Vietnam, bungled the Bay of Pigs invasion and the Iran hostage rescue attempt, wallowed in political indecision and hand wringing on the eve of the first Gulf War, failed to see the troubling signs in Somalia, and pulled U.S. Navy warships from Haiti's harbor when confronted by a band of ill-mannered hoodlums early in the Clinton years. Republicans Nixon and Ford failed to achieve the "peace with honor" they had promised in Vietnam; Reagan's national-security team ran afoul of the law with Iran-Contra (and cozied up to Saddam Hussein in a manner that seems clearly mistaken in retrospect); and President George H. W. Bush failed to stop the carnage in Bosnia.

By the same token, as difficult as the post–9/11 era has been for Democrats, it has also been no picnic for seasoned Republican centrists mentioned earlier, like Brent Scowcroft, James Baker, Richard Lugar, Colin Powell, Richard Armitage, and perhaps even George Herbert Walker Bush. Several of these experienced, thoughtful public servants and national leader have been marginalized or alienated from the decisionmaking core of the Bush presidency on foreign-policy matters.

This book was inspired by a desire to provide hard-headed ideas and intellectual ammunition to both Democrats and those Republicans prepared for a new approach to foreign affairs and national security. We hope that the quality of the national conversation on these vital subjects rises considerably and that at least a modicum of bipartisanship or inter-party cooperation can be restored on the big issues confronting the country.

In addition, for the broader good of its foreign policy, the United States needs a stronger voice on national security from a group we would describe as Hard Power Democrats (though moderate Republicans and independents might find a similar worldview appealing). This group believes that military force is often needed to defend the nation's interests, and that decisions about employing the American armed forces will therefore remain a central aspect of governance for decades to come.

Hard Power Democrats and other moderates prefer to work through alliances and the U.N. Security Council if possible, and would heed the views of others much more than the Bush administration has, but would not insist on U.N. approval or international popular support before carrying out certain military missions. They would avoid the extreme casualty aversion of much of the 1975–2000 period in American politics, being willing to risk American lives to deal with serious threats to the country before those problems get worse. Recognizing that failed states can provide sanctuary for terrorists and weaken the international system in general, they would support the use of force for stabilization and reconstruction missions—and take these missions much more seriously than the Bush administration has done. They would be attentive to military advice yet willing to challenge the uniformed services as well, taking a page from Secretary of Defense Rumsfeld without going to the extremes that have characterized his tenure at the Pentagon.

And finally, they would seek to emulate part of the broader neo-con playbook as well, focusing on big ideas and vision in developing their foreign policy agendas—though without the unilateralist tendencies and the sloppiness in execution of policy that have often characterize the Bush administration. Unlike the case with many on the left, however, for Hard

Power Democrats multilateralism is a means to an end, not a sacrosanct principle or an endpoint in and of itself. Their vision for foreign policy is grounded first in thinking about how to keep America safe, while also addressing new and longer-term security threats—issues that we develop in the pages ahead. [8]

The title *Hard Power* is inspired by our friend and former assistant secretary of Defense Joseph Nye. He coined the term "soft power" and developed the argument that a modern superpower cannot lead through brute strength alone, but must entice and attract followers around the world through its culture, values, and democracy. Nye was certainly right. It is in these areas that Democrats and moderate Republicans already generally have a greater feel for the textures and tolerances of global politics than their traditional conservative, as well as more visionary or neo-conservative, Republican colleagues.

Nye was emphatically not advocating that the United States base its foreign policy on soft power alone. He favored a combination of hard and soft power. Many other Democrats, who tend to be more comfortable with diplomacy and dialogue than with military might, have had to learn the hard way that understanding soft power is not enough to wrest control of the political machinery of government in the complex post–9/11 domestic environment. Democrats must regain their confidence and establish their bona fides on matters of hard power if they are to govern effectively in the years ahead. Internationalist Republicans will have to be attentive to this matter as well, especially because they don't want the inevitable criticisms that they—and the Democrats—will continue to levy against the Bush administration's Iraq policy to come across as symptoms of an allergy to the use of force more generally. This book is thus, we hope, a natural and necessary complement, in both substantive and political terms, to Nye's earlier contributions.

"Hard power" is meant to convey two meanings. In traditional foreign-policy parlance, hard power has meant the application of military power to meet national ends—that is, the deployment of ground troops, naval assets, and precision munitions to secure a vital national objective. Some Democrats in particular have tended to get a little squeamish when the nation goes to battle stations. Often this has been for good and honorable reasons. But at other times it has resulted from a deep belief in the philosophy found frequently on blue-state bumper stickers: War is not the answer. Yet, for most Americans, it depends on the question. Sometimes war is the answer. There have been and will continue to be periodic reasons to take up arms and march toward the sound of the guns. In this sense, our book aims to provide a primer on how to think about the difficult decisions associated with military power and national security.

We argue for going back to basics on defense and national-security priorities—decisions about guns, bombs, difficult military missions, and tough Pentagon budget issues—and build outwards to the more comfortable issues of multilateral diplomacy and international regimes. Without a solid defense and national-security core, Americans are likely to perceive even the most sophisticated aspects of a non-military Democratic or moderate Republican platform as being hollow at the center.

Yet, by using the term "hard power," we are also underscoring that the enterprise is difficult. The underlying conceptual question of when an issue becomes a matter of national security is extraordinarily complex, and framing such matters is a primary challenge for this generation of foreign-policy practitioners. There have been numerous attempts, primarily by Democrats, to broaden the conception of national security or to appropriate the urgency, language, and imagery of war, from Lyndon Johnson's "war on poverty" to Jimmy Carter's famous dictum that achieving energy security was the "moral equivalent of war" to the common refrain of the 1990s that regaining economic competitiveness was as important as addressing traditional threats to our national security. And throughout the last decade, U.S. officials and activists attempted to rally support for a broad range of issues—including improving our schools and dealing with the health challenges of the disadvantaged and the intractable problems of global poverty—by suggesting that these were national-security matters. Even if often right, this line of reasoning created the perception that many Democrats were distracted from the most urgent and direct threats to the country's physical safety and security.

Republicans, and especially conservatives, largely countered by going back to first-order basics. They suggested that 9/11 provided an essential wake-up call and reminder about the *real* national-security challenges the nation is confronting—in this case, they argued, radical Islamic fundamentalists, as well as Saddam Hussein. Under their watch in the opening decade of the twenty-first century, two wars have been launched at a cost that could approach a trillion dollars based on a belief that military power was the most useful tool—and, to some, the only requisite instrument—for dealing with the problem of global terrorism. America cannot continue to rely predominantly on the martial aspects of foreign policy. When it does employ military power, moreover, it must do so with a keen understanding of the importance of gaining international legitimacy for its actions and carrying the policy through to its logical conclusion. That means effective stabilization and reconstruction efforts are of paramount importance when hard power is used the way it was in Afghanistan and Iraq. This is something the Bush administration dismally failed to appreciate. The United States also must redirect attention to other rising national-security challenges—from energy security to China's rise—that have achieved a new urgency while attentions have been directed elsewhere.

What is needed, whichever party prevails in the coming elections, is a more sophisticated approach to this broad array of rising transnational issues. Within the "hard power" issues, traditional uses of force must be complemented by adept diplomacy as well as responsible follow-on operations involving military power and other instruments of the state. Further, promotion of America's own national security now depends acutely on complementing hard power with softer power on issues such as the ascendance of China and the rebuilding of our alliances. Yet Democrats and indeed moderates will not have the chance to apply such a nuanced approach unless they can master the first-order matters of traditional national security—that is, how and when to put force on targets.

This book is also divided into two parts. The first section provides a general overview of the state of American politics when it comes to national security. In this section, we examine the Republicans'—particularly conservatives'—successful strategy of linking perceptions of national-security prowess with their party, as well as the corresponding challenges plaguing Democrats who attempt to offer a countering view. We explore the new politics of national security, asking how hardheaded Democrats, moderate Republicans, and genuine independents must respond to regain their own confidence and that of the public on the essential question of defending the nation from harm. We also examine how the decision to go into Iraq and its many costly consequences will provide an essential, and in some ways limiting, context for what comes next in American foreign policy and national security.

The book's final chapters detail how the next administration will need to do it differently. We attempt to offer a compelling, competing strategy for better managing the military, protecting the homeland, conducting the war on terror, dealing with China's rise and Asia's new significance, developing a serious energy policy informed not only by global climate concerns but also by the connections between energy and the terror nexus, stemming proliferation and generally running an effective foreign and national-security policy for the twenty-first century.

As such, *Hard Power* goes beyond the now familiar critique of Bush administration mistakes and mismanagement to identify three essential features for an alternative that should have appeal across party lines. First, a fair-minded assessment of what the incumbent Republican administration has gotten wrong but, perhaps as important, an honest account of what it has gotten right in the difficult period since 9/11. Second, an equally blunt critique of where Democrats and, to a lesser extent, many moderate Republicans have struggled or stumbled on national-security issues—and why they have done so. And third, most importantly, a concrete set of policy recommendations for dealing with both the traditional and nontraditional national-security challenges confronting the country.

As Democrats' electoral failures and ominous poll numbers (at least around matters of confidence in national security) have mounted, many of them have begun to take a hard look at their own shortcomings—as well as their successes—with an eye toward tackling the problem directly. An essential element for Democrats in recovering their mojo on national security will be rediscovering the many things Democrats have done well when it comes to hard power. They are doing so not only for their party's sake, but also for the sake of the nation, which needs a robust competition between the parties.

While the Bush administration has indeed mastered the politics and perceptions around national security and achieved some impressive accomplishments in this area, it has not consistently acted in the strongest traditions of the United States or the GOP. More political voices need to master the *new* politics of national security that Karl Rove understands so well, in order that the country may make its choices about future foreign policy based on substantive debate rather than the simple symbolisms of political campaigns and public anxieties.

CHAPTER 1

IT'S THE WAR, STUPID

Why National Security Is the Essential Electoral Issue

HOW COULD A decorated war hero, experienced senator, and outstanding debater lose a presidential race that focused largely on national security to an incumbent who had profoundly miscalculated both the urgency of the war he pursued and the way to win the peace? Given the demands the Bush administration had placed upon the U.S. armed services, how did Republicans find their most loyal demographic not among the Bible Belt voters of the South and West or the wealthy businesspeople along the country's coasts, but rather among the country's nearly 2.5 million current military personnel and 25 million-plus military veterans?

The 2004 election made clear that key segments of the electorate feel a profound anxiety about how Democrats in general, and Senator John Kerry in particular, would manage issues of war and peace. If Democrats learn anything from the electoral shutout dealt by President Bush and the Republicans, we hope it is that the party must grapple differently and more substantively with issues of national security and military policy.

This imperative is two-fold. First, the practical: National security is now the dominant electoral issue. During the 2004 presidential election, about 34 percent of the electorate cited either Iraq or the war on terrorism as the policy issue they were most concerned about. This marked a significant jump from the 12 percent that cited "world affairs" as the issue that most concerned them in 2000.[1] Democrats can willingly embrace this shift in electoral priorities, seeing it as a popular mandate, or they can grudgingly accept it, viewing it as a political ultimatum that sets the terms for regaining control over Congress or the presidency. Either way, if party leaders are to avoid further marginalization, they must acknowledge that the electorate's current national-security focus deserves prima facie attention.

The second, more important rationale behind this imperative is that Democrats should prioritize national-security concerns not just because so many voters do, but also because *those voters are right.* International stability is needed for Americans to live in security and prosperity; it is just that simple. When we have forgotten this simple truth—most notably in the 1920s and 1930s, but also to some extent in the late 1940s and 1970s—the United States has paid dearly for our oversight—and so have the political leaders associated with these times.

Moreover, the origins of overseas dangers are often difficult to predict. Who would have thought that Germany, defeated so resoundingly in World War I, would be the main cause of World War II just twenty years later? Or that the physically small island nation of Japan could dominate much of its region and set the United States back on its heels for several years in that same war? Or that a guerrilla movement in another geographically small and underdeveloped Asian country, Vietnam, could defeat first France and then the world's most powerful country in combat? Or that one of the world's poorest nations, Afghanistan, could serve as the base of operations for the most deadly attack on U.S. soil in the history of the United States? The only constants running through these and other cataclysmic events of the last century are the inevitability of being surprised and the centrality of national security in ensuring the well-being of American citizens.

Somehow, Democrats have missed the recent shift in electoral priorities toward national-security issues, despite a century's worth of warning. Among the 34 percent of voters who put Iraq or the war on terrorism at the top of their priorities list, 60 percent favored President Bush in 2004; an overwhelming 86 percent of those most worried about the war on terror favored the incumbent.In the electorate at large, 58 percent said they trusted President Bush to wage the war on terrorism effectively, whereas only 40 percent trusted Senator Kerry to do the same.[2] Iraq policy was effectively a draw in the election, despite steadily negative trends throughout 2004, and despite Paul Bremer's admission in the weeks just before the election that the Bush administration had not, to his mind, deployed enough troops to stabilize the country.

Voters can often tell when a candidate takes national-security positions out of political expediency rather than core belief and conviction. Let's return to the initial question of how a decorated veteran could lose to an incumbent whose failures in planning and executing war were recognized across political boundaries. Democrats understood the political argument for prioritizing national-security issues, but not the more essential fact of the real-world importance of these matters. Subtle as it may seem, this distinction is the difference between checking a national-security box and building a convincing national-security platform.

Mentions of Kerry's military background may have paid deference to the issue of national security in form, but the substance of Kerry's platform gave very little import to hard security issues. In the public discourse leading up to the election, Kerry opted to emphasize other, traditionally Democratic topics such as energy and the environment that line the security periphery. But even assuming that there was, and remains, a sizeable constituency for these traditional Democratic issues, the Kerry campaign failed to link them to pressing security questions surrounding, for instance, Iraq or terrorism. As a result, although he focused on perfectly reasonable issues, Kerry sounded flat (or even somewhat contradictory) to an American electorate seeing its sons and daughters' being sacrificed and slogging it out in an ongoing war. Some of the more memorable utterances from the campaign include "no nation will have a veto over us"; "preemptive strike must pass a global test"; "I will never take my eye off the real dangerous threats"; "America should lead by extending a hand, not a fist"; and "America's power comes from respect, not weapons."[3] Statements such as "offer a military-modernization plan for the troops" and "need to be smarter about how we wage war-on-terror efforts" failed to outline a clear, coherent, and positive program. While every campaign contains numerous examples of empty rhetoric, Democrats could scarcely afford to have their instances of political filibustering come in that most vulnerable of areas: national security.

A smaller but still telling example of how Democratic Party heads have tended to think about national security: When Democrats thought they had a chance of winning the recent presidential election, they got far more excited about filling the post of secretary of State than secretary of Defense. The contrast was such that a military officer asked one of us, "Don't you find it surprising to be a member of a party that at a time of war spends no time thinking about who the secretary of Defense should be?"

The problem went deeper than the Kerry campaign. In the national discourse leading up to the 2004 election, Democrats as a party stood for little more than international cooperation and multilateralism on matters of national security. The problem extended beyond Democrats, in fact, to many independents and moderate Republicans, including what might be termed the "Powell wing" of the Bush administration. Cooperation and multilateralism are important matters, but they are means for achieving a successful foreign policy, not objectives in themselves. Democrats', moderate Republicans', and other internationalists' focus on the necessity of a broader foreign-affairs agenda (to include civil conflicts, HIV/AIDS, and other matters) cannot substitute for a direct and well-communicated approach to the "hard" security problems of the day. It did not require the ample help from Republican political strategists for Americans readily—and aptly—to note the deficiency in Kerry's security platform. Whatever the candidate's strengths, and however good a president he might have become, he and his advisers did not manage to present a national-security agenda that was cogent and compelling to the country.

Yet for all of the Kerry campaign's missteps on security, the 2004 elections were nothing new. Since the late 1960s, a major public-opinion gap has emerged over how the country sees the two parties on matters of national security, with Republicans typically enjoying a 30 percent edge in terms of public confidence. The numbers have generally fluctuated by approximately 10 percentage points over that period, but the gap has been striking for almost four decades.[4] The fact that it may have closed somewhat in the course of 2005 and 2006, during a difficult time for the Bush presidency, provides an opportunity for Democrats to change this reality—but only if they demonstrate more competence and confidence in their own ideas. Otherwise, their improved position will quite likely be a temporary phenomenon. If the situation in Iraq improves even modestly, or U.S. troops there are withdrawn in large numbers, the Republican position could revert to recent norms. And in any case, the year 2006 is the last time Democrats can plausibly base their own political strategy on a comparison with George W. Bush.

This pattern has been called "issue ownership," meaning that voters, to the extent that they consider policy issues, "are less influenced by the substance of candidates' platforms than with their perceived competence (as representatives of their party) to 'handle' the issues of importance."[5] Perceptions, especially those cast and re-cast over more than three decades, are stubbornly resistant to change.

TABLE 1.1 Griffith's Chart on National Security Preferences

SOURCE: Loren Griffith, "Where the Democrats Went Wrong," Truman National Security Project, Washington, D.C., May 2005, p. 3, available at www.trumanproject.org.

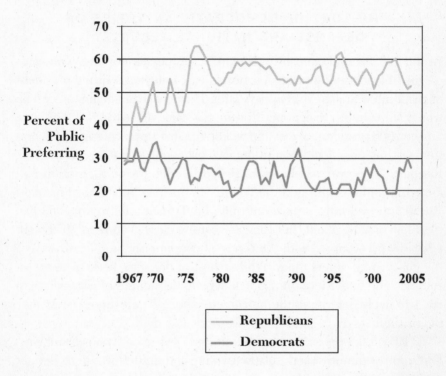

Little in politics is permanent, and the security gap is far from immutable. Nonetheless, it is striking how resilient the gap proved in 2004—even when the Democrats ran a much-vaunted combat veteran against a president whose Iraq policy, measured by the very standards he himself had created during the planning and opening stages of the war, was flailing. It is that Democrats lost amid these prevailing circumstances, more than the simple fact of their defeat, that makes the case for a radical rethinking of the party's approach to national-security affairs. If the party is to revitalize itself—and, for the good of the country, revitalize the national debate—in the post–9/11 political landscape, Democrats must reassess wholesale how they perceive the substance of national security and how they present its politics to voters.

Crucially, any such reassessment must include a way to reconnect with the military, for the party's ability to reconcile its current rift with the military is essential to the health of not only the country's Democrats, but also its democracy *writ large*.

A HISTORY OF DEMOCRATIC ANXIETIES ON DEFENSE AND NATIONAL SECURITY

In the 1952 New Hampshire primary, a Tennessee populist who campaigned by dogsled, wearing a coonskin cap, defeated a sitting president of the United States. Twelve days later, Harry S. Truman announced he would not run for reelection, throwing the race wide open.[6]

The 2008 presidential election will be the first since 1952 in which neither a sitting president nor a sitting vice president is running. As in 1952, the party in power has been tarnished by charges of corruption and cronyism and has engaged the country in an unpopular war. President Bush's approval ratings have not quite hit Truman's February 1952 historic low of 22 percent, but they are getting close. Voters in 1952 were primarily preoccupied with the threat of communism, and terrorism is a top concern for voters today. While a host of domestic and economic issues will rise to the level of national debate, the politics of national security will likely determine the outcome of the 2008 election, just as they did in 1952.

In 1952, the opposition Republican Party bypassed its powerful, virulently anti-communist and isolationist wing and drafted war hero Dwight Eisenhower to run, with a campaign focused on "Korea, communism, and corruption." He won in a landslide. Today's Democratic opposition undoubtedly faces a similar opportunity, but has yet to find a unifying figure, comparable national-security agenda, or rallying cry.

This shortcoming should come as no surprise. Democratic weakness and relative Republican strength on national security have become well-established electoral facts in the last thirty years. This situation has historic roots, but takes a unique form in the political climate of the moment, which is defined by extreme partisan rancor and post–9/11 fears.

Up until the Vietnam War, Democrats were comfortable with hard power. The Democratic Party was, after all, the party of Woodrow Wilson and Franklin Roosevelt, who led the nation to victory in two world wars. This was the party of Harry Truman, who ushered in the era of containment and deterrence before the threat from the Soviet Union was obvious. This was the party of John F. Kennedy, whose claims of a "missile gap" helped him get elected to office. Indeed, the Republican Party traditionally has been more dominated by isolationists, right up to Pat Buchanan's "America First" campaigns in 1996 and 2000.

In fact, it was a Democratic president's exercise of hard power that would lead to a thirty-year credibility gap on national security for the Democratic Party. Although he came into office with ambitious plans to create a New Deal–inspired legacy with his "Great Society" programs, Lyndon Baines Johnson's decision to step up military operations in Vietnam undermined his domestic agenda—and public confidence in the Democratic Party.

After this, the Democrats retreated from hard-power military policy. But the "Come Home, America" theme of George McGovern's speech accepting the Democratic Party's 1972 presidential nomination, with its cautionary tale about American imperialism, was not a complete departure for the Democrats. In fact, McGovern's speech had deep roots in the Democratic Party establishment. After World War II, for example, a significant wing of the Democratic Party, led by former vice president Henry Wallace, saw communists as important allies in the struggle for progress. He advocated for a more cooperative than confrontational stance toward the Soviet Union.[7]

And while Henry Wallace never had the opportunity to test his approach in a national election, George McGovern did. In accepting the Democratic presidential nomination in 1972, McGovern vowed an immediate unilateral withdrawal from Vietnam, adding "this is also the time to turn away from excessive preoccupation overseas to the rebuilding of our own nation."[8] Despite antiwar protests across the country and polling that showed overwhelming public support for ending the war,[9] McGovern lost the election in a landslide, winning only 13 electoral votes. The lopsided vote demonstrated that Americans not only blamed the Democratic Party for getting the country into the Vietnam War, but they also had no confidence in the Democrats' ability to get the country out of the war. This latter historical point should be seen as something of a cautionary tale for Democrats now confronting what to do in Iraq. Just because it was the Republicans that took the country into Iraq and made a general mess of the post-invasion planning does not translate into meaning that Americans will trust Democrats more with managing our departure from that ill-fated place.

The McGovern loss started something of a pattern for the Democratic Party over the next two decades; in fact, when he ran for president in 1984, Walter Mondale also received just 13 electoral votes. The one exception to the rule was Jimmy Carter, elected in 1976 after the Watergate scandal. In his inaugural address, Carter sounded the Wallace-McGovern theme of leading overseas by leading at home:

> "Our nation can be strong abroad only if it is strong at home. And we know that the best way to enhance freedom in other lands is to demonstrate here that our democratic system is worthy of emulation."[10]

While Carter's emphasis on human rights, nuclear cutbacks, and negotiation did produce results, such as the Israeli-Egyptian Camp David Accords, his presidency would end with dramatic foreign-policy failures. Carter's inability to muster a robust response to either the 1979 Soviet invasion of Afghanistan or the Iran hostage crisis solidified a public perception of Democrats as weak.

Bill Clinton did not overturn this perception as much as he sidestepped it. His 1992 presidential campaign famously emphasized the slogan, "It's the economy, stupid." With the Cold War over, Americans did not place a high priority on national security—and those few who *were* concerned about national security did not support the Democrats. Among voters who said foreign policy was important to them in the 1992 election, 92 percent favored Republicans.[11] Nevertheless, domestic and economic concerns trumped military matters in the 1992 election and, along with a third party candidate that arguably hurt the Republicans more than the Democrats, Bill Clinton came to power with an initial agenda that was heavily inclined towards challenges at home.

Clinton did make important advances in America's international position during his two terms in office, including the enlargement of NATO to include former Warsaw Pact countries, the successful negotiation of the North American Free Trade Agreement, and the NATO victory in the Balkans. However, these successes did not appear to alter the underlying perceptions about Democrats.

In 2000, national security still did not rate high on the list of voters' concerns. A 2000 exit poll asked voters what they thought the top four priorities should be for the new president. National security did not make the list.[12] If national security had rated higher in voters' minds, George W. Bush certainly would have won the race by a larger margin. In an August 2001 Gallup poll, 59 percent of respondents thought the Republican Party "would do a better job [on] . . . national defense," and only 32 percent thought Democrats would. Party affiliation did not completely account for the discrepancy. In that particular poll, 91 percent of the Republicans surveyed felt their party would do a better job on defense; 58 percent of the independents agreed, as did 35 percent of the Democrats.[13]

That discrepancy only widened after the terrorist attacks on September 11, 2001. An early 2002 poll showed 52 percent of respondents expressing confidence in Republicans' ability to fight terrorism; only 16 percent had confidence in Democrats' ability in this area. Even respondents who identified themselves as Democrats were split in terms of their confidence in Republicans versus members of their own party, with an equal number (33 percent) expressing confidence in each.[14] Those numbers would stay more or less the same for the 2004 election.[15]

After the March 2003 invasion of Iraq, the Democratic Party saw the resurgence of an antiwar coalition that strongly echoed the Henry Wallace and McGovern tradition. This coalition is having an effect on Democratic politics, including posing significant primary challenges to established hawkish Democrats such as Connecticut senator Joe Lieberman and California representative Jane Harman.

In addition to expressing strong antipathy toward President Bush, many antiwar activists reject the overall struggle with terrorism. Filmmaker Michael Moore pointed out that while terrorists do exist, Americans are far more likely to die in a car accident or suicide attempt. "You need to calm down, relax, listen very carefully, and repeat after me: There is no terrorist threat," he wrote in 2003.[16] This is a foundation neither for a viable foreign policy nor a viable political campaign. On its Web site, the antiwar organization Code Pink notes that it "rejects the Bush administration's fear-based politics that justify violence, and instead calls for policies based on compassion, kindness, and a commitment to international law."[17] This is a more noble and principled view than Moore's. But it also fails to pass the common sense test of showing how kindness could plausibly affect the calculations of a megalomaniac mass murderer such as Osama bin Laden.

A LEGACY OF MISCOMMUNICATION

The U.S. military today is a highly politicized—some would even say Republican—institution. This political proclivity appears to have intensified even amid the various failures of Republican military planning and follow-through since 2001. This now-accepted political fact in American life carries much broader significance than many Democratic strategists have yet appreciated. But if, as "issue ownership" theory predicts, perception rather than substance guides the military's recent voting habits, it is worth a brief look at how the Republicans' deft handling of that perception compares to the Democrats' failures.

Most political scientists and national commentators agree that the humiliation suffered by the military in Vietnam, "the ill-advised war conceived by Robert McNamara and his Whiz Kids,"[18] serves as a useful marker to begin tracking Democrats' current difficulties with the military as an instrument of foreign policy. It would be too simplistic to ascribe sole responsibility for the Democrats' struggle with the military to the "culture wars" of the 1960s, but the truth remains that, by and large, the Democrats have not been able to shake their antiwar image since. This is a handicap in a culture that holds agonistic virtues of combat and victory in near universal regard.

The 1972 presidential election illustrates how the rift between Democrats and the military began to become institutionalized. While Nixon combined rhetoric of pride in the military with a promise to restore dignity and respect, George McGovern favored withdrawal from Vietnam, which opened him up to charges of defeatism. It was a sore miscalculation, as the perceived isolationist tenor of the Vietnam protests proved more apparent than real—or at least more complex than images suggested. Tracking public opinion on whether or not the United States should concern itself with world problems, the University of Michigan's 1972 ANES poll showed that 77 percent of those polled disagreed with the statement that "[t]his country would be better off if we just stayed home and did not concern ourselves with problems in other parts of the world."[19] Despite the failure in Vietnam, it would seem that Americans were still eager to be a positive force in the world and were not, as has been claimed, inclined to indulge a "deep-seated popular American urge to turn inward."[20]

In the military's view, the Vietnam experience had been nearly lethal to its integrity. The time was ripe for reform, and the result was a hardening of the perimeter around the military establishment itself. If fault for a demoralized military after Vietnam could be laid at least partially at the feet of mendacious Democratic civilian leadership, then the remedy would be to make it harder for civilian Democrats to carry the country to war in the first place. Toward this end, Creighton Abrams, who directed Vietnam operations between 1968 and 1972, initiated the Total Force policy that rendered the operations of the active army dependent upon the reserves.[21] This amounted to a warning to the civilian leadership that they could not wage war without the consent of those they called upon to fight, since the politically difficult task of taking America to war would be almost infeasible without the active support of those in uniform. Combined with Nixon's institution of the all-volunteer force and fresh infusions of cash, the stage was set for the rise of a newly empowered, tightly knit core of military professionals.

And yet the next Democratic president continued what was becoming a party tradition of alienating the military. Despite important advances in military technology during Jimmy Carter's presidency—including cruise missiles and stealth aircraft—the overall period did not elicit military confidence in the Democratic party. During these four years, the Soviet military buildup continued while America's reversal of the post-Vietnam defense budget cuts was belated and halfhearted. The problems showed vividly in 1980, when the Desert One hostage-rescue attempt in Iran never got close to Tehran and eight American servicemen died in what became that era's most shocking symbol of post-Vietnam American military misfortune. (Although Carter bore ultimate responsibility, the tragedy reflected problems within U.S. military command and training structures as much as within the Carter administration; those military problems were later addressed through the 1986 Goldwater-Nichols bill and other reforms.)[22]

Carter's "Crisis of Confidence" speech did not win him any favor among members of a military institution characterized by a can-do attitude and a spirit of optimism. In that famous address, Carter called upon the nation to look inward for the source of freedom, to make daily sacrifices to mitigate the negative effects of a materialist culture.

> We've discovered that owning things and consuming things does not satisfy our longing for meaning. We've learned that piling up material goods cannot fill the emptiness of lives which have no confidence or purpose . . . For the first time in the history of our country, a majority of our people believe that the next five years will be worse than the past five years.

Carter's grim warnings stood in stark contrast to the more positive equations of sacrifice with military commitment made by John F. Kennedy and others at the height of the Cold War. Unlike these earlier, more patriotic conceptions, Carter's negative vision of sacrifice as privation offered Americans little hope for improvement, and even less hope for improvement through military means. As a result—even though, in retrospect, Carter's call for alternate energy sources, his focus on the Middle East as a looming problem, and his support of the Rapid Deployment Forces (the forerunner to CENTCOM) were prescient—his vision and its lack of any corresponding role for the military was not robust enough to convince the public that his party was capable of handling the perceived threats.

Ronald Reagan, with an actor's instinct for winning over an audience, picked up the question right where Carter left it: "Are you better off now than you were four years ago?" And with that, his strategists gave Americans the vision of themselves they wanted, turning to the military for the imagery of hope and being a force for good on the world stage. The electorate responded, and Reagan carried forty-four states in 1980. Despite such an overwhelming defeat, Democrats failed to appreciate how Reagan's success had hinged on his ability to translate military strength into a positive message of national pride and possibility. The Democratic Party thus repeated mistakes in 1984, allowing nominee Walter Mondale to be cast as weak on defense for his opposition to Reagan's Strategic Defense Initiative. Whatever his political motivations, Reagan's 35 percent increase in defense spending over his two terms helped not only to exhaust the Soviets, but also to buoy national pride in the military that had led the country in its victorious homestretch in the Cold War.

The change in the country's mood was dramatic. The renewed surge in defense spending and renewed sense of pride and excellence among the troops reconnected Americans to their military and made them feel good about their place in the world. Andrew Bacevich notes how this was reflected in popular films and books celebrating military virtues: *An Officer and a Gentleman, Rambo, Top Gun, The Hunt for Red October, Red Storm Rising, Patriot Games*. Bacevich then contends:

> By the time Reagan left office, Republicans had managed to brand Democrats as national-security wimps. Democrats had gotten the United States into Vietnam, had made a hash of things, and then washed their hands of the mess they had made, leaving it to the Republicans to clean up. When it came to military matters, therefore, the Democratic Party was untrustworthy. Worse, among the party rank and file, undercurrents of antimilitary sentiment persisted. Democrats didn't understand and didn't much like soldiers—so at least the story went.[23]

A look at the voting demographics of the 1984 and 1988 elections turns up some interesting evidence supporting Bacevich's claim. Reagan's victory in 1984 was due not to the working class, whose vote, if measured by labor-union affiliation, was 52 percent Democratic, but rather to voters who were college-educated (61 percent of this group supported Reagan), under thirty (60 percent), Southern (63 percent), and/or independents who swung to the Republicans (67 percent).[24] Similarly, in 1988, George H. W. Bush took 63 percent of the under-thirty vote, and his support dropped only slightly with the other groups that had supported Reagan. The presence of such a solidly Republican cohort of young people throughout the 1980s suggests that the positive and vigorous military images so pervasive in popular culture, deployed in tandem with a rising sense of political hope, indeed helped shape public perception.

In fact, the link between popular culture and the new military had become so strong during the Reagan years that it compelled even the most unlikely of Democratic candidates to attempt a military display during his campaign. But such artless and unconvincing pandering left the Democrats with a mortifying image of wimpishness: a helmeted Michael Dukakis emerging from the hatch of an Abrams battle tank looking more like Elmer Fudd than a soldier. How in Heaven's name could the public trust these guys? The antiwar party dressed up in a tank?

The real challenge for the Democrats' relationship with the military, however, was yet to come.

THE CLINTON YEARS: DEEPENING THE DIVIDE

Bill Clinton's troubles with the military began as early as his declaration of candidacy in the 1992 campaign. Back in the 1960s, he had avoided the draft, written a letter expressing his "loathing" for the military, and, at Oxford, demonstrated against the Vietnam War. Clinton's campaign advisers, aware of the liabilities caused by their candidate's lack of foreign-policy and military experience, were eager to mitigate Clinton's antimilitary image. They sought and received the endorsement of some twenty retired officers, among them a former chairman of the Joint Chiefs, Admiral William Crowe, and the deputy commander of the U.S. forces in the Persian Gulf, Lieutenant General Calvin Waller. Most of these retirees supported Clinton based on his domestic agenda, which involved matters on which they were not usually experts, but much to the consternation of their active-duty counterparts, their endorsements were used by the campaign "not to justify [Clinton's] economic or social programs, but to legitimize his claim to be an effective commander in chief."[25] The distaste of active service personnel over Clinton's antimilitary background was compounded by his campaign positions on military issues. Candidate Clinton promised to accelerate cuts to an already declining defense budget, to integrate openly gay men and women into the military, and to scale up the country's military posture in Bosnia.

At the time of Clinton's inauguration, a *Los Angeles Times* survey found that "only 12 percent of the active-duty force had a great deal of respect for the president."[26] The military expressed their distaste during the Clinton transition by engaging in what President Eisenhower called "legalized insubordination," with soldiers of all ranks "letting the media know about their opposition to Clinton's social, foreign policy, and budgetary proposals, implicitly questioning his ability to be commander in chief."[27] On a NATO base in the Netherlands, for instance, Air Force Major General Harold Campbell referred to Clinton before an audience as a "gay-loving," "pot-smoking," "draft-dodging" womanizer.[28]

In fairness, Clinton himself did little to improve the situation. His attempts to change his antimilitary persona were halting at best, and when they occurred, could scarcely have been more counterproductive. One of the most uncomfortable images of this came "a few days into his administration . . . as an honor guard saluted the president on the White House lawn, [and] Clinton brought his hand up in a startled half wave before scurrying up the steps of a waiting helicopter." As one commentator observed at the time, "the wobbly salute seemed symbolic of the tenuous relationship between the new commander and his troops."[29] And not one hundred days into his tenure, Clinton was met with near hostility when he donned an ill-fitting green flight jacket and addressed the crew onboard the *Theodore Roosevelt* aircraft carrier off the coast of Norfolk, Virginia. Brad Owens, a twenty-two-year-old Marine lance corporal from Grand Rapids, Michigan, summarized the feeling that day: "Put it this way: Bush knew the military. With Clinton, it's all politics."[30]

President Clinton's ample follow-through on campaign promises that were perceived as antimilitary did not help his image with the armed forces. Still, the fallout was disproportionate to the actual substance of Clinton's military reforms, some of which—such as his initial rejection of the fatally flawed Vance-Owen plan to stop fighting in Bosnia—were well advised. Clinton's National Security Cabinet and political team allowed his critics to carry the microphone. Among a litany of distorted complaints, critics charged that Clinton doubled his proposed defense cuts (despite the fact that his Republican predecessor, George Bush Sr., had slashed military spending by $50 billion, and that some amount of defense downsizing was natural after the dissolution of the Soviet Union); "reduced military pay by 10 percent in real terms" (in fact, real pay held steady in Clinton's first term and went up substantially in his second term); "tampered with the military retirement system" (in reality, Clinton reversed reforms made under Reagan that were unpopular with troops and that had reduced benefits for most); and "appointed an analyst to run the Pentagon." (That "analyst" was Les Aspin, who, aside from having served with distinction at senior levels in Congress, had actively served in both the U.S. Army and the Department of Defense. He did not have the formal, traditional personal style that tends to play well in the Pentagon and that served his successor, Bill Perry, so well. His downfall, however, was due primarily to the fact that he made his big mistakes in the use of military force during his first year in office, unlike Secretary Rumsfeld or Secretary Weinberger, whose main operational tragedies occurred in 1983 and 2003, respectively.)[31]

The administration's failure to rebuff unfair criticism was matched by its reticence to herald Clinton's earnest military successes. The White House made little mention of the Pentagon's demonstrable victory in Kosovo, its belated and partial but still real successes in Bosnia, or its successful deterrence of conflict through prudent military steps in Korea and Taiwan.

Clinton's record on hard defense issues notwithstanding, it was his push to reform cultural aspects of the military that elicited the bulk of popular criticism. In what was probably his most public fray with the military, Clinton's efforts to incorporate gays into the armed forces brought him into particular conflict with the Joint Chiefs, including the much-acclaimed General Colin Powell, who was one of the plan's most forceful and articulate opponents. Powell began meeting with Clinton and Secretary of Defense Aspin on the issue even before the inauguration, and in the several meetings that followed Clinton's taking office, he "emphasiz[ed] each time the threat that lifting the ban would pose to 'good order and discipline' in the ranks."[32]

Still, Aspin and Powell successfully worked out a compromise. President Clinton unveiled his "don't ask, don't tell" policy in a July 6, 1993, speech at the National Defense University:

Our military is a conservative institution, and I say that in the very best sense, for its purpose is to conserve the fighting spirit of our troops, to conserve the resources and capacity of our troops, to conserve the military lessons acquired during our nation's existence, to conserve our very security, and yes, to conserve the liberties of the American people. Because it is a conservative institution, it is right for the military to be wary of sudden changes. Because it embodies the best of America and must reflect the society in which it operates, it is also right for the military to make changes when the time for change is at hand.[33]

Powell and the Joint Chiefs remained mum, but the announcement sparked outrage among several senior officers who had been under the impression that they would be consulted prior to any decision to repeal the ban. Concerned that "repealing the ban would wreck morale, undermine recruiting, force devoutly religious service members to resign, and increase the risk of AIDS for heterosexual troops, these leaders were furious to learn of the new approach from a news article."[34]

The polls at the time showed widespread public disagreement with the president; as President Clinton later wrote in his autobiography, 16 percent approved of lifting the ban, while 33 percent very strongly disapproved.[35] Perhaps not surprisingly, Aspin bore most of the political fallout. When these attacks on military tradition were joined by turmoil over the decision not to reinforce American troops fighting in Somalia in the weeks before eighteen American soldiers died on a tragic October day in Mogadishu, Aspin was left with little recourse. In late December 1993, concluding that President Clinton had lost confidence in his leadership, Aspin resigned, and in so doing, laid bare the strains between the military and their chief commander.

When the 1995 Monica Lewinsky affair and subsequent attempts to conceal it became public in 1998, Clinton sunk to new lows in the eyes of the military. The outcry among officers and enlisted personnel raised enough concern within the Pentagon that the Marine Corps and the Air Force each took the unusual step of reminding officers that Article 88 of the Uniform Code of Military Justice explicitly prohibits them from speaking "contemptuous words" about the president and other civilian leaders of the military.[36] In one particularly well-publicized debate, the Marine Corps ultimately opted not to punish Marine Major Shane Sellers for publicly calling President Clinton an "adulterous liar" and "criminal" who should be impeached.[37]

Likewise, reserve major Daniel J. Rabil, writing in a *Washington Times* op-ed column, called for the president's removal, labeling Clinton a "lying draft dodger" and a "moral coward" who has "always had contempt for the American military."[38] The publication of Rabil's column was noted prominently in the *Congressional Quarterly Weekly* of January 5, 1999.[39]

Ironically, probably the least publicized of Clinton's fissures with the military was in reality the most taxing on their partnership. Throughout Clinton's tenure, the military's budget remained *the* vexing issue for the Pentagon. Complaints aired before Congress in 1993—policy and programming issues, weapons delays and cost increases, difficulties over the F–22 program, and a "declining operational readiness among deployed forces"—were echoed at the end of 1999. The Pentagon's top political appointees, however, regarded the complaints as baseless and politically charged. Defense Secretary William Cohen and others "believe[d] the Navy, Air Force, and Army could be more gracious in victory. President Clinton and Congress this year approved a five-year, $112 billion increase, making the military the biggest beneficiary of the budget surplus."[40]

Admittedly, this came after a previous period of cutbacks under the first President Bush and President Clinton. But the post–Cold War defense drawdown was the most successful post-conflict drawdown in the nation's history, as evidenced by the excellent performances of U.S. armed forces in Bosnia starting in 1995, Kosovo starting in 1999, and Afghanistan starting in 2001. (Previous drawdowns were followed, for example, by the rise of Nazi Germany and Imperial Japan in the 1930s, by debacle in Korea in 1950, and by the operational failure in Iran in 1980.) By 1996, real defense-spending reductions under Clinton had effectively ended, and when Clinton left office, spending was back up to about $300 billion—90 percent of the inflation-adjusted Cold War average.[41]

Moreover, the 1999 Kosovo war, while it got off to a very poor start, was ultimately successful—and historic. It was the first time NATO had gone to war as an alliance. Some observers viewed the need to work with nineteen nations as a major reason the conflict got off to a poor start, and this may have colored some Bush-administration officials' thinking about the purported perils of multilateralism. But in fact, the operation's initial difficulties had more to do with incorrect assumptions about how Milosevic would behave that were shared in Washington as well as other NATO capitals. As such, what is most notable about the Kosovo experience, apart from its botched initiation, is how well the alliance—led by the U.S. military—recovered and performed in the end.[42] It is largely because of this type of impressive performance of the American armed forces that most analysts favor retaining the all-volunteer force, rather than taking the advice of distinguished military sociologist Charles Moskos and the highly respected Congressman Charles Rangel and a few others that military conscription be restored—a subject to which we return in Chapter Three.[43]

Even so, as the 2000 election approached, the leading Republican presidential candidates were returning to their most loyal base, again citing the bread-and-butter issue of military reform. Both Senator John McCain and then-governor George W. Bush insisted that, even with the 1999 budget increase, the American military remained woefully underfinanced. According to the *New York Times*, "one candidate, Senator John McCain of Arizona, a highly decorated veteran and former prisoner of war, has routinely derided the military for paying such low salaries that record numbers of service members have to rely on food stamps."[44] (Had Democrats engaged in any friendly fact-checking, the heir-apparent Gore campaign could have countered McCain's claims as patently false; the 20,000 U.S. troops on food stamps under Bush Sr. had fallen to 5,000 by the end of Clinton's tenure.)

The military also figured prominently into Governor Bush's campaign; he promised to "add $5 billion to the annual military budget to give the armed forces another pay increase and to pay research costs to develop new, modern weapons systems that would 'skip a generation of technology'."[45]

On September 23, 1999, at The Citadel, presidential candidate George W. Bush laid out an ambitious but ultimately pragmatic vision of American power:

> For America, this is a time of unrivaled military power, economic promise, and cultural influence. It is, in Franklin Roosevelt's phrase, "the peace of overwhelming victory." Now a new generation of American leaders will determine how that power and influence are used . . . Our challenge is not as obvious, but just as noble: To turn these years of influence into decades of peace.[46]

To achieve this overarching goal, Governor Bush vowed to "renew the bond of trust between the American president and the American military . . . defend the American people against missiles and terror . . . and begin creating the military of the next century." He also underlined the importance of "strong alliances, expanding trade, and confident diplomacy," as well as "tough realism."

Bush's victory in 2000 set the stage for Republicans to pick up where Ronald Reagan had left off; once again the Democrats could be painted as inept on defense, and again Democrats played into Republican hands. Advisers to Vice President Al Gore, referring to public-opinion polls, counseled their candidate to avoid the defense issue. In so doing, they failed to appreciate what seems a truism to us: that when Americans choose a president, even when the polls do not predict or reveal it, they *always* rate defense matters high. Even if Americans' security does not seem imminently imperiled, they understand the special place of America in the world as well as the special national-security powers entrusted by the Constitution to the chief executive. They also look to discussion of defense issues, which have a certain gravity and concreteness, as a way to assess the character and steadfastness of any would-be commander in chief.

Partially because they recognize the truth of this insight, Republicans generally are experts in the art of defining the current environment and the politics of the recent past as well. Not only have President Bush and his lieutenants expertly defined the current security environment in ways favorable to dominant Republican thinking and interests, they have also successfully shaped public perspectives about the past, particularly the Clinton era. This contemporary conservative interpretive commentary is one of the essential features of modern Republicanism, and significant resources have been devoted not only to the shaping of future debates but also to the rewriting of old ones.

Take, for instance, President Bush's characterization of the 1990s during his second inaugural address, just as the hopes of a new bipartisan approach to the global challenges confronting the country were fading in the wind: "After the shipwreck of communism," Bush declared, "came years of relative quiet, years of repose, years of sabbatical—and then there came a day of fire." The language captures Republicans' essential critique of the Democrats: that they are elitist in their university cocoons, unfocused on the dangerous challenges confronting the country, and essentially unprepared to meet and make the hard choices necessary to keep the country safe.

Yet this picture of Democrats' lollygagging in the 1990s, enjoying a holiday from history, ignores some of the drama that played out almost exclusively in America's favor during this supposedly relaxed decade. Indeed, the 1990s involved some important successes on the international scene and helped set the stage for continued American power on the global arena. Increasingly, the administration of Bush Sr. and the Clinton administration—despite coming from different parties and somewhat differing perspectives—can be seen in retrospect as essentially fitting together to complete a decade of accomplishment in a way that paints President George W. Bush's subsequent term in office as an outlier.

Together, George H. W. Bush and Bill Clinton labored to create a Europe "whole and free" through three essential efforts: the unification of Germany, the enlargement of NATO that knitted the newly free states of Central and Eastern Europe into the security mechanisms of the West, and the belated but ultimately successful efforts to stand up to ethnic cleansing in Bosnia and Kosovo. In Asia, North Korean nuclear efforts were rebuffed and largely stymied. The United States deployed aircraft carriers to the western Pacific to send a clear message of resolve and resolution to Chinese leaders in the midst of their military saber rattling against Taiwan.

The North American Free Trade Agreement was negotiated by President George H. W. Bush and secured by President Clinton to improve hemispheric trade and American competitiveness in the face of rising Asian manufacturing challenges. Both administrations sought to contain Saddam Hussein's Iraq—a policy that despite its flaws and failings looks much better in retrospect. President Clinton also took the politically difficult route of trying to equip and prepare the American people for the enormous challenges and opportunities wrought by globalization and the revolutionary spread of technology and information.

Clinton's Treasury Department also navigated the overheated global economy through the dangerous shoals of the Asian financial crisis and the Mexican peso devaluation. Perhaps most importantly, presidents Bush Sr. and Clinton both restored fiscal responsibility and put in place the financial preconditions for an economic renaissance that was virtually unmatched in American history.

Yet Karl Rove, Vice President Cheney, and Republican National Committee head Ken Melman have all aggressively castigated Democrats for having a "pre–9/11 worldview" that was insufficiently vigilant to the onerous task of protecting the nation from terrorist threats and rogue nations. This has proven a devastatingly successful line of attack against the generally long-winded, nuanced, and complexity-laden language of Democrats who speak on national-security matters, particularly on Capitol Hill. It plays right into stereotypes about the post-Vietnam Democratic Party. The situation has not been helped by Democrats' general reluctance to trumpet several of Clinton's hard-power accomplishments.

But finally, after more than thirty years, the Republican narrative may be in jeopardy. The Bush administration, whatever its early successes in rehabilitating the military's morale, has neglected several key aspects of the Iraq operation. It ignored counsel from the Army chief of staff and most outside analysts, who urged it to plan for a difficult post-Saddam environment. It hastily celebrated a "mission accomplished" while the president himself taunted the Iraqi insurgency with his call to "bring it on." These charges can hardly be dismissed as partisan. Richard Kohn, despite his public support for several of Bush's military policies, admits that "the Iraq war may be what forces the officer corps to return to the old . . . model of nonpartisanship."[47] In fact, the most damning evidence of the Bush administration's lack of postwar planning hails from the military's own Third Infantry Division, whose after-action report finds: "Higher headquarters did not provide the Third Infantry Division (Mechanized) with a plan for Phase IV. As a result, Third Infantry Division transitioned into Phase IV in the absence of guidance." A broader Department of Defense report on the war similarly observed that "late formation of Department of Defense [Phase IV] organizations limited time available for the development of detailed plans and pre-deployment coordination."[48]

So, chaos ensued after the fall of Saddam; early chances to build on positive momentum were lost; political and economic reconstruction plans were patched together hastily and shoddily and then revamped; former lower-level Baathists were fired and then rehired; Iraqi military personnel were cut off from pay and then put back on the state payroll; and the United Nations, after initially being kept at arm's length along with the international community writ large, was asked to help rescue a mission headed in the wrong direction. By 2004, with the Abu Ghraib prison scandal and Fallujah uprising dominating the images coming from Iraq, the situation was clearly going south. It has improved little since. As of March 2006, more than 77 percent of the U.S. public viewed civil war in Iraq as either an already present reality or an imminent prospect.[49] Poll numbers vary on Iraq, of course, based on recent trends in the mission there, not to mention the wording of the question. But as of this writing in the summer of 2006, Americans continued to describe America's saga in Iraq as the nation's top problem, at a time when the overall national mood has clearly remained sour (with only one in three satisfied with the state of the country).[50]

The revolt of the recently retired general officers who have spoken out against Secretary Rumsfeld and his role in the conduct of the war, combined with ongoing concerns about stresses on U.S. fighting forces, suggest that the long Republican honeymoon with the military may be coming to an end. The perceptible decreases in the president's second-term approval ratings among the military shown in 2006 polls might well represent a window for the Democrats. To put it differently, and less partisanly, the nation's current problems require new ideas on national security—and the whole purpose of competitive politics in democracies is to provide new ideas for voters to consider. We need a competition.

The simple fact that the military and the public may be tiring of one party, however, does not automatically imply their allegiance to the other party. Whether the Democrats will capitalize on this narrow shift depends on the extent to which they appreciate not simply their own failings since Vietnam, but also the amount of ground they must regain as a result of those failings. And in our view, the American body politic, left and right and center, should be rooting for them to succeed. The country needs a stronger debate on national-security matters at this time of listless performance by a conservative Republican administration on the core issue of the day.

Internationalist, moderate Republicans face their own challenges. While they have been less plagued than Democrats by a public perception that they are allergic to the use of military force, they have been consistently outmaneuvered by neoconservatives during the Bush years. They need to retain their own credibility on the use of military force while projecting a fuller understanding of how to use hard power effectively in the twenty-first century—for example, by following through in situations that require stabilization and rebuilding after the kinetic phases of war. Like Democrats, they also need a bolder and bigger vision on related security matters such as the long-term struggle against terrorism and development of an alternative energy policy for the United States.

OF POLLS—AND COMMON SENSE

A September 2004 *Military Times* survey showed President Bush the preferred candidate among active-duty military personnel by a rough magnitude of 73:18, a staggering ratio that was found not only among active-duty troops but also among reservists. The survey was not a scientific poll, and likely overrepresented older and more senior military personnel, but it did include enlisted ranks as well as officers. In any case, that it showed a 4:1 dominance for the president was astonishing.[51] Further,

TABLE 1.2 Conservative Ideological Self-Identification Among Military
Officers in the FPLP Surveys of American Opinion Leaders (1976–1996):
The Effects of Time and Age

Generation (Date of birth)	% Very Conservative + % Somewhat Conservative (N)					
	1976	1980	1984	1988	1992	1996
Post-Vietnam War	—	—	—	—	—	—
(born after 1954)	—	—	—	—	—	—
Vietnam	62	68	78	78	71	67
(born 1941–54	(383)	(19)	(50)	(97)	(136)	(52)
Interim	58	76	68	77	89	76
(born 1933–40)	(59)	(86)	(44)	(32)	(9)	(21)
Korean War	71	78	82	81	83	95
(born 1924–32)	(18)	(38)	(22)	(17)	(6)	(19)
World War II	50	80	80	0	—	—
(born before 1924)	(23)	(5)	(10)	(2)	—	—

SOURCE: Ole R. Holsti, "A Widening Gap between the US Military and Civilian Society? Some Evidence, 1976-1996," International Security, Vol. 23, No. 3 (Winter 1998/1999), p. 11

NOTE: Percentages are based on respondents who identified year of birth, excluding those who did not do so.

despite some serious gaffes in the Bush administration's defense policy over the last few years, predictions that the Republican sway over the military vote would diminish in the 2004 election did not come to pass. More than 60 percent of today's military leaders self-identify as Republicans, as do 59 percent of military personnel overall. (Meanwhile, only 13 percent identify as Democrats, and 20 percent as independents.)[52] This continues a trend charted by Ole R. Holsti in a 1999 issue of *International Security*.

The military membership has skewed toward Republicans and away from Democrats since 1976. This is troubling for those who value a non-politicized, or at least politically balanced, military. There are also fewer independents in today's military, reinforcing the overall trend towards the GOP. Democrats found reason to take notice of this new pattern when, after the 1986 Absentee Voting Act was made law, the resulting increase in the military vote turned into a windfall of additional votes for Republicans. The ultimate rightward slant of the military's "undecided" vote stems from the interplay of several factors, including the resurgence of social conservatism in the decades since the free-spirited 1960s and 1970s and its overlap with the necessarily conservative nature of an institution that must maintain the discipline required to throw itself into war. Considering these parallel trends toward conservatism, together with Democrats' poor record of mediating these two forces, it seems logical that Republicans, "the standard bearers of social conservatism,"[53] have won over this swing constituency, at least through the 2004 presidential election.

As the Iraq war has dragged on, however, support for President Bush's policies has dropped even among the military population. By late 2005, according to another *Military Times* poll, only 54 percent of those responding to the survey assessed the administration's Iraq policy favorably. The president's overall favorability rating among this population declined to 60 percent, an 11-point drop from the previous year.

Even so, 73 percent of respondents still expected some type of success in Iraq, and many blamed the media for disproportionately emphasizing the bad news from Iraq.[54] However, critique of the media's performance in Iraq needs to be tempered by the indisputable reality that the media are, in fact, covering a war there, and a war that is not going particularly well.[55] Research on the effect of media coverage on public opinion indicates that the media merely reinforces already held ideas.[56] This news should enliven Democrats based on the logic that if opinion is changing, it is due not to media manipulation but to a public desire for good leadership and clear policy goals, two requisites for support of military operations, according to a 1996 RAND study.[57] A 2006 *Military Times* article accompanying the above-mentioned poll provides Democrats, many independents, and some moderate Republicans additional reason for political optimism—even if much of the precipitating cause is a tragically difficult war abroad. The piece shares findings by David Segal, a military sociologist, who maintains that the drops shown in the poll are "real drops, but [are changes] reflecting the tone of the country . . . People in the military talk to folks back home. Eventually the military does catch up [with public opinion]."[58]

Democrats cannot assume that the president's troubles will help them make major inroads among military personnel—especially at a time when defeatist language from some, including the current head of the DNC, Howard Dean, gives an impression of a Democratic Party that views the state of the military in significantly bleaker terms than the institution views itself. Democratic stalwarts describe 2006 as a "year of transition" when Iraqi government and security personnel will begin to take up much of the burden from American and other coalition forces. Yet there

TABLE 1.3 Support for Military Spending, 1980–2004 (7-point scale)

		'80	'82	'84	'86	'88	'90	'92	'94	'96	'98	'00	'02	'04
Greatly Decrease	1	3	8	8	9	8	11	8	10	4	**	3	**	3
	2	2	8	9	10	9	11	12	10	8	**	3	**	5
	3	5	12	11	14	12	15	20	14	14	**	7	**	8
	4	15	26	28	27	29	29	29	33	28	**	22	**	23
	5	21	15	16	17	15	11	10	16	18	**	22	**	24
	6	20	7	9	7	8	4	4	6	9	**	14	**	13
Greatly Increase	7	20	4	7	5	6	4	3	3	5	**	9	**	9
Undecided		15	20	13	11	14	14	14	8	15	**	20	**	14

SOURCE: The American National Election Studies. The Anes Guide to Public Opinion and Electoral Behavior. Ann Arbor, MI: University of Michigan, Center for Political Studies, Generated November 2005. (Accessed 2/2/2006)

are undeniable political pressures for some Democrats to entertain a more precipitous withdrawal from embattled Iraq.

Despite Democrats' several missteps, there are also numerous reasons for the military's overwhelming Republican tilt that are endogenous to the military itself. So long as the military outlook is governed by the charge to guard the nation against military threats, conservative values of discipline, loyalty, obedience, and duty will command central importance and will continue to shape the military frame of mind.[59] The military thus already shares an underlying cultural affinity with Republicans and their drumbeat emphasis on "values." And, of course, as already noted, recent Republican administrations have tended to support big defense budgets, appealing not only to a military desiring to stay in business, but also to a nervous voting populace that believes national security requires such expenditures. As the following chart detailing a recent poll on defense spending shows, the public supported greater increases in both 2000 and 2004, up several points from 1982 (but not nearly as high as in 1980).

Another contributing factor to military Republicanism may be the fact that large percentages of military recruits—particularly for the Army and Marines— come from rural and Red State America, where the conservative "values" issue has become a battle cry. As already noted, both Reagan and Bush I carried the south by large margins, and much of what was left of the Blue State Midwest fell in 2000.[60] Along similar lines, voting habits within military families have been shown to pass from parent to child in stronger numbers than in civilian families, which further consolidates a block within the larger group. And finally, religious observation, often linked to conservatism, is also higher than the national norm among active-duty military personnel. This comes at a time when Democrats are perceived as the more secular of the country's two major parties.

While it may be tempting, given these institutional reinforcements, for some in the Democratic Party simply to "write off" the military or "hard core" national-security vote as unattainable, a quick review of the size of this voting cohort should cause one to reconsider such a shortsighted view. So should the fact that there are many, including top leaders, in the Democratic Party who would not yield an inch to Republicans on matters of values, religion, or commitment to the nation's traditions. And so should the Clinton Administration's national security legacy, which in operational terms had several important accomplishments.

A BATTLEGROUND DEMOCRATS IGNORE AT THEIR PERIL

The military vote is important politically. While the current uniformed military only includes about 2.5 million people (in broad terms, 1.5 million on active duty and another million in the reserve component), or less than 2 percent of the voting public, it could still act as an important swing constituency. That is especially true considering that the two most recent presidential contests were effectively decided by a single county in Florida and 50,000 votes in Ohio, respectively. The overwhelming Republican edge among active military personnel makes for a daunting challenge for Democrats as they seek to win back some of this vote. Perhaps the best that can be hoped for in the short run is a return to a larger independent vote among the military—something that we argue should be seen as healthy for the country as a whole regardless of one's politics. (There has been a growing number of independents among civilian voters in the last several elections.[61])

But the problem is far deeper and more serious than even these voting figures for active-service personnel suggest. Democrats, and in fact politicos of all stripes, often forget that there are more than 25 million military veterans alive today in the United States (as well as 4 million civilians currently employed full-time either by the Department of Defense or by defense contractors working for DoD). Former soldiers, sailors, Marines, airmen, and airwomen are conscientious participants in the American democratic system. They dramatically widen the pool of voters who rank military matters near the top of their list of electoral priorities. Military members' spouses and children further widen this pool.

Another hidden multiplier for the military cohort are the communities surrounding military bases. These townships and urban areas have vested interests often inextricable from those of the military installations that so frequently constitute the fabric of their regional economies. The political significance of these town-tank ties transcends mere economic interests. As Benjamin Wallace, editor of *The Nation*, powerfully observed after attending a deployment ceremony for Army National Guard soldiers in Jacksonville, North Carolina:

> In this section of coastal Carolina, fewer than thirty miles from the Army's Fort Bragg, the Marines' Camp Lejeune, and the Air Force's Seymour Johnson Base . . . it is the presence of the military and their willingness to sacrifice that give this town its sense of its own values, that it is more than just another section of sprawling, strip-malled blacktop. It gives citizens the sense that everything they do to support the troops has deep import. In this deeply Southern town, a visitor comes across the unlikely sight of a white grandmother volunteering to pay for the meals of a couple of off-duty black enlisted men who are eating in the local . . . fried chicken joint. At the mobilization ceremony I attended, an old man with a veteran's cap told his grandson importantly, "Four companies in a battalion, four battalions in a regiment." And a sergeant acting as usher asked a lanky young man whether he was here with any families or friends with whom he wanted to sit, but the young man said no, "Just here to support."

So strong is the bond between the military and its surrounding community that a perceived slight to the former, even of a budgetary nature, comes across as a personal affront to both. This issue assumes whole new political significance for Democrats when these military communities are mapped against a breakdown of the country's electoral college votes. Among the states with the greatest concentration of military installations are California, Texas, Florida, Virginia, Georgia, and Pennsylvania—all holders of key electoral votes.

The point stretches even beyond the military's outermost social or geographic periphery. The military is now among the most trusted institutions in the country. Gallup has tracked confidence in the military and shows that it remained fairly constant in the late 1990s, when around 33 percent of those polled claimed a "great deal" of confidence in the military. Confidence rose to 37.6 percent in 2000, dipped in June 2001 to 31.6 percent, and jumped again to 42.5 percent in 2002. It has remained roughly there, with Americans always placing the military first or second among major American institutions in terms of public confidence.[62] This suggests that the public not only trusts the military, but also regards it as a source of pride. Younger generations of voters are every bit as inclined to view it favorably as those born prior to the baby boom, even though, as a group, younger generations show limited proclivities to join the armed forces themselves. On matters of leadership in general, and on matters of national security specifically, Americans hold members of the armed forces in high regard.

All of these factors—the voting habits of active-duty personnel, veterans, and members of surrounding communities, as well as the national image of the U.S. armed forces—combine to make defense a key political issue even in times of relative international tranquility. These factors, combined with an astute public awareness of the military's overwhelming Republican preference, means that even those who have never served are influenced by the military's position. The resulting de facto endorsement by the military acts as a powerful validating source for Republicans. Unless they find at least a partial remedy for their current disadvantage among service members, Democrats can anticipate continued political setbacks with reverberations that extend well beyond the obvious groups of veterans and others close to the armed forces.[63]

The same argument can be put even more starkly in regard to the 2000 presidential elections, when Al Gore was told by his political advisers that defense issues did not rank in the top ten of voters' major concerns that year, and therefore that he did not need to discuss military matters at any length. This political advice, to be blunt, demonstrated a remarkable lack of awareness about the nature of American national-security politics. It was an extreme example of how polling results can mislead, and of how badly political consultants can be out of tune with the public they purport to understand.

WHY THE DEMOCRATS' PLIGHT IS THE NATION'S PLIGHT

Clearly, this electoral picture should—and does—worry Democrats. It should also concern all citizens, whatever their party affiliation. Independent-minded voters, whether they are registered with one of the two major parties or not, want and deserve a strong set of choices on all major issues when going to the polls. Many thoughtful Republicans believe their party is stronger when it has to compete vigorously on national-security matters—and that means having Democrats who recognize that their plight in recent years and decades is largely self-inflicted (and hence remediable).

Why should all Americans see it this way? First, because of the risks of politicization of the nation's armed forces. The United States rightly values its strong historical tradition of an apolitical military and should want to maintain that tradition. But given Republicans' image of being much tougher and smarter on defense than Democrats, and with the military leaning increasingly further to the right, this tradition is in jeopardy. It would be far healthier for the country if the broader military community were not inherently inclined to vote predominantly for one party over the other.

Today's picture bears little likeness to the proud tradition of General George Marshall, the first career soldier to become secretary of state. As Truman's chief diplomat, "Marshall stood high with Republicans on the Hill in a way almost no one else did, and this irrespective of the fact that he had worked so closely through the war with the Democrat they all liked least, Franklin Roosevelt."[64] His ability to finesse both sides with honesty gained Marshall enormous respect. But as James Traub has pointed out, "The line of descent from those mid-twentieth-century heroes was shattered thirty-five years ago [with Vietnam], and the question of patrimony remains bitterly contested."[65]

In the generation since Vietnam, society has not reflected seriously enough on the implications of highly politicized armed forces; we simply take it for granted that the military will be equally obedient to Republican and Democratic administrations alike. Clinton's travails, however, raised the specter that it could easily be otherwise. During his tenure, much of the military establishment challenged Democrats using tactics similar to those of Republican political operatives: leaks, questionable channels to Capitol Hill, and scripted opinions expressed by retired officers in media debates. Ironically, Republicans including Donald Rumsfeld may be experiencing some of this treatment themselves, with public calls from retired general officers urging the firing of the secretary of defense. This is another sign that things may be changing.

The second reason Americans should be concerned with the partisanship of the military vote relates to the optimal functioning of democracy. The existence of a Democratic Party that is perceived as weak on national security deprives the nation of vigorous debate on subjects that must be analyzed in depth if successful policies are to be developed. Such debate is especially crucial during times of war. It also helps establish the right tone for thinking about future policy, which, though largely absent from candidate Kerry's rhetoric on Iraq, was what voters most wanted to hear, since the decision to invade could not be undone. The fact that the 2001 terrorist attacks continue to pervade American politics, combined with the related fact that national-security issues will remain salient for a long time, should further focus the attention of strategists from both parties on matters of hard power. Republicans need to face up to the fact that the war in Iraq has not, to put it mildly, helped win the war on terrorism, and Democrats owe the electorate a serious alternative to the current security paradigm that is not simply the opposite of George W. Bush's.

DEPOLITICIZING THE MILITARY

This mandate will not prove easy for Democrats. Any honest attempt to fulfill it will force the party to confront the increasingly Republican institutional memory guiding day-to-day policy inside the Pentagon. Further, given the Pentagon's expanded reach under the Bush administration, pushing the necessary reforms with any success will require that a Democratic administration add forceful leadership atop clear policy goals, backed at times with a bit of creative diplomacy.

Campaign agendas and platforms really do matter—they shape how the public views candidates and, by all accounts, affect subsequent policy a good deal.[66] Campaign statements on foreign policy and national security affect not only a candidate's prospects for winning the election, but also—and more importantly—what transpires once the election is won.

Two particularly pressing reform issues beg a place on this agenda. First, the responsible action for Democrats and Bush-administration critics within the GOP as well with regard to Iraq is not simply to decry administration failures, but to renew the U.S. military's long, solid record of post-conflict stabilization (seen most recently in the Balkans). Relatedly, they should strongly support the creation of additional capacity for stabilization and reconstruction missions within the State Department and other parts of the government to improve our ability to help "win the peace." Second, as the debate on Iraq during the 2004 presidential election so emphatically attested, Democrats must make clear that they, like Republicans, understand that effective diplomacy must often be backed by the credible threat and sometimes use of military force.

For U.S. forces, what began as two months of formal conflict in Iraq has since devolved into more than three years of civil-political mishandlings, halting counter-insurgency operations, and difficult reconstruction efforts. Foreign as many of these challenges seem to U.S. troops, current Democratic leaders should remind the military that they were not always so unaccustomed to post-conflict stabilization. Throughout the twentieth century, the military had a strong tradition of performing stabilization tasks, which by any realistic assessment continue to be undeniable aspects of modern military conflict. To pretend otherwise, as Republicans have done over several decades, puts American troops at greater risk and lengthens their stay in post-conflict zones. Rachel Kleinfeld and Matt Spence aptly trace this phenomenon:

> [U.S.] civil affairs units were integral to the success of stabilizing and democratizing Japan and Germany after WWII. In fact, civil-political affairs work has been a key part of military action since the time of the Monroe Doctrine. But beginning in the 1980s, military action to govern countries following conflict came under concerted attack by conservative think tanks. They called such work "soft," and said that it "distracted" from the real work of our military—which was redefined as simply fighting battles, not winning wars.[67]

The result, according to Kleinfeld and Spence, is that conservative discourse has given our military an ever-larger role in foreign policy, while simultaneously stripping the military—and the government, and the nation more generally—of the tools needed to carry out the job. Years of repeating this message "have made even the military itself forget its proud history. Our subsequent lack of preparation for nation-building in Iraq shows the price, in flag-draped coffins, of the narrow conservative view of security."[68] However, the need for change is hardly limited to the U.S. armed forces. As we argue in Chapter Three, a major (though targeted, and relatively economical) increase in the nation's civilian capacity for helping stabilize and rebuild failed or defeated states is also urgently needed.

THE LEGACY OF IRAQ AND THE USE-OF-FORCE QUESTION

Democrats of all stripes also need to become comfortable with American military strength (as their predecessors were) and reconnect it with party values. Let's return to this chapter's opening question: How did Democrats lose an election that was largely a referendum on Iraq?

The answer has less to do with the actual position of the Kerry/Edwards ticket than with the way the candidates and the campaign presented it. The Kerry/Edwards stance was perceived by many as unclear at best, opportunistic and political at worst. Kerry's unfortunate "flip-flopper" image was engineered by the Bush/Cheney campaign, but was exacerbated considerably by the senator's own statements on Iraq. Less mentioned, though perhaps more to blame, however, was his voting record. Had Kerry not wavered in the face of the rising clamor of the antiwar wing of his party, he might have steadfastly voted yes in 2003 on the $87 billion supplemental-funding bill, and thereby escaped what later became the Republicans' flip-flop cudgel (which he reinforced in saying he had voted for the bill before voting against it). He might have offered and emphasized alternative legislation to support the troops in their efforts, perhaps emphasizing a better reconstruction plan than the Bush administration had devised, rather than issuing an apparent rebuff to the military. Again, this was a matter of leadership.

What resulted was the appearance of a "leftward tilt" meant to enliven the Democratic base. But the base was already enraged at Bush over his Iraq policy and hardly needed a rallying point. Despite a number of good specific suggestions, some of them adopted by the Bush administration as it accelerated the transfer of Iraqi sovereignty and brought the United Nations back into the equation, Kerry's treatment of Iraq became perceived as a nostalgic look backward rather than a forceful declaration of a positive way forward. The lesson for Democrats: Positions on matters of war and peace cannot simply be political fodder with which to pound the opposition. Of course, many prominent Democrats understood this all along, among them Senator Joe Biden, House Democratic Whip Steny Hoyer, and Senator Hillary Clinton.[69] Their voices, however, do not always transmit as the party's public image.

The Kerry/Edwards team was not wrong to have complex and nuanced views on the subject of Iraq. And they pushed many of the ideas—more multilateralism, a greater role for the United Nations, more reconstruction efforts designed to create employment for Iraqis, a better training program for Iraqi security forces—that the Bush administration ultimately adopted. But the senators' wavering on so many issues, combined with their antiwar language, alienated crucial swing voters. In addition, their approach also complicated Kerry's efforts to show strong support for the troops deployed abroad and their mission. As President Bush fairly asked, how can you elicit more allied help in Iraq—or the confidence and support of American troops and those who strongly support them—when you are describing the mission as "wrong war, wrong time, wrong place"? Or, to put it differently, looking back, what simple message about Iraq did Kerry manage to convey to the public? It is hard to know, and not clear that the candidate himself had a consistent answer to the question. His statement in the summer of 2004 that he would have done "nearly everything differently" than George W. Bush had done it was not a clear answer to this question.

This is not to suggest that Democrats, any more than all Republicans, need to support the war on Iraq in order to be serious about national security. There was, and continues to be, a serious antiwar argument. The Iraq invasion was a tough call, and the beginning of wisdom on the issue is to recognize as much. By the same token, Democrats seeking to recapture public confidence in their ability to handle national security would do themselves a great disservice in reflexively supporting whatever use of force comes under consideration. While Dean frequently slipped into inappropriate mockery of the Iraq invasion, the substance of his or General Wesley Clark's antiwar stand was as strategically reasonable as Kerry/Edwards' reluctant support for the war or, for that matter, Senator Lieberman's unflinching endorsement of it. At issue between these Democrats was not the appropriateness of this particular manifestation of American military might. It was the appropriateness of U.S. military might itself, as well as resoluteness, conviction, and consistency when applying it.

The Republican view of modern times reasons that the best means of keeping the peace is through military strength.[70] (Traditionalist conservatives lean toward seeing the military as a tool for deterrence, whereas neoconservatives are more activist in their willingness to employ it, but both groups share a strong commitment to the "peace through strength" approach.) This is in part a product of the long-standing Republican tendency to regard strength as the means through which America can propel its values into the world.[71] Democrats could learn from the larger Republican example about the importance of force, taking caution not to divorce Democratic values from any pragmatic and, yes, sometimes even military means of achieving them. In the context of national security, this would mean that Democrats could come to admit, comfortably and unambiguously, that military strength constitutes a critical element in maintaining peace.

What more often transpires in Democratic circles, as Kleinfeld and Spence note, is that "those who work for human rights bask in moral approbation, while those brave souls who work with the military are treated as curiosities. Intelligence remains the field that dare not speak its name."[72] This point of view is not only shortsighted, but also flatly incorrect. Robust military and intelligence services offer more than just an effective last resort of force. They give U.S. diplomats their bargaining power. Without encouraging needless risking of military lives, history warns us that Democrats must be mindful that weakness invites aggression. American servicemen and -women suffer a great disservice when their leaders "are overly fearful of using them intelligently for the missions they were trained to do. [Democrats] owe it to them to accept the critical part power plays in promoting our security, and the security of other nations."[73]

The United States owns no more important asset than its military force. But using force well, using it judiciously, and ensuring maximum international collaboration in the effort are all key. As the current predicament in Iraq painfully demonstrates, there is a distinction between victory as a force for progress and victory as the last man standing—a distinction that is not always decided strictly according to sheer preponderance of power. Jeffrey Record argues that the United States is at a disadvantage against materially weaker foes such as the Iraqi insurgents for two reasons:

> The first is the American tendency to separate war and politics—to view military victory as an end in itself, ignoring war's function as an instrument of policy. The second is the U.S. military's profound aversion to counterinsurgency. Both combine to form a recipe for politically sterile uses of force, especially in protracted hostilities against weaker irregular opponents . . . Approaching war as an apolitical enterprise encourages fatal inattention to the challenges of converting military wins into political successes. It thwarts recognition that insurgencies are first and foremost political struggles that cannot be defeated by military means alone—indeed, that effective counterinsurgency entails the greatest discretion in the use of force. Pursuit of military victory for its own sake also discourages thinking about and planning for the second and by far the most difficult half of wars for regime change: establishing a viable replacement for the destroyed regime. War's object is, after all, a better peace.[74]

The problem has become even more acute in Iraq with the rise of the jihadi element of the insurgency. This and the victory of the Shia Muslim majority in the December 2005 election have combined to turn that initial "cakewalk" of simple "regime change" into a fantasy of fantastic proportions. The mission is still "winnable," if winning is defined very modestly and soberly, as we discuss in the next chapter. Indeed, it is critical for American security that Iraq achieve at least a reasonable degree of stability and political coherence. But the Bush administration predictions of where we would be by 2006 (proudly viewing an idyllic democratic bastion in the Middle East and a shining example of a successful military campaign) have become among the most demonstrably wrong of any prognostications on any major issue in modern American history. It's now up to the Democrats to begin to offer a different vision for the future, one that appreciates that hard power and military matters remain at the core of what's important to Americans in the years ahead.

CHAPTER 2

IRAQ, THE MYTH OF REPUBLICAN SUPERIORITY, AND THE FUTURE

O NE OF THE REIGNING features of Republican governing philosophy has been the notion of their supremacy in matters of foreign policy and national security. The annals of history indeed include examples of deft diplomacy and military prowess under Republican leadership, including the broad opening to China in the 1970s, elements of the Reagan defense buildup, the conduct of the first Gulf War, and the management of the end of the Cold War in Central Europe.

Of course, Republican administrations have had setbacks as well, such as the Iran-Contra scandal, the failure to prevent the bloodshed in the Balkans, and the slaughter of Shia in southern Iraq by Saddam Hussein after Operation Desert Storm. But by selecting Dick Cheney as his running mate in 2000, and giving Colin Powell a nod as his secretary-of-state-to-be, George W. Bush successfully sought to project the same aura of foreign-policy excellence that the public had long associated with the Reagan and Bush I administrations. As one prominent Republican touted after the contested 2000 election was finally decided, "The A team is back in the business of foreign policy, and the amateurs have been sent home."[1]

Perhaps there really was something to the theory that Republicans "got it" in foreign policy, that their inner circle of top officials had figured out how to establish and maintain a quasi priesthood of excellence from decade to decade and administration to administration, that GOP leaders were smart enough to know to keep turning to this elite group of individuals who had helped restore America's military and win the Cold War and who were now ready for equally great things in a new millennium.

In one fell swoop, however, the invasion of Iraq and its fractious aftermath have dispelled any notion of innate Republican superiority in matters of international hard power—particularly in relation to that brand of Republicanism championed by the Bush administration, which often claims (rightly or wrongly) the confident, assertive mantle of Ronald Reagan. This should hardly be a revelation. No American political party has ever had any intrinsic advantage on any issue, and even when one party has dominated a given issue for a lengthy period, the situation has always changed over time.

The Bush administration undoubtedly oversimplified and overstated the case for war in Iraq. It tried frequently, by direct statement or implication, to link Saddam to al Qaeda although the evidence never supported any operational link (as documented by the 9/11 Commission Report[2]). For example, the administration played up a possible meeting between a 9/11 hijacker and an Iraqi intelligence operative in Prague that appears not to have happened; claimed a strong tie between Saddam and al Qaeda based on the simple fact that one key al Qaeda operative was known to have been in Baghdad at one point during Saddam's tenure; and called the Iraq invasion part of the same global war on terror that targeted bin Laden and company in Afghanistan. The Bush administration also overstated the significance of uncertain intelligence, later proved wrong, that Saddam was making major progress toward nuclear-weapons capability.

That said, there was a real case for overthrowing Saddam, even with the benefit of crystalline hindsight. Compliance with sanctions had eroded significantly over time. Saddam was interested in nuclear weapons and might someday have attained them, even if not imminently. His refusal to allow proper weapons inspections except at the point of a cocked gun (which could not be kept cocked indefinitely) made it likely that someday he would resume or accelerate illicit weapons programs. His overdeveloped sense of vengeance and hatred made him a source of genuine worry in terms of potential terrorism, if not directed against the American homeland then at least against Israelis (and the occasional American citizen, such as former President Bush). So while the haste and hubris that characterized the Bush administration's march to war in Iraq can and should be castigated, the basic decision to confront Saddam was not unreasonable (even if it was debatable). And in fairly judging the effectiveness of the Iraq operation, it must also be noted that—despite prewar predictions of a cakewalk from some administration cronies (and officials), and despite overly optimistic and breathless rhetoric about how a new Iraqi democracy could purportedly spark deep reform throughout the region—any effort to build a democracy in a large Arab state that had no democratic traditions was bound to be exceedingly difficult.[3]

But the litany of key mistakes made in the course of the Iraq operation has been extensive and profound. Mistakes that had been anticipated by many, if not most, outside critics were committed by the administration. Its theory of easy victory left it woefully unprepared for the almost inevitable difficulties of stabilizing and rebuilding a country whose politics and security institutions had been decimated. The execution of the Iraq war has verged on incompetence, and the lessons of this experience for the United States have been both dramatic and traumatic.

There is a consistent theme in Bush-administration talking points about waiting for historians to decide about the conduct of the entire Iraq war. However, there is ample evidence to begin that process of accounting and establishing accountability now. The Iraq mission, even if we manage to attain a degree of stability and earn an honorable redeployment of U.S. forces, has been tragic in myriad ways for the nation and for its soldiers, sailors, and Marines. Moreover, while we can never know what might have been, most of the major mistakes in formulation and implementation were not only predictable but also predicted. Had some of these now well-known errors in planning and preparation been avoided, the post-Saddam period in Iraq might well have gotten off to a far better start and allowed the building of a positive momentum that could have deprived insurgents and terrorists the witch's brew of anger, chaos, economic malaise, and political uncertainty that they have thrived upon since.

The first explanation of what happened is the president's own personal proclivity for absolute certitude on policy issues that are core to his political makeup and worldview. The second is that Bush team members probably believed their own press clips and spin about their masterful status in the making of American foreign policy and did not question (or allow others to question) their assumptions about the world in general and Iraq in particular. Further, they tended to dismiss virtually every aspect of the Clinton-administration legacy, even on issues such as nation building where the Clinton administration had considerable experience.

With much less effort than the Clinton administration had employed in the Balkans, they thought they could achieve even more sweeping results—a wave of new democracies that would redefine the geopolitics of the broader Middle East region. They disagreed sharply with many aspects of the previous Bush administration's worldview, including its focus on multilateralism and building useful coalitions. The George W. Bush team also largely shunned bipartisan approaches to difficult international problems, seeking instead to play for domestic advantages on foreign policy rather than painstakingly building domestic support across political lines. Finally, even while the Bush team had some deep talent on its national-security roster, it has been one of the most divided and contentious governing groups in modern history. Divisions within the administration seriously impeded overall effectiveness—especially because on several key issues, President Bush resolved the disputes by siding with the wrong people making the wrong arguments.

The objective in making the case for Republican fallibility is not to encourage voters to immediately and reflexively reward Democrats at the polls. Indeed, the very notion that the Bush administration's poor performance and weak approval ratings will inevitably produce political gains for the minority party in 2006 and beyond should be treated with the same skepticism that the original plans to rebuild Iraq deserved. Some Democratic political consultants have argued that, in the 2006 elections, Democrats should allow Republicans to fall of their own weight and the Democratic Party should work toward producing a new vision for American power and security only in time for the 2008 elections. The strategy of waiting until the 2008 presidential campaign to unfurl and run on a new platform of ideas gained common currency in 2006. But this course of action is dangerous. It presumes that good ideas and vision can be turned on like a switch, when the truth is that smart policy proposals take time, testing, and perseverance. Indeed, most of the subjects requiring good ideas and fresh leadership today are extraordinarily complex and contentious. Political leaders need the practice of wrestling with them, and campaigning seriously about them, to develop and project expertise, convey a sense of confidence, and communicate a constructive agenda to the nation.

At a time when Republicans, particularly neoconservative Republicans, have been brought back to Earth by their own historic miscalculations and mistakes, the United States needs new ideas and inspirations in foreign policy and national security. This need presents opportunities for Democrats as well as moderate Republicans such as Nebraska senator Chuck Hagel who have been out of favor with many in their own party in recent years. It also creates responsibilities for all political candidates and those who advise them. The country needs their ideas, their inspiration, and their leadership.

The Iraq experience also constitutes a warning about how to understand and employ hard power. It is not enough to invoke kinetic military instruments when undertaking a campaign as ambitious as the overthrow of an enemy regime. U.S. technology, revolutions in military affairs, and a neoconservative confidence about the value and effectiveness of the American armed forces do not by themselves a foreign policy make. Hard power is effective only when used legitimately and comprehensively. The United States needs substantial international support for major military operations, especially wars of choice. Together with the rest of the international community, it also needs the full range of stabilization and reconstruction capabilities that are so critical to ensuring a sustainable peace after conflict.

The United States and its partners may still achieve some very modest success from the dangerous morass in Iraq—helping build a new nation that, while violent and strife-ridden and plagued by enormous economic and social challenges, may still become something approximating a democracy that lives in peace with its neighbors, eschews weapons of mass destruction, and gradually stabilizes. In fact, many Americans still hope and believe in the possibility of this outcome, however difficult and distant it might currently seem. But even this admittedly modest set of societal accomplishments will only be achieved if the United States remains an active player—and this will entail, among other things, maintaining at least some component of military power on the ground in Iraq—for years to come. This is an unwelcome reality for a nation growing weary of the war, but it is a reality born out daily on the dangerous urban battlefields of Iraq. Iraq would not long hold together without an armed American presence there.

Still, despite the best hopes for a passable outcome, the overall U.S. performance in Iraq has been a profound disappointment. The costs have been exponentially higher, the plausible benefits of the invasion much more limited, and the prospects for even a belated, partial success substantially worse than should reasonably have been expected.

THE EXTREME NEGLIGENCE OF
PLANNING FOR POST-SADDAM IRAQ

Simply put, the U.S. defense planning system did not work in Iraq. Indeed, it failed badly in preparing for the aftermath of Saddam's fall from power at several levels, including the most important ones. The first three phases of the operation, including the buildup, initial preparatory actions (largely carried out by covert teams), and the main air-ground thrust, were conducted with impressive professionalism. But what is now commonly called Phase IV—an umbrella term that covers several steps in any stabilization effort, such as the initial period of international trusteeship as well as subsequent periods when sovereignty and responsibility are transferred increasingly to indigenous actors—was handled so badly that the downsides associated with the armed campaign have now outweighed the virtues of the earlier parts of the operation. In other words, while Operation Iraqi Freedom, or Cobra II, achieved a worthy goal in the removal of Saddam, on balance the entirety of the U.S. operation in Iraq must be seen as falling far short of what was required.

The problem with the Iraq mission was not Secretary of Defense Rumsfeld's decision to become heavily involved in the war planning per se. Indeed, Rumsfeld was fulfilling his responsibilities in demanding a fundamental reassessment of a plan for invading Iraq that, when last formally approved in the mid–1990s, would have required half a million troops and more than half a year of preparation.[4] Rumsfeld also allowed himself to be talked out of some of the bad ideas he and other top Pentagon civilians may have initially held about how to win such a war. Notably, the initial hopes among some civilians that a war plan could be executed with only a few tens of thousands of American troops were ultimately dashed by a responsible military planning process. By this standard, at least, the invasion force that was ultimately employed was in fact not tiny, though it was still small.[5] Rumsfeld and, to an even greater degree, CIA director George Tenet had usefully involved themselves in war planning in Afghanistan as well.[6]

Yet even as Rumsfeld's involvement in war planning was perfectly reasonable, he would ultimately end up bearing the lion's share of responsibility for a plan that lacked the necessary elements to ensure success. The essential problem, of course, was with the part of the operation after Saddam was overthrown. The plans were constrained by Pollyannaish assumptions about what Iraq would be like after Saddam was gone.[7]

As a result, only minimal policing capability was secured. This left the operation vulnerable to a debilitating loss of public order.[8] Military force levels were not adequate to guard weapons caches and key infrastructure and maintain presence on the streets, as Ambassador Paul Bremer himself quickly noted upon arriving in the country.[9] Former Secretary of State Powell has now revealed that he too objected to the modest force levels.[10] Even worse, perhaps, the U.S. military had no guidance on how to reestablish order after major conventional combat operations were over because Pentagon leaders starting with Rumsfeld had assumed, incredibly, that order would not be severely disrupted.

Invading another country with the intention of destroying its existing government, but without a serious strategy for providing security thereafter, defies logic and falls far short of proper professional military standards of competence. That the Bush administration did this in Iraq was, in fact, unconscionable.

This lack of proper planning, and the failure to confront the Saddam Fedayeen when opportunities presented themselves during the invasion (which allowed them to escape and reconstitute as a guerrilla force), have been thoroughly documented by George Packer as well as by Michael Gordon and Bernard Trainor.[11] The latter authors quote a telling comment made by Secretary of State Condoleezza Rice: "The concept was that we would defeat the army, but the institutions would hold, everything from the ministries to police forces." This was a reasonable aspiration, a desirable goal. But as an *expectation* of what would occur in post-Saddam Iraq, it was naively optimistic to the point of being irresponsible.[12]

Why did the Bush administration fail to recognize that overthrowing Saddam could shatter Iraq's security institutions and thus leave responsibility for maintaining civil order in the hands of the American-led coalition? It is not hard to hypothesize. The explanation surely includes the administration's desire to rally domestic and international support by portraying the Iraq war as a relatively easy undertaking; the administration's disdain for nation building; and the Pentagon leadership's unrealistic hope that Ahmed Chalabi and the generally distrusted and weak Iraqi National Congress might somehow assume control of the country after Saddam fell.[13] Accordingly, Pentagon leaders publicly predicted that U.S. forces would be mostly out of Iraq by the fall of 2003; that the U.S. costs of reconstruction would total in the low billions; that it did not matter if the United States failed to pay Iraqi civil servants and military personnel because their own country would be able to take care of them soon enough—or because it would be easy enough to recruit and train new military personnel.[14]

Many people outside the Pentagon did recognize, and emphasize, the centrality of the post-Saddam security mission. Some were at the State Department, though State's Future of Iraq Project produced an extremely long and somewhat unfocused set of papers that attempted to identify the key features of post-conflict stabilization inside the country rather than a workable game plan.[15] Other analysts were also prescient, and much more cogent, in their emphasis on the need to prepare for peacekeeping and policing tasks. One of the more notable efforts was a study published in February 2003 by the Army War College, which underscored the importance not only of providing security but also of taking full advantage of the first few months of the post-Saddam period, when Iraqi goodwill would be at its high point.[16] Some mid-level officials at CENTCOM also recognized the importance of post-Saddam planning, even if they were not authorized to carry it out.

These think-tank studies and reports did not develop precise estimates of how many troops would be needed to stabilize post-Saddam Iraq or lay out detailed rules of engagement for restoring security. But General Erik Shinseki, the Army chief of staff, provided the Congress with its clearest advice on the former point when he estimated in response to a question during a Congressional hearing that "several hundred thousand" troops might be needed for the overall operation. And formal planning mechanisms were available for such purposes, notably the large planning staff at Central Command in Tampa, Florida. But they were not properly instructed to develop detailed plans.

Previous CENTCOM plans for overthrowing Saddam had indeed given attention to this critical issue, but throughout much of the 1990s, these plans relied on a brute-force approach to seizing Iraq that had its own set of potential downsides, such as the likelihood that surprise would be totally sacrificed during a lengthy buildup period. A major revision of the war plan begun late in the decade by General Tony Zinni was never completed.[17] But these previous efforts laid a groundwork that could easily have been built upon in the year leading up to the March 2003 invasion. Instead, they were effectively discarded. According to General Tommy Franks, while planners spent many hours in discussions about Phase IV, and while Franks himself always cautioned that this stage of the operation could take years, it was ultimately assumed that many soldiers from the regular Iraqi army would be promptly available to play a large role in keeping postwar order.[18]

Recent American actions in the Balkans provided modern-day experience with the challenges of post-conflict stabilization missions, making naïveté about or unfamiliarity with their typical nature an unacceptable excuse for the lack of planning for post-Saddam Iraq. To be fair, it should be noted that many aspects of the Balkan peace plans and the effort to ensure stabilization and reconstruction there could be developed sequentially—after battlefield victories were achieved in the more classic sense. That is because there were still cohesive, if battered, indigenous security forces in place in Bosnia and Kosovo, which allowed for something akin to a classic surrender and transfer of responsibility—as opposed to the profound power vacuum that resulted in Iraq.

Still, the United States had learned much from prior post-conflict experiences that should have been applicable to Iraq. Instead, many basic tasks that should have been seen as necessary in Iraq—policing the streets, guarding huge weapons depots, protecting key infrastructure, maintaining public order—were simply not planned for.[19] The minimal planning that did occur was taken out of CENTCOM's hands, placed under the control of Under Secretary of Defense Douglas Feith and retired general Jay Garner, and did not seriously commence until January 2003. That effort was not only way too late, but reportedly unfocused, shallow, and too dependent on wildly optimistic scenarios that saw Ahmed Chalabi (or perhaps some of Saddam's more moderate generals) taking charge without the need for strong U.S. involvement.[20]

Even as it became apparent that the initial assumptions were wrong, the Pentagon was unresponsive, even dismissive of the new realities taking shape on the ground. The initial post-invasion chaos was famously attributed by Donald Rumsfeld to the fact that "freedom's untidy," not that Iraq had become an anarchic environment that only U.S.-led coalition military forces were in a position to stabilize.[21]

How much did it matter that the coalition got off to a poor start in securing post-Saddam Iraq, allowing chaos to reign in much of the country for weeks before fully responding? In fairness, it cannot be known for sure. In a country rife with weapons, and plagued by the continued presence of thousands of Baathists from Saddam's various elite security forces who had melted into the population rather than fight hard against the invading coalition, violent resistance was probably inevitable. Porous borders and foreign fighters exacerbated the situation, as did serious sectarian divisions, a long Iraqi history of colonialism and anticolonialism, and a strong disdain for occupiers.

There are, however, several powerful counterarguments to the claim that post-Saddam Iraq was destined to be chaotic. First, porous borders and large unprotected weapons caches were to a large extent preventable. A more complete Phase IV operational blueprint would have done much to secure them through better planning and, quite probably, more troops. As the head of the Coalition Provisional Authority, Ambassador Paul Bremer later argued, "The single most important change . . . would have been having more troops in Iraq at the beginning and throughout." Bremer claimed to have "raised this issue a number of times with our government" but was overruled.[22] Beyond the issue of troop numbers is the question of specific rules of engagement for those troops. Without clear guidance, soldiers do not know whether to shoot looters, try to block them, or stand aside; they also cannot know where to employ their limited resources most effectively. The absence of a plan, and of clear rules and regulations, for the post-Saddam period was in fact a more egregious oversight than the shortage of troops. There was a military logic to using a relatively small force and moving fast to unseat Saddam—and therefore ending up with temporary troop shortages in the stabilization period. There was, however, no logic in failing to tell these American soldiers and Marines what to do with their local monopoly on military power once Saddam had fallen.

Second, although violent resistance from hard-core Baathists and jihadists was perhaps to be expected, the willingness of Iraqi "fence sitters" to take up arms against the U.S.-led coalition out of frustration appears to have increased over time. Indeed, while estimates of the strength of insurgencies are never reliable, it is nonetheless striking that the Iraqi resistance was estimated to number only 5,000 hardened fighters in mid- to late 2003, but was thought by some U.S. officials to approach 20,000 in size by mid–2004. The passivity of the U.S.-led coalition during those precious first weeks, combined perhaps with mediocre counterinsurgency techniques in places (as Tom Ricks has documented), gave Iraqi fence sitters a rationale to take up violence alongside Baathists and jihadists.[23] It created a dynamic in Iraq in which high levels of street crime combined with the growing insurgency to increase the population's insecurities, which then also impeded economic-recovery activities. With the security environment and the economy both stagnant, dissatisfaction grew, and the resistance had more potential recruits to draw upon.[24]

Finally, opinion polls in the occupation's early months showed a general happiness among Iraqis that Saddam was gone. That translated into a certain goodwill toward the occupation forces, or at least a willingness to tolerate their presence as a necessary means of ensuring stability.[25] Wasting this moment of Iraqi cooperation meant losing something that could never be recovered. This was not just a matter of losing a popularity contest. The general population's willingness to provide intelligence on the resistance—a key ingredient in any successful counterinsurgency—is a function of the perceived risks of doing so. Citizens are more likely to provide information when they are convinced that doing so will help defeat an insurgency; they are less likely to take such risky steps if they see the tide of battle favoring the rebels. If a major effort had been taken to nip the resistance in the bud, that effort could have developed a self-perpetuating momentum.

None of these arguments are conclusive. But, especially when taken together, they strongly suggest that establishing early momentum would have made a huge difference in the subsequent course of the coalition's counterinsurgency operation.

THE STATE OF IRAQ IN MID-2006

In theory, getting off to a bad start in Iraq might not have been disastrous if the situation had been properly diagnosed and operational policies had been improved soon thereafter. Many U.S. wars have started badly but still been won. This was certainly the story of the 1999 NATO war over Kosovo, the first desperate months of the Korean War when U.S. forces were overmatched against the invading North Korean Army, and indeed the U.S. military operations in Africa during the early part of World War II. Even the Afghanistan invasion had bogged down for a few weeks before the Taliban was overthrown in 2001.

Tragically, the United States and its partners may not be able to truly reverse the mistakes of that bad first year and more in Iraq. The enormity of the initial miscalculations was matched only by the administration's stubborn refusals to recognize troubling developments on the ground, including the facts that the United States faced a determined insurgency rather than just a "handful of dead enders," that our early training program for Iraqi security forces was woefully inadequate, and that our presence was increasingly perceived as a clumsy and ineffective occupation force that did not provide security to the Iraqi people. While the administration clung obstinately to its initial judgments, Iraqi perceptions quickly moved on.

It is clear now that too much momentum was lost; too many Iraqis became cynical about America's intentions and hateful towards its soldiers and Marines; too many weapons were leeched out of arms caches; and too many radical jihadists from abroad snuck into the country. The security environment deteriorated so much that it became impractical to restore it, especially with the modest numbers of coalition forces available. As of mid–2006, an overview of the situation in Iraq might begin like this: On the battlefields of Iraq's streets, the war seems to have stalemated. Overall levels of violence have hardly changed in two years (and are worse than in 2003 or even the latter years of Saddam's rule). Economic recovery, after impressively bouncing to 2002 levels, has stagnated since 2004. Despite it all, there is still some hope, reflected most clearly in the Iraqi political process and in the indomitable optimism of the Iraqi people—or at least Iraqi Shia and Kurds. But the positive feelings are not shared by the country's Sunni Arabs, and even the optimism of Kurds and Shia is now being threatened by political disarray and increased sectarian strife.

A more detailed examination of trends in Iraq underscores the frustration involved in efforts to stabilize and rebuild the nation. Iraq's economy continues to disappoint in almost every sector. Although Iraq had a fairly quick recovery in 2003 and early 2004, when gross domestic product was restored to Saddam Hussein–era levels, violence and instability have slowed further progress, and critical setbacks in some areas have led many Iraqis to conclude that some economic conditions were better under Saddam. Although subsidies for gasoline and other goods that have been costing the Iraqi government about $10 billion a year (or a third of gross domestic product) have been reduced, projections that the country's economy will grow by 10 percent a year for the rest of the decade look increasingly suspect. Current growth sputters along at less than 5 percent, despite sky-high prices for oil exports. Most utilities (except telephones and Internet services) are still performing below Baathist-era levels. Unemployment remains very high.

Politically, the opportunity offered by democracy may slip away as sectarian battle lines become entrenched. In the first part of 2006, the most difficult task seemed to be forming a coalition government. But the anger of Sunni Arabs—the group primarily responsible for Iraq's insurgency—has deeper roots than these recent challenges. They remain deeply troubled by halting efforts to reintegrate lower-level former Baathists into society, gain fair compensation for disputed property taken from them (and returned to those Kurds who claim to be its rightful owners) in and around Kirkuk, and, perhaps most of all, ensure fair and equitable access to Iraq's future oil revenue. The loya jirga model that was used so well in Afghanistan to create some level of consensus and national support for the new government there was discarded in Iraq by Ambassador Paul Bremer. The constitution that was negotiated and then approved by voters in 2005 creates a framework in which Kurds and Shia are both claiming exclusive rights to future oil revenues from new wells. This outcome, combined with the less rational Sunni Arab sense of both superiority and paranoia vis-à-vis Shia and Kurds, has created a psychology of anger and of support for violence. The lack of real progress on the ground since the transfer of sovereignty reinforces the widespread Sunni Arab sense of estrangement. It contributes to remarkably high levels of Sunni Arab approval for violence against coalition troops (almost 90 percent in early 2006, according to pollsters at the Program on International Policy Attitudes)[26] and even against their own government.

To put it differently, and starkly: After failing to maintain the invading coalition's monopoly on the use of force in the weeks and months after Saddam fell, the Bush administration also failed to develop or implement a viable political strategy for rebuilding Iraq. Confusing the mechanics of holding elections with the development of true democracy, it compounded its initial errors and largely squandered three critical years. Because it did not combine its initial application of military force with an integrated civilian plan for transition, it botched one of the most fundamental tests of wielding hard power in the twenty-first century.

There have been a few hopeful signs on the security front. For example, in the first months of 2006, American troop fatalities in Iraq declined substantially. So did car bombings. Unfortunately, civilian casualties have been as high as ever and sectarian strife has increasingly become a severe problem, which it remains as of this writing in the summer of 2006. Not only does the country now face a protracted insurgency, it also confronts the specter of possible civil war. By late March 2006, according to the International Republican Institute (an American outfit loosely linked with the GOP), only 30 percent of Iraqis expressed positive views about the future, and most rated the security environment and the economic situation mediocre or poor.[27]

Iraqi security forces continue to improve, with far higher percentages having reached the upper half of the four-tier readiness rating system—

meaning that they can take the lead on most types of operations. These statistics may point to the possibility of a troop-drawdown strategy for the United States. But the worsening of sectarian violence means that even some Sunni leaders now realize a precipitous and complete American troop withdrawal would risk plunging the country into all-out civil war.[28]

Coalition troops have proven unable to suppress the insurgency or establish an effective Iraqi government. The insurgents, however, have not yet defeated any major American or British units in battle. Nor have they gained substantial active indigenous or foreign support. It is still possible that a more effective and integrated U.S. approach could weaken the insurgency, diminish the sectarian violence, create more capable government institutions, and reinvigorate the Iraqi economy sufficiently to allow U.S. field commanders to declare a dubious "victory" of sorts and withdraw. But the opportunity for even a new strategy to reverse the situation is rapidly fading.[29]

Most of the current U.S. public discourse around the war in Iraq revolves around conditions and timelines for the withdrawal of our troops. Congressional critics in both parties have focused on this subject somewhat exclusively, and there has been too little attention paid to how best to rescue a bad situation with innovative policies and better oversight.[30] Democrats have focused mostly on missteps in Iraq. But there has been a less vibrant debate about the potential downsides of a precipitous American military withdrawal and how the dangerously eroding U.S. position in Iraq might somehow be made more promising.

CASUALTIES, COSTS, AND OTHER CONSEQUENCES

The Iraq operation has been enormously costly for the U.S. military, American taxpayers, America's reputation around the world, and U.S. national-security policy. Unfortunately, the litany of mistakes helps set the context for the next U.S. administration, which will see some aspects of its global power diminished as a result of Iraq. A key challenge for future leaders will be to overcome these constraints with a positive new vision and strong leadership, rather than allowing them to set the tone for America's future global role.

Any assessment of costs must begin with the human toll. As of mid–2006, more than 2,500 U.S. troops have died in Iraq. Nearly 20,000

American troops have experienced combat-induced wounds, roughly half of them serious. Improvements in military medicine have resulted in miraculous achievements on battlefield operating tables, and many people have survived wounds that would likely have been fatal in earlier conflicts. Whereas during the Vietnam War, about 25 percent of the seriously wounded died, in Iraq, only approximately 10 percent have been lost.[31] Yet better medical technology and practices have meant that hundreds of Iraqi veterans have survived injuries so severe that military doctors have generated a new term: "polytrauma."[32]

Besides physical wounds, many soldiers also have experienced severe mental trauma. An October 2005 study found that more than one-quarter of U.S. troops who had deployed in Iraq and Afghanistan between October 2003 and February 2005 sought treatment in Veterans Administration hospitals for various maladies. More than 30 percent of these suffered from some type of mental disorder or severe psychological stress. Doctors diagnosed almost an equal percentage with "ill-defined conditions."[33] The tripling of the divorce rate among U.S. Army officers from mid–2002 to mid–2005 provides another likely indicator of psychological stress—and highlights another aspect of the serious human toll that has already resulted from the war.[34]

To be sure, the Iraq operation has taught the U.S. military a great deal and produced a generation of battle-tested officers and enlisted personnel. It has also debunked the dangerous myth of the 1990s: that somehow American forces could prepare almost exclusively for a future of high-tech warfare in which traditional infantry skills and other such capabilities would be of diminished importance. But the cost for this education has been enormous.

Other members of the international coalition and foreign workers in Iraq have suffered substantially from the war as well. More than one hundred British soldiers have died in Iraq, as have a comparable number from other coalition nations in aggregate. About one hundred journalists have died in Iraq as well.[35] The Committee to Protect Journalists said Iraq in 2005 had the distinction of being "the most dangerous place in the world to work as a journalist."[36] Furthermore, more than three hundred civilian contractors working for the coalition have been killed since November 2003, when they became clear targets of insurgents.[37] The number of Iraqi casualties since the 2003 invasion is harder to determine, but the reputable range is roughly 50,000 to 100,000 fatalities.

Whatever the exact number, this range certainly represents far fewer deaths than occurred during any given three-year period in the bloodiest phases of Saddam's rule (in all, some 1 million died from 1980 to 1991). But the number of Iraqi deaths since 2003 is probably higher than in most three-year periods from 1992 to 2003.[38] On December 12, 2005, President Bush himself said that about 30,000 Iraqis had been killed since the war began.[39]

The direct financial costs of the Iraq war will surely exceed $300 billion by the end of 2006.[40] (Operations in Afghanistan cost about $1 billion a month.) The long-term costs of the war in equipment replacement, health care, and reconstruction expenses will be many tens of billions of dollars more. Since the Bush administration has persisted in cutting taxes despite the war—dangerously perpetuating a view that war is possible without some societal sacrifice—the United States has experienced its largest budget deficits in history. The Congressional Budget Office has forecasted that the president's proposed budget for fiscal year 2007 will lead to a budget deficit of more than $300 billion; that projection is an improvement upon earlier expectations but still very large by historical and macroeconomic standards.[41] Whereas during the Clinton administration, economists were contemplating how to manage multiyear budget surpluses, they now debate how quickly interest rates need to rise to compensate for the inflationary effects of out-of-control federal spending. The war's costs have deprived the nation of the fiscal cushion that would be helpful for responding adequately to unplanned emergencies such as Hurricane Katrina or a possible avian-flu pandemic. They also have complicated efforts to manage the coming retirement wave by making it more difficult to restructure Social Security and other major entitlement programs. Over the long term, the fiscal problems engendered by the war may undermine a key pillar of American power—the health of the U.S. economy.

The costs of the war are, of course, even broader than such figures can convey. Relations with major American allies have been harmed—though perhaps the damage is reparable if the United States makes a major shift in the way it engages its allies over Iraq and other issues. However, damage to the U.S. reputation has been extensive in the Islamic world beyond Iraq, and this has had severe and even deadly consequences. Although this is hard to measure, the U.S.-led invasion and occupation of Iraq probably has motivated scores of people to join anti-American terrorist groups. Analysts Peter Bergen and Alec Reynolds note that "the year 2003 saw the highest incidence of significant terrorist attacks in two decades, and then, in 2004, astonishingly, that number tripled."[42] The December 2004 report of the National Intelligence Council (NIC), "Mapping the Global Future," warns, "The al-Qa'ida membership that was distinguished by having trained in Afghanistan will gradually dissipate, to be replaced in part by experienced survivors of the conflict in Iraq." According to the authors, "Iraq and other possible conflicts in the future could provide recruitment, training grounds, technical skills, and language proficiency for a new class of terrorists who are 'professionalized' and for whom political violence becomes an end in itself."[43] Polls show that millions of Iraqis accept the legitimacy of suicide attacks against coalition military forces, a sentiment tragically bolstered by their almost universal belief that the presence of these troops has not improved Iraqis' security.[44] The skills guerrillas develop to attack military targets in Iraq could assist them to assault civilians in other countries.

Besides generating more terrorist threats, the war has increased other signs of anti-Western and especially anti-American sentiment. In many countries, opposition to the Bush administration's policies has metamorphosed into hostility toward American values, American culture, American companies, and even the American people.[45] The sympathy that much of humanity felt for Americans after September 11, 2001, has largely vanished. According to the June 2006 Pew Global Attitudes Survey, foreigners' views of the United States plummeted after the Iraq war began in March 2003 and have yet to recover in most cases. In most major European countries, China has a better image than the United States. Majorities in every country surveyed besides the United States wanted to see another country challenge U.S. global military supremacy.[46] In fairness, America's reputation had suffered in some parts of the world before George W. Bush came to office—in large part, undoubtedly, due to the simple fact that as the world's only superpower, the United States engenders resentment among many. But the degree to which post–9/11 sympathy for the United States has been squandered since that tragic date is stunning.

Concern about the extraordinary rendition and subsequent treatment of people identified by U.S. authorities as suspected terrorists at Abu Ghraib, Guantanamo Bay, and other detention and interrogation facilities has tarnished the image of the United States as a leading supporter of international human rights. Vice President Dick Cheney's prominent lobbying of Congress to oppose rules banning torture of detained terrorism suspects has only exacerbated the problem. Representatives of other nations have cited these practices in response to U.S. criticisms of their human-rights policies, and the United States has arguably lost some of the high ground that once supported its attempts to influence other states on their handling of political prisoners.[47]

Former Secretary of State Colin Powell has said that the Abu Ghraib scandal created a "terrible public diplomacy crisis" for the United States.[48] The abuse of Iraqi prisoners at Abu Ghraib—partly caused by civilian Pentagon leaders' poor prewar planning, lax oversight, brutal standards for interrogation procedures, and use of civilian contractors and inadequately trained reservists to support overtaxed active-duty forces—has aroused particular ire among foreigners. In the movie *Valley of the Wolves: Iraq*, the most expensive Turkish film ever made, a Jewish doctor cuts out the organs of detainees at Abu Ghraib and sells them to wealthy clients in London, New York, and Tel Aviv. This is only the latest crude manifestation of anti-American sentiment in a country whose population had generally been favorably disposed toward the United States before the Iraq invasion.[49]

Other American interests have suffered too. The Bush administration's sustained preoccupation with Iraq has resulted in its giving short shrift to other vital U.S. foreign-policy priorities. A telling example is the administration's lack of active work to curb the spread of nuclear weapons. Although President Bush justified invading Iraq by citing the need to prevent Saddam Hussein from sharing weapons of mass destruction with terrorists, his administration has chosen to rely primarily on other governments to persuade Iran and especially North Korea to desist. Since Bush assumed office in January 2001, Pyongyang has quite possibly built eight or more nuclear weapons while Washington, distracted by Iraq, largely has stood aside in the vain hope that China might help curb North Korea's nuclear ambitions. By making it more difficult for the administration to threaten military force or even strong economic coercion against Iran, the Iraqi quagmire also has led the administration to rely on European and Russian initiatives to circumscribe Tehran's nuclear program. Furthermore, officials in Washington have yet to devote sufficient attention to developing a comprehensive strategy for managing China's growing strength and increasing sophistication.

The latest quadrennial survey conducted by the Pew Research Center and the Council on Foreign Relations of 520 prominent Americans in foreign affairs, the media, the military, and other fields found that 88 percent of the respondents blamed the Iraq war for what they saw as a precipitous decline in American prestige in recent years.[50] These foreign-policy elites also feared that the Iraq war had hurt rather than helped the U.S.-led war against terrorism.

Many of the above costs of war have been well documented and discussed before. But another cost has not yet been sufficiently appreciated—America's will to engage confidently and assertively in the world. This U.S. strength, developed over the course of a century, is now threatened—and future leaders will have to work hard to mitigate the damage.

The Pew survey mentioned above also suggests that the Iraq war has made the American elite less inclined to see their nation pursue an activist role in world affairs. For example, these opinion leaders expressed declining support for the United States' being either the "single world leader" or "most assertive of the leading nations." They also showed profound skepticism about U.S. efforts to promote democracy abroad, suggesting that the war might undermine a core tenet of American foreign policy.[51] A February 2006 article in *The Economist* similarly rued the fact that opposition to the Iraq war was contributing to rising isolationist sentiment among Americans on a range of foreign-policy issues.[52]

IRAQ AND THE FUTURE

We are at a critical juncture in Iraq. Defeat is not inevitable and a defeatist attitude will be both self-reinforcing and self-fulfilling. An early, inauspicious exit from Iraq is likely to trigger another bout of isolation similar to the post-Vietnam malaise that took the country nearly a generation to recover from (some would argue that the nation has never fully recovered from the trauma). Isolationism, too, is not inevitable, and the tendency toward withdrawal from global affairs must be strenuously resisted. So must the temptation to assume that, since Iraq is the Bush administration's project, we can count on the incumbent administration to solve the problem (and in the process to absorb all the negative public sentiments and onerous political consequences for the debacle). Preserving America's global interests and avoiding a potentially disastrous withdrawal from global affairs requires avoiding a stinging defeat in Iraq—and for that, an enduring American commitment is indispensable, as is a policy for at least some modest level of success.

In March 2006, when asked how long American troops would remain engaged in Iraq, President Bush stated that his successor and future Iraqi governments would make that decision. He was almost surely right. Although it was the first time Bush had spoken so plainly, Secretary of Defense Donald Rumsfeld had been saying for months that stabilization and counterinsurgency campaigns typically take a decade—even when successful. Some hark back to U.S. experiences in Japan and Germany after World War II, remembering that it took a half decade in each case to help a new government get on its feet. But for Iraq, a nation that lacks strong democratic traditions, Korea may be a better model. There, the United States needed to help defend South Korea from North Korea, and then help Seoul inch its way toward true stability and democracy for more than three decades. A more optimistic but still sobering analogy would be the experiences of Central Europe after the Cold War, where about ten years was required to achieve a general sense of stability, or of NATO operations in the Balkans, where foreign troops have already been present for more than ten years in Bosnia and more than seven in Kosovo. This is not what many Americans want to hear, but to suggest that the United States can soon wash its hands of the realities and enduring responsibilities of Iraq and still cheat defeat would be the height of political irresponsibility.

BROAD GUIDELINES FOR POLICY

What, then, should be America's broad policy guidelines in Iraq in the future? First, the United States, working increasingly in a supporting role to the Iraqi government and people, must strive resolutely to win this war. Defeat would set back democracy in the Middle East, embolden terrorists, likely further destabilize the oil-producing regions of the Middle East, make other nations question American staying power, and shake public attitudes and confidence here at home. These dangerous consequences could be mitigated with considerable effort and over time—consider how the United States recovered from defeat in Vietnam—but it would be far better for the United States to stay a difficult course in Iraq until some level of stability is attained.

Second, it is still probably possible to achieve a flawed victory on the ground in Iraq, though it would not nearly approach the level of success initially expected and predicted by the Bush administration. Iraq will not soon be a beacon of stability and prosperity to inspire the region and the world; instead, its people have essentially exchanged tyranny and some limited measure of stability for democracy and instability. To date, however, that is a trade that most Iraqi Shia and Kurds seem prepared to accept, even as they resent the actions of insurgents and terrorists—as well as the mistakes made by the United States—that have made Iraq by far the most violent and unsettled country in the region. The United States, meanwhile, has traded a country that had been a source of regional insecurity for a country that can no longer plausibly develop weapons of mass destruction or attack other nations—but in the process, we have risked triggering a sectarian conflagration in the Middle East and have provided al Qaeda a much greater foothold in Iraq than it had before, at huge costs to our military, budget, and international popularity and prestige.

Third, Iraq cannot soon hold itself together. Its security forces are improving fast in technical terms, but their loyalty to the state generally remains suspect, and they could easily splinter along ethnic and sectarian lines if civil strife intensifies in the future. The "glue" of a foreign coalition presence of tens of thousands of Americans will therefore be required for some time—as even some Sunni Arab leaders, despite the visceral distaste most feel for the United States, have begun to agree.[53]

In light of these realities, it would be a profound mistake for the United States to carry out a complete military withdrawal from Iraq on any fixed timeline. America should not give up in other ways either. In particular, it should continue to work hard to help Iraqis rebuild their economy and their government—not, at this point, out of any obligation to Iraqis (though such an obligation does exist), but primarily because America's own national-security interests require it.

The need for steadiness and resolve does not, however, demand blanket support for Bush-administration policies. (On a related point, we would argue that senator Joe Lieberman's difficulties against challenger Ned Lamont in the August 2006 democratic primary in Connecticut had more to do with the fact that Lieberman sounded "too close to Bush"— even in the face of mounting difficulties with the Iraq mission in recent months—than because he had voted to support the invasion per se.) In fact, Democrats and moderate Republicans have been critical in pushing the administration to make several needed policy changes in Iraq already: hastening the transfer of sovereignty, involving the United Nations more fully in Iraq's reconstruction, and modifying the economic-reconstruction plan so that it does not rely as much on large infrastructure projects. And there is ample room for debating how *large* the U.S. military presence in Iraq should be, even if there should be no doubt about the need for some serious, sustained presence.

Specific Suggestions

The situation in Iraq is changing too quickly for a book written in the spring and summer of 2006 to be fully current even in the fall and winter of that year. But it is possible to comment generally on today's problems and priorities within Iraq.

Begin with Iraq's politics. Beyond the question of forming a multiethnic government, which absorbed leaders for much of 2006, there is the question of what that government must strive to accomplish in order to gain Sunni Arab support. Without that support, there will likely be no end to the resistance. A key issue is how oil will be allocated in the future. One problem in the arena of oil is found in Kirkuk, an oil-rich northern Iraqi city inhabited by Kurds, Sunni Arabs, and others. The Kurds believe the city and its environs are historically theirs, and resent that the Arab population living there now originally settled there at the behest of Saddam Hussein to weaken the Kurds' influence over a key part of Iraq's oil economy. The Kurds want not only the Kirkuk land for the Kurdish families who once owned it—a reasonable enough proposition—but also virtually all of the rights to and revenue from the oil produced in the area.[54]

However, the temporary constitution promulgated in early 2004 under Paul Bremer specifically assured Sunnis that Iraq's natural resources belong to "all the people of all the regions and governorates of Iraq." It further underscored that oil revenue would be distributed equally and fairly through the national budget. Effectively, the Kurds are demanding all of the autonomy protections afforded them by that interim document, and the 2005 constitution, while trying to remove the key resource-distribution provision important to the Sunnis. If successful, this Kurdish action will establish a precedent that Shiites may seek to emulate in the south, where almost all the rest of Iraq's oil is found. The Sunnis would likely see any constitution that allowed this to happen as representing a deal struck between Shiites who will eventually dominate Iraq's central institutions and Kurds who covet eventual separation. Further, Sunnis would feel deprived of their fair share of Iraq's national resources. This might provoke Sunni Arabs to intensify their attacks on Shiite-dominated security forces and mobilize against Kirkuk or other oil-rich sectors of the country. In other words, the insurgency could become a civil war. Bosnia-style ethnic cleansing could result, along with major damage to Iraq's oil infrastructure. And since the Sunni Arabs would probably lose the conflict, their region might become a miniature version of what Afghanistan was in the 1990s—a failed, radicalized, largely ungoverned state that could become a safe haven for jihadists.

There are various models for how to allocate oil revenue. One thoughtful concept offered by Brookings scholar Kenneth Pollack would create several pots of money—one to be shared directly with Iraqi citizens, one for the federal government, one for sharing with provincial governments, and so on.[55] As Pollack points out, another key requirement is to track production, transport, and use of oil (as well as electricity) to reduce theft as well as waste. The main point is that for Sunni Arabs to feel that the new Iraq is protecting their rights, all oil revenue should be seen as a national asset and allocated (at least roughly) on a per capita basis.

Another important political issue is the matter of de-Baathification—or, more specifically, reincorporation of lower-level Baathists back into Iraqi society. The Baathist Party had about 1.5 million members and supporters, but only about 25,000 people were active within it.[56] Many professionals joined the Baathist Party because they had to, if they wished to have successful careers. Most should not be seen as directly culpable for the misdeeds of the previous regime; instead, in keeping with the truth-and-reconciliation processes created in countries such as South Africa, a process for quickly rehabilitating and forgiving lower-level Baathists makes sense, particularly if they are prepared to renounce their past associations with the party. A plank in Iraq's constitution, approved in the October 2005 referendum, makes clear that only those Baathists who committed crimes will be punished, but this notion needs to be developed further, clarified, and made operational so that most Baathists (a disproportionate number of whom were Sunni Arab) can feel confident that the new Iraq is for them too. This pursuit of accountability coupled with forgiveness has been a key feature of successful post-conflict reconstruction efforts the world over.

Beyond oil, the Iraqi economy requires much more concerted attention than it has received to date. The successive waves of spontaneous looting, criminal lawlessness, and increasingly well-organized guerrilla attacks against the occupation forces—unforeseen in the U.S. administration's rosy pre-invasion plans—have driven up the costs of reconstructing Iraq's critical infrastructure and forced a reduction in programs that might have helped win popular support for U.S. policies among Iraqis and others. According to the U.S. State Department, security-related expenditures represent 16 to 22 percent of the overall costs of major infrastructure projects in Iraq. Persistent attacks against Iraq's core energy, sanitation, communications, and transportation infrastructure, as well as the foreign contractors hired to maintain them, have largely prevented their rehabilitation despite the more than $18 billion the U.S. Congress appropriated for that purpose in 2003 and other funds.[57] Most critically, Iraq has generally been producing less oil and electricity than it was before the March 2003 invasion.[58] Prior to the war, Bush administration officials argued that Iraq's oil resources would largely finance its reconstruction.[59] Although Iraq's oil infrastructure survived the Anglo-American invasion largely intact, guerrilla sabotage against the more vulnerable pipelines has kept exports to a modest level.[60] The inability to revive oil exports, which account for more than 90 percent of the Iraqi government's direct income,[61] deprives the government of the revenue it desperately needs to rebuild its security forces, revive other crucial sectors of the Iraqi economy, or even maintain U.S.-funded infrastructure projects after they have been completed.[62]

To be sure, the United States has poured huge amounts of money into Iraq since 2003. Of the $21 billion in total reconstruction aid that Congress has appropriated since the invasion, about $14 billion had been exhausted, with $7 billion still unspent, as of May 2006. But security demands have drained at least $3 billion of the overall total from the projects for which it was intended. Planned funding for electricity has declined $1.3 billion even as workers struggle to return average electricity production just to Saddam Hussein–era levels. Funding for water and sewage projects has been cut severely, from just over $4 billion to just over $2 billion, even though at least half the population remains badly underserved by these utilities.

Some would argue that with the United States spending, on average, at least $5 billion a month in Iraq since 2003, Americans don't owe the Iraqi people any more help. Their own oil, after all, provides an important source of revenue that helped the economy grow by nearly 50 percent in 2003/2004. If one looks just at aid levels, this is a fair point. The $21 billion that the United States has already committed in Iraq compares surprisingly well with per capita spending on Western Europe during the Marshall Plan years, even after accounting for inflation, and it dwarfs what any other country or group of countries has provided in terms of true aid (as opposed to loans, which are often unwelcome) to Iraq. But American generosity toward Iraq is not what's at issue. What is at issue is the safety and well-being of our own troops—and the prospects for at least some strategic success in the overall mission. Indeed, the "Pottery Barn" rule of foreign policy made famous by Colin Powell may best summarize what the United States is required to do at both a moral and strategic level: You broke it, you pay for it and have it fixed.

As noted earlier, Iraq's economy is generally in mediocre shape. The failings of the economy foster resentment and support for the insurgency among the Iraqi people. While there has been some notable progress in areas such as telephone and Internet service, the availability of automobiles, and the number of students in school, progress in water and sanitation has been slow, and bitterness about the electricity situation is palpable. Meanwhile, an unemployment rate of perhaps 35 percent—probably much higher in Sunni Arab regions—translates into legions of bored, impoverished youth who have become prime targets for insurgents' recruiting campaigns.

Despite generous assistance and the intrepid work of many dedicated Americans, most Iraqis remain unimpressed by U.S. efforts. According to figures provided to the *Washington Post* by the U.S. Army Corps of Engineers, fewer than 50 percent of Iraqis had seen any direct evidence of U.S. efforts at reconstruction as of early 2006.[63]

In addition to fully funding existing plans for infrastructure and health care in Iraq, the United States should work with the Iraqi government (and other donors, if possible) to develop a massive job-creation program. To some extent, military commanders have been doing this on a piecemeal basis with their emergency-response-program funds, but these efforts have been, for the most part, underfunded and implemented ad hoc. What is needed is a Roosevelt-like pledge that any honest Iraqi who wants a job can have one, at a modest wage, for at least the next five to seven years. While this would cost some $2 billion to $3 billion a year, it may be the only way to engage a growing body of alienated and disenfranchised Iraqis in something other than the insurgency.

And while a jobs program designed largely to put money in Iraqi people's pockets for the next few critical years would probably neither appeal to the Bush administration's free-market faithful nor be what members of Congress would most wish to trumpet to constituents smarting from high energy and health-care costs here at home, such an initiative need not and should not be cast as philanthropy. The goal, pure and simple, would be to reduce the number of Iraqis willing to fire grenades at passing police officers, plant explosives along the routes of troop convoys, or otherwise aid and abet the insurgency. In other words, the purpose of a jobs program would be to fight this war preventively by giving Iraqis an option to work for a stronger Iraq in whose success they have a stake.

It is true, as a number of Bush-administration critics have argued, that this American president should announce that he seeks no permanent military bases in Iraq. While the base option could always be reconsidered by future U.S. and Iraqi leaders, a clear and unambiguous statement of American intent in this regard will help considerably to dispel lingering suspicions about American territorial designs on Iraq—particularly suspicions about the Bush administration. America should make no apologies for its long-term security partnerships; it is a good military ally that helps other countries maintain their security—and that leaves when asked to leave (e.g., the closing of the Clark and Subic bases in the Philippines in 1992, and the K2 base in Uzbekistan in 2005). But the level of mistrust about American motives in Iraq is so great—with festering rumors exacerbating the tendency of Iraqis to view the United States as an illegitimate occupier—that the United States must make a straightforward, high-level denial of plans for an enduring security presence.

However, the security agenda should not stop there. A much stronger penitentiary system is required to ensure that Sunni Arabs are not summarily arrested, tortured, and/or killed. Stronger oversight programs are needed throughout the Iraqi security and legal system to ensure fair treatment of citizens and to assess rigorously the integrity and the capabilities of police, judges, prison guards, and soldiers. Regional leaders should be given more influence in vetting police forces and controlling their operations to reduce the strength of militias; if that fails, police capabilities may have to be organized on a regional rather than a national level.[64] The principal purpose in trying to improve Iraqi human and political rights along these lines in the short term is not to create a Western-style democracy in the land of the Tigris and Euphrates; it is, rather, to dampen Sunni Arab collective anger and thereby give Iraqi and American forces a better chance of ultimately defeating the insurgency while also preventing all-out civil war.

CONCLUSION

There is ample room for debate about bringing home substantial numbers of U.S. troops over a certain time period to counter the image of America as an occupier and keep pressure on Iraqis to build and take responsibility for their own country. But there is not a serious case for scheduling a complete withdrawal on any fixed schedule. While American troops may be part of the problem in Iraq, stoking the insurgency and breeding resentment, they are also a necessary part of the solution for the foreseeable future because Iraqi security forces are not yet capable of handling the situation on their own.

This conclusion applies to the main problem of the last three years: a strong insurgency with a core of Sunni Arab nationalists and former Baathists reinforced by a small, violent group of al Qaeda extremists. It also applies to the possibility of all-out civil war. If civil war begins in Iraq, it will likely consist of increasingly active vigilante justice— as well as random, pointless acts of violent rage—by Iraq's powerful militias. They will attack defenseless mosques, homes of important figures from other ethnic and religious groups, and defenseless citizens. They will begin to perpetrate ethnic cleansing with cold, premeditated purpose. As time goes on, they will hear about similar behavior by other militias from other sectarian groups, and they will increasingly be motivated by a desire for vengeance—not just for Hussein's atrocities of yesteryear but for what happened last week and last night. And they will seek to protect their own unarmed families and friends, to preclude the possibility of further attacks against their own kin, by stepping up ethnic cleansing in neighborhoods where they live. Large ethnic-group relocation efforts will become prevalent in much of Iraq, and retributive violence will become a growing cycle. Indeed, all these things are happening to a degree already.

These are the typical dynamics of civil conflicts, as analyzed by scholars such as John Mueller, Barry Posen, Steve Stedman, and Chaim Kaufmann. Civil wars with a heavy ethnic dimension do not typically begin as full-blown conflicts but rather develop from an internal dynamic in which hate, rage, and fear increasingly influence the actions of a growing number of people.[65]

In such a situation, stemming the early signs of violence is of critical importance. Checkpoints need to be manned, curfews enforced, vigilantes arrested or shot, mosques and schools and hospitals protected. Iraqi forces can and should do many of these things. But Iraqi security forces are at present politically untested. Most units are dominated by one ethnic group or another. If the country continues to descend toward civil war, the temptation of many will be to take sides in the sectarian strife rather than stop it.

The foreign coalition can do a great deal to discourage this. By deploying with Iraqi police and army troops on the streets, it can provide enough manpower to do the labor-intensive work required to restore order as anarchy begins to spread. It can help give Iraqi security forces the backbone they need to hang together and do their job for the country rather than fight for their Kurdish or Shiite or Sunni Arab interests. It can help to hold them together by working with them and providing an example worthy of emulation. The Bush-Maliki plan of July 2006 for Baghdad correctly, if very belatedly, recognizes as much. We must try to make it work.

It is for this reason that, whatever drawdown trajectory American forces embark upon, the U.S. military presence must not quickly drop to zero. Further, however important the drawdown debate may be, and however salient it may be for American voters, it is not the be-all and end-all of the Iraq policy debate—and the United States must never act as if it is.

In debating future Iraq policy, Democrats and other Bush-administration critics need to be careful. On balance, this mission has very clearly not been successful, and it could prove a failure. This sorry picture is due largely, though not exclusively, to Bush-administration mistakes. There is thus a temptation for political critics to declare the whole undertaking illegitimate and failed and to counsel immediate withdrawal.

Yet Iraq is a paradox. It is a botched operation, but one that nonetheless still must succeed—and that probably still can do so, at least up to a point. This assessment could change in the course of 2007–2008. But it would be premature and strategically mistaken to conclude now that we have already failed. Even as voices and political aspirants across the spectrum of American politics demand political accountability from the Bush administration, they must be constructive—not only on Iraq, but also on America's broader national-security agenda.

CHAPTER 3

MANAGING THE MILITARY

QUESTIONS ABOUT HOW to manage the U.S. military are among the most central in any U.S. national-security platform and any attempt by American political leaders to wrestle with the challenges of hard power. These questions address a number of absolutely critical matters for the Department of Defense and the country: When and how should the United States use force? How much money should the United States spend on its military? How assertive should the nation's political leadership, most notably its president and secretary of defense, be in challenging the armed services on questions related to the use of force? In other words, what is the proper role of civilians in this decisionmaking process? And what changes are needed in specific elements of the nation's defense posture—the size and structure of the military services, the domestic and overseas base networks, policies for modernizing weaponry in an era of rapid technological change and (according to some) a defense revolution?

This chapter addresses these matters, which are of fundamental importance not only for the security of the United States, but also for the political fortunes of any candidate for national office. We argue that there is no case for cuts to the defense budget, though there may be room to economize in specific and carefully chosen ways in parts of the military. But added capabilities are needed, starting with larger ground forces and regional planning centers for the National Guard, which will probably require slight increases in the inflation-adjusted defense budget. A much more muscular State Department response force for aiding in the reconstruction and stabilization of countries that have recently experienced warfare is also necessary. But before getting to such specific subjects, we begin with the broader question of civilian-military relations, an issue that has bedeviled Democrats in the past.

This chapter begins the forward-looking policy agenda we advocate for hard-power Democrats and kindred spirits from the GOP and the nation's independent and third-party traditions. On philosophical grounds, it does not represent a radical contrast with previous policy. It is close in many ways to the main traditions of the Clinton administration and the first Bush administration. Substantively at least, it does not depart widely even from some aspects of the current Bush administration's stated views.

At the rhetorical level, this fact makes our recommended future agenda harder to advertise as a clear alternative to the Bush administration. Some would see that as a liability. We believe, however, that this is the right approach for Democrats in particular, who sometimes try too hard to sound like anti-Republicans—and wind up weakening themselves more than their political opponents in the process. Rather than trumpet multilateralism, or the "new" security agenda, or the purported need to focus on domestic matters rather than foreign policy, or the alleged need to get out of Iraq now, they need to compete less in terms of sweeping ideology and more in terms of good specific ideas on the big questions of the day. This view will clearly be unpopular among some elements of the Democratic base. But we believe it is both smart politics and good policy. It is also consistent with much of the argument made in the first part of this book—that Democrats and others looking for a new approach need to project the kind of resolve and seriousness over the use of force that the Bush administration has conveyed (at times misleadingly) to the public. It is not a matter of instinctively rejecting existing policy ideas; it is rather a question of being thoughtful, credible, well-informed, and serious.

In fact, Bush administration policy in terms of broad vision has had strengths in many important ways. Promoting democracy, defeating terrorists, upholding traditional alliances, advancing trade, developing relationships with new strategic partners like India—these are all sound concepts as far as they go, and are generally situated within strong American foreign policy traditions. The administration has at times even talked about the importance of a stronger long-term war on terror (the battle of ideas, or the war for hearts and minds) and about mitigating our energy dependence through development of alternative fuels. In other words, it has laid out talking points that describe much of the agenda we develop in the remainder of this book. Even preemption doctrine, controversial as it has been, makes a case for an option that most past U.S. administrations have supported and most future ones would want to retain.

But talk is cheap. And the Bush administration, despite some successes, has often allowed a yawning chasm to develop between rhetoric and policy follow-through. Hard-power Democrats, independents, and moderate Republicans should therefore not run against the Bush legacy on matters of ideas so much as of seriousness, competence, and execution. They also need to maintain some of the boldness of this administration while tempering its frequent disdain for allies, institutions, and treaties (not to mention a few too many of its predecessor's ideas). If there is a single sound bite to introduce the rest of this book, it is that the United States does not need a radically new vision for its role in the world. It needs to get serious about building on the best of ideas that already exist while giving more meat and substance to some newer notions. We now proceed to explain how this challenging agenda might be pursued.

RELATIONS BETWEEN THE CIVILIAN LEADERSHIP AND MILITARY BRASS

The subject of how elected and appointed civilian leaders interact with the nation's war-fighting professionals in uniform is among the most important any new team at the Pentagon will have to confront. However, it is not a subject to ignore until they take over at the Pentagon, at which point it may be too late to establish the framework for healthy civil-military relationships. The time is ripe to consider it now.

Democrats and moderate Republicans need to recognize that they have a challenge in this area. During the Clinton administration in particular, many Democrats seemed intimidated by the military brass. This not only hurt their political standing, it may have affected their ability to assess policy options thoughtfully. The two most glaring instances may be the Clinton administration's relative unwillingness to confront Osama bin Laden assertively after the August 1998 Africa embassy attacks (largely due to the objections of Joint Chiefs chairman General Hugh Shelton) and the administration's non-intervention in Rwanda during the 1994 genocide at a time when humanitarian missions were out of favor with much of the military establishment.[1]

Secretary of Defense Donald Rumsfeld will likely be remembered for his excessive willingness to buck military advice, particularly on the Iraq war plan, as we have already documented. But Democrats have often had the reverse problem.[2] Recognizing the discomfort many in their party feel with military matters, and knowing that they are not the preferred political choice among most military personnel today, they may allow the military slightly too much influence over key matters of defense policy. Ironically, such an approach is not only at odds with the Constitution, and at times the nation's best interests, but as a mindset it can hurt the Democrats politically—reinforcing their public image of national-security meekness. It can also hurt them in the eyes of uniformed leaders. Generals and admirals naturally expect a certain amount of influence over military matters. But they also know that the Constitution gives civilians ultimate authority, and they respect civilians who wield that authority with confidence.

The Democrats' problem should not be exaggerated. For one thing, the Clinton administration's challenges in this regard were partly tied to President Clinton himself and his own vulnerabilities and weaknesses. In addition, the administration improved over time at balancing military advice with its own instincts and policy priorities in the Balkans, Taiwan, and Korea.[3] Where the Clinton administration gave in to the military on matters of military pay and defense budgeting, moreover, the military argument was generally right. Defense-budget cuts had indeed gone somewhat too far in the early Clinton years, and it was appropriate for the administration to compensate thereafter. Finally, a healthy respect by civilians for the advice of professional soldiers, sailors, Marines, and air personnel is clearly desirable; they are, after all, the nation's professionals in the conduct of war. Moreover, U.S. civilian leaders and military personnel are all clearly on the same team when it comes to protecting the nation and marshaling a broad strategy to defeat radical jihadism and other threats to the country. It is therefore critical that each listen to, work with, and attempt to help the other. While Democrats have not exactly become the favorite among the majority of men and women of the U.S. armed forces in recent years, one increasingly hears at least an element of nostalgia among many military leaders for the greater weight their advice typically carried—and the greater respect they were often accorded by top officials—in the 1990s.

That said, the overall point remains—and at least some of what Donald Rumsfeld has done in reasserting strong civilian control of the military was justifiable. Even on Iraq, where Rumsfeld deserves much more criticism than praise for his poor post-invasion planning, some of his ideas were sound—and his challenges to military thinking appropriate. Rumsfeld was on solid ground in demanding a fundamental reassessment of a plan for invading Iraq that was last formally approved in the mid–1990s. He also wisely promoted greater use of special forces in the war's opening days (and beyond) than what previous plans had apparently anticipated.[4] Rumsfeld and, to an even greater degree, CIA director George Tenet had usefully assisted war planning for Afghanistan as well, as noted earlier.[5]

Uniformed leaders are not always right on matters of war simply because they are professionals in that arena. Often they are wrong—or at least in need of balancing viewpoints from civilian leaders, who, after all, bear ultimate responsibility for leading the nation into any war.

Eliot Cohen's book *Supreme Command*, which dramatizes several periods in history in which civilian leaders have usefully challenged their military establishments not just on military strategy but also on operations and tactics, is convincing in its main thesis.[6] It is of critical importance to the United States that civilians and military personnel share responsibilities. They must not pretend that their jobs can be neatly separated into two broad and distinct bins—high strategy, primarily the province of civilians, and military operations, where the experts are uniformed members of the armed services. There are usually no clear red lines separating strategy from operations. Clausewitz depicted war as a continuation of policy by other means; Sun Tze wrote that the greatest form of military victory was the one that required the least battlefield action. What these observations made by two great yet very different military theorists share is a recognition that broad strategy and military operations are inherently intertwined.[7] There can also be a creative tension between civilians and military leaders on matters that concern them both.

So civilians and military personnel must encroach on each other's policymaking territory. The question of how wars are conducted—at what cost, with what prospects of success—affects decisions on whether to fight them. That means that civilians must concern themselves with the technical subjects in which the armed forces specialize. Likewise, the political goals of the nation's conflicts—and the political assumptions on which plans for them are based—fundamentally affect the tactics and operational plans available to the military, meaning that military planners and commanders must also think about and understand strategy.

Even on the pure domestic politics of defense issues, Democratic and moderate Republican civilians must be assertive in their relationship with the military to succeed. There is an unstated belief among some Democrats that if you defer to the military on most occasions, give them plenty of space, and leave them to their military pageantry and ceremonies, co-existence is possible. There were numerous instances during the Clinton administration when the White House sought to avoid a confrontation with the uniformed military at all costs. When a senior Air Force officer drunkenly criticized the president overseas and his superiors recommended severe penalties and even dismissal, President Clinton intervened and essentially said, "all is forgiven." This approach, designed to curry favor, is misguided, as the military respects a firm and at times unsympathetic hand. Democrats would have been better off simply firing the Air Force general and sending a message that disrespecting the commander in chief is never tolerated—even when the commander in chief is a Democrat.

Relatedly, whatever one thinks of the substance of the dispute, it would have been wrong for President Bush to fire Secretary Rumsfeld in April 2006 when seven or eight retired generals called for his ouster based on past performance. Had the retirees linked their suggestions to ongoing catastrophic policy mistakes that Mr. Rumsfeld was purportedly committing, it would have been harder to decline their counsel. But the U.S. Constitution does not give retired or active generals the power to demand the dismissal of a secretary of defense, especially over disagreements about past decisions or personal style. We believe the generals voiced important and legitimate criticisms of the Bush administration's policy and performance in Iraq, but the call for a belated Rumsfeld resignation went too far. No political leader should be expected to heed such advice.

Of course, it would be foolish for Democrats to prioritize establishing dominance over the armed forces. They need to broaden respect for the institution and its people within their party. Recent elections have seen both Democrats and Republicans gathering together prominent retired military officers to speak out for their candidates. For many reasons, the line of military officers behind the Republican candidates is longer. Democrats have recently recruited a number of prominent military men and women, including General Jack Keane, Admiral William Crowe, General Claudia Kennedy, and General John Shalikashvili. Indeed, a retired four-star general, Wes Clark, was a Democratic candidate for president in the 2004 election. Outside of election periods, however, retired military people are rarely involved in the political dynamics or the strategic thinking of the Democratic Party. This situation must change if the Democrats want to increase confidence among military people about serving with and for them on matters of national security. Accomplishing that objective will involve a long-term cultivation of personal and political ties with current military leaders as well as junior officers and prominent military officials who have recently left the service.

To be successful, politicians must understand how to use the language of the military. In the last two campaigns, both Senator Kerry and Vice President Gore spent surprisingly little time dealing with specific issues associated with the military and national security. This approach contrasts with that of Governor George W. Bush, who prior to his first presidential run in 2000 gave several speeches specifically devoted to the military and national security. Most notably, the 1999 Citadel speech provided a blueprint for what he wanted to achieve when he came to power. Although many elements of the speech later proved in need of major adjustment, Bush got a lot of credit for demonstrating his understanding of the idea of military transformation, emerging military technologies, and national security.

Gore and Kerry also gave speeches on subjects related to the military and national security, but these issues were not core messages of their campaigns. When Democrats have spoken out forcefully on policy issues involving the military, it has often been over matters of social inclusiveness, such as gays in the military or women in combat billets. This has prompted many members of the armed forces to believe that some Democrats view the military primarily as a vehicle for social change and fair representation, as opposed to an institution that serves to inflict grievous harm upon the nation's enemies.

THE DEFENSE BUDGET, POSTURE, AND PROGRAMS

In planning future defense forces, it is important to identify the broad goals and responsibilities of America's military. To be sure, it must fight and win the nation's wars—but which wars are those, exactly, and what military tools are needed to prevail?

In answering these questions, the United States can begin with the assumption that it must directly protect its own territory. But doing so is principally a challenge of homeland security (discussed in the next chapter) and certain specific instruments of the military such as missile defense. The primary tasks of the country's defense forces are to protect key allies, prevent or limit the proliferation of dangerous weaponry, ensure global economic stability, and foster the growth of a community of peaceful, democratic states that together compose a fundamentally secure international system.

These broad goals must be translated into concrete policies to shape military choices. In the coming years, U.S. armed forces will likely remain engaged in Iraq and Afghanistan. These missions pose a huge challenge.The strain they have placed on the all-volunteer force has put its general viability in far greater jeopardy than any other operation of the last quarter century. On the one hand, the military is holding up remarkably well despite the strains; this is due, at least in part, to the exceptional commitment of the men and women of the armed forces. Most members of the military are strongly committed to mission success and to each other. On the other hand, signs of severe strain are evident in divorce and suicide rates, periodic problems with recruiting, and a general fatigue among military personnel. Predictions of plummeting morale, mass departures from the military, and a crisis of confidence in the ranks have proven wrong to date—and will probably continue to prove wrong. But a prudent planner must begin with the assumption that the all-volunteer force is under serious pressure and look for ways to provide it some measure of relief.

At the same time, the American military will also need to maintain deterrence missions in the western Pacific, most notably in regard to Korea and the Taiwan Strait. The United States will also wish to remain strongly engaged in European security because most of America's main security partners are located in Europe. The strength of the NATO alliance has important global implications for the United States.

The United States does not know which, if any, major new wars it may have to wage in the coming years. It cannot predict whether relations with the People's Republic of China will continue to improve or deteriorate; nor can it divine if the odds of war over Taiwan will increase or decrease. The United States also does not know if the current nuclear crisis with North Korea will be resolved peacefully. It cannot foresee whether any other countries will allow their territories to be used by terrorist organizations bent on attacking the United States. And it cannot predict other military scenarios that may arise. A nuclear-armed Pakistan could wind up in civil conflict or a war against nuclear-armed India. Iran could threaten shipping operations in the Persian Gulf or a nuclear attack against Israel. Saudi Arabia's stability could even be called into question.

The future is unpredictable, yet defense planning must be based on assumptions and plausible scenarios. It is important to postulate circumstances that are realistic but not imprudently optimistic.

It is also important to remember that much about today's global security environment is desirable. The United States leads a remarkable alliance system. Never before has a great power elicited such support from the world's other powers and provoked so little direct opposition. This situation is in some jeopardy as a result of the Bush administration's internationally unpopular decision to go to war against Saddam Hussein in 2003, but on balance it holds.

Some fear American military strength. But the United States is far from omnipotent. Past historical eras such as those during which European colonial powers could easily conquer distant lands are gone.[8] In today's world, the United States may have impressive ability to wage traditional warfare, but it also has a great deal of trouble contending with many land-based conflicts, particularly those that involve irregular resistance fighters. This has been underscored in Iraq (and Somalia, Lebanon, and Vietnam).[9]

America's high sensitivity to casualties limits its inclination to use military force. And given its highly open and democratic political system, it need not be so feared.[10] Even in Iraq, where the legality of the invasion was shaky, the Bush administration acted only when it could point to more than a dozen U.N. Security Council resolutions that Iraq had violated, and it only sought regime change in a place where the existing government had slaughtered more than a million people during the previous two decades. American power is, we would argue, generally a force for good in the world, and not one likely to be systematically overused.

Holding together a major alliance network and preserving stability in the global system offer great benefits to the United States and the world. But they also cost money. The United States presently accounts for about half of all global military spending. (Any specific estimate is imprecise given uncertainty about true military spending by China and several other countries.)[11] But arguments for or against the current level of American military spending cannot be based on an international comparison of defense budgets; they must more specifically consider the missions of the American armed forces.

The 2006 Quadrennial Defense Review (QDR)

Secretary of Defense Donald Rumsfeld completed his second major military review in 2006.[12] In that document, he reaffirmed his own earlier position, and the basic view of his three immediate predecessors, that the U.S. armed forces should:

- number about 1.4 million active-duty troops
- have the capability to fight two wars at once (though only one that could result in the overthrow of a government and subsequent occupation of the country, as with the Iraq war)
- maintain three major fighter-jet programs, a major attack-submarine program, several surface-combatant programs, a new type of tilt-rotor transport aircraft for tactical uses, and intense focus on improving precision weaponry as well as the command, control, communications, and computer networks that make precision weapons so effective

Although it is not expressed so precisely in the QDR, this basic defense program leads fairly directly to a peacetime defense budget in the range of $400 billion to $500 billion. Combining the costs of a high-quality all-volunteer force with those of high-technology weaponry and the expectation that most forces will be well-trained and ready to deploy with little notice, it is difficult to escape this range of cost. There is room for variation within this range as a function of specific policy decisions, to be sure, but the basic magnitude of the defense budget is determined by the broad parameters of this American defense posture.

While there is a temptation to critique severely Secretary Rumsfeld's latest defense plan and call for a major overhaul of the armed forces, this critique is overdone. Just as President George W. Bush was wrong to adopt an "ABC" (anything but Clinton) foreign policy on several key matters early in his tenure, it would be equally wrong to fall into an ABR (anything but Rumsfeld) mentality. For all his talk of dramatic change, Mr. Rumsfeld actually preserved much of what the Clinton administration had done in the realm of military planning, which was itself a logical follow-on to much of what the first Bush administration planned after the Berlin Wall fell and the Soviet Union collapsed. There are sound reasons to have a military of roughly the current size, shape, and posture. The United States does not know what enemy it will fight next or what type of military operation will prove most taxing in the coming years, so it needs a range of capabilities. There is also a strong premium on continuity in the nation's armed forces; absent a powerful case for change, it is generally wiser to go slowly, preserving what has worked and ensuring high standards that have served the nation well in the past.

Many criticized the 2006 Quadrennial Defense Review for failing to make tough decisions on canceling weapons or increasing U.S. ground forces, which are facing their most severe strain since the all-volunteer military was created in the 1970s. And it is true that, despite its worthy initiatives to increase support for unmanned aerial vehicles, special-operations forces, and weapons-of-mass-destruction (WMD) response teams, the review fell short. But that does not mean that radical reform is called for. There has actually been a fair amount of substantial change in defense policy in recent years. In the Bush era alone, the litany includes a new style of warfare in Afghanistan, a new global basing posture, major changes in how the Navy and Air Force deploy their forces, the Shinseki/Schoomaker modernization and restructuring of the Army, and a successful base-closure process. All but the new global basing posture had important antecedents in the Clinton administration, but the rate of change has remained vigorous, and the Pentagon has not been stuck in old ways.[13]

The United States has badly overstrained the Army and Marine Corps. Their ranks should have been increased substantially in 2003 (or 2004 at the latest). Alas, it is getting late to introduce such a policy, at least on a major scale. Even if we started a crash effort now to expand the size of the ground forces, little could be accomplished before 2008, when the U.S. presence in Iraq will almost certainly have been substantially scaled back.

When Rumsfeld is judged a historical context, the decision not to increase ground forces in 2003 or 2004 will probably be judged a major mistake. But not calling for a major increase in the 2006 QDR is a less serious oversight. In fairness, it must also be said that, due to the incredible patriotism and commitment of our men and women under arms, the ground forces—while enormously strained—are holding up better than might have been expected. We still favor an increase in the size of the Army and Marine forces, but the notion that this will fundamentally relieve an overstretched force is harder and harder to sustain.

As for weapons systems, it is true that virtually everything survived the review—the F–22 and F–35 jets, the DD(X) Destroyer, the V–22 Osprey tilt-rotor aircraft, the Virginia-class submarine, and so on. This is regrettable; there is not enough money to fund them all. However, two counterbalancing points need to be made. To begin, there is a serious military argument, even in today's world, for every weapon listed above. For example, although the F–22 is often described as a fighter designed to defeat Soviet combat aircraft and air defenses that no longer exist, it is insurance against a rapidly improving Chinese military that may someday wind up in conflict with Taiwan (and thus, quite likely, America). And the

F–35 provides stealthy attack options for carrier-based operations, as well as operability from land-based runways that may be damaged by accurate enemy missiles in future wars. Still, the F–35 program could be cut substantially, perhaps even in half—but then something else costing at least 50 percent as much (e.g., new F–16s) would have to be bought to replace aging fighter inventory, so any savings created by the hypothetical cut would be reduced significantly.

A corollary of these arguments is that Democrats and moderate Republicans should not promise to cut the defense budget. Indeed, it will be important to sustain funding in this age of major security challenges.

Not even counting the costs of wartime operations, which have been adding about $100 billion a year to the military budget since the invasion of Iraq, the U.S. military budget totaled about $430 billion in fiscal year 2006. The Bush administration's request for 2007 was $460 billion (including the nuclear weapons–related costs of the Department of Energy). In inflation-adjusted dollars, these numbers are broadly comparable to spending at the height of the Vietnam War or the Reagan defense buildup. (As a fraction of the nation's economy, today's defense spending represents about 4 percent of GDP, in contrast to Vietnam levels closer to 9 percent and Reagan-era levels closer to 6 percent).[14]

These numbers are big, to be sure, and some of these dollars are spent for purposes of debatable merit. That said, it will take work, and tough choices, simply to hold the defense budget roughly steady in inflation-adjusted dollars. Any savings created by cuts to expensive plans for future weaponry will do little more than keep the procurement budget roughly where it is, obviating the need for further large increases. Operating costs are likely to keep growing. The other large component of the defense budget, military compensation, is now generally competitive with the private sector. But that is as it should be in an era when so much is asked of our men and women under arms; while large additional increases in real compensation are generally unneeded, pay cuts would be unwarranted.

Key Questions About the Modern U.S. Defense Program

A number of key defense questions that are on the minds of policymakers and citizens deserve individual attention.

Should we restore the draft?

As the number of U.S. casualties in Iraq has mounted, active forces as well as troops from the National Guard and Army Reserve have been heavily deployed. This has placed unusual strains on many of the nation's citizen soldiers. In response, some political leaders have called for a return to military conscription. Congressman Charles Rangel of New York and former senator Fritz Hollings of South Carolina even introduced a bill in Congress that would restore the draft.[15] And one of Congress's most respected military veterans, Senator Chuck Hagel of Nebraska, called for a serious national debate about the idea.[16] There has certainly been no real planning for the possibility of a draft within the Department of Defense in the modern era, despite some allegations to the contrary by activist organizations during the last presidential race.[17] But the question remains: Does it make sense to restore the draft? The short answer is no, given the outstanding quality of the all-volunteer force, which would surely be compromised by any plan to restore military conscription, as we explain below.

It is important to note that America is making far greater demands on some individuals and institutions—most notably, its soldiers and Marines, active-duty as well as National Guard and Army Reserve—than others. Of course, at one level, this is always true. Those who are killed in war, and the families they leave behind, make the ultimate sacrifice; those who are physically and psychologically wounded in combat and their caretakers also suffer an enormous burden. Current policies amplify this set of circumstances. Of particular concern are the facts that the military is all-volunteer and certain regions of the country and certain parts of society contribute disproportionately to that force. Some argue that policy elites, less likely than U.S. leaders of past eras to have served in the armed forces or to have children who are presently serving, have become less sensitive to the human costs of the use of force.

There are indeed reasons to worry. It is problematic for the country when an increasing share of total military personnel comes from certain geographic regions, ethnic groups, or economic sectors of society.[18] On the whole, a much smaller percentage of today's population shows any interest in ever considering military service than during the Cold War.[19] And, of course, far fewer lawmakers today have military experience than then.[20] The modern American military is smaller than it has been in decades although the U.S. population has continued to expand, so there is not room for everyone within the armed forces. But having large swaths of the country's population effectively elect out of military service cannot be good for the nation's cohesion. It is also troublesome that, even in the aftermath of the September 11 attacks, most Americans have made little or no sacrifice in financial terms for the sake of national security—in fact, they have seen their taxes *cut* in the face of large war appropriations and mounting deficits.

That said, the draft is not the answer. For one thing, the fact that certain groups serve disproportionately in the military also means that the military offers opportunities to people who need them. Society asks a great deal of its military personnel, especially in the context of an ongoing war in Afghanistan and another in Iraq. But it also compensates them better than ever before—with pay, health care, educational opportunities, retirement benefits, and the chance to learn skills within the armed forces that are often highly marketable in the broader economy. These various forms of compensation are quite high by historical standards, and have eliminated any hint of a military-civilian pay gap except in relatively rare cases. Indeed, today's enlisted military personnel are generally compensated considerably more generously than are individuals of similar age, experience, and educational background working in the private sector, once health and retirement benefits are factored in.[21]

The military, while not without its problems of discrimination and prejudice, is also now among the most progressive institutions in America in terms of employment opportunity, providing many of the best opportunities for minorities and the economically disadvantaged.[22] Enlisted personnel in the current American military are about 62 percent white, 22 percent African American (reflecting a fairly steady level since the early 1980s), 10 percent Hispanic, and 6 percent other races. But it is important to note that minorities do not make up a disproportionate share of the personnel in the most dangerous jobs. For example, of the Army's 45,600 enlisted infantrymen in early 2003, only 10.6 percent were African American.[23]

Moreover, one must be careful not to break an institution in the process of attempting to fix it. The U.S. military is extraordinary —not only in terms of its technology, but also in terms of the quality of its personnel, their basic soldiering abilities, and their other skills in fields ranging from piloting to computing to equipment maintenance to engineering to linguistics to civil affairs. Those who doubt this assertion need only review the decisiveness of recent American military victories in a range of combat scenarios, as well as the professionalism of U.S. forces in post-conflict environments.[24] It is true that the Army has had to modestly lower its standards in recent years (e.g., about 2 percent more of its recruits now come from those scoring poorly on its aptitude tests in 2006 than in 2001). But overall standards remain high.[25]

With no disrespect intended to those who served in earlier generations, we maintain that today's U.S. military is far superior to the con-
scripted forces of the past. Today's soldier, Marine, airman, airwoman, or
sailor typically has a high-school diploma and some college credits, several years of experience in the military, and a sincere commitment to the
profession he or she has chosen. Contrast that with the type of soldier
produced in most draft systems, where ten- to twenty-four-month tours
of duty leave only a small fraction of time to train soldiers for deployment. This results in mediocre armed forces, as evidenced by a number
of European militaries still dependent on the draft.

It is important to maintain a link between society and the military. But
that link is not so tenuous today as some assert, given the important role
of the National Guard and the Army Reserve in any overseas mission.[26]
Their contribution in Iraq has been remarkable, with tens of thousands of
Army Reserve forces deploying at a time, and many combat brigades
coming from the Army National Guard. Even after the completion of the
current reconfiguration of the National Guard, Army Reserve, and active
force, the role of the National Guard and the Reserve will remain important in any operation of significant scale and duration.

Moreover, the frequently heard assertion that policymakers have become casualty-insensitive is exaggerated. Only a decade ago, the nation
was purported to have the opposite problem: an extreme over-sensitiv-
ity to casualties that prevented the country from considering decisive
military actions that its national security required. This helped to create
a perception of American weakness that allegedly emboldened some
adversaries.[27]

We do not mean to categorically reject the idea of mandatory national
service of some kind, with military service being one option among several from which individuals could choose. That could be necessary if another major war breaks out during the Iraq operation, or if the Iraq operation drags on for so long that military morale breaks and the
all-volunteer force can no longer be sustained. But even in that unlikely
event, only certain types of military jobs should be filled by those performing mandatory (and, presumably, short-term) service. The most demanding military professions should be reserved for the professionals, as
is the case today.[28]

A better policy than mandatory national service would be an all-out
effort among political leaders to encourage voluntary military service.
They should press the notion of service and sacrifice when it comes to

national-security issues, and make service more affordable and attractive to young Americans.[29]

Further, Democrats in particular must think creatively—and courageously—about how to break down civil-military barriers that are arising in our society. For instance, on many elite campuses, Reserve Officers' Training Corps (ROTC) programs are still banned because of the military's policy on homosexuality. Regardless of what one thinks of the "don't ask, don't tell" policy, the banishing of ROTC from the university setting is a punishment disproportionate to the purported crime, and it hurts not only the armed services but also the nation's centers of higher learning. Given that the United States is in a desperate fight with a vicious enemy, it is time that these universities again encourage Americans to join up. As Larry Summers so eloquently said in his speech at Harvard's ROTC commissioning ceremony in June 2004, "We as a nation are strong because we are free . . . But I would say equally to you . . . that we are free because we are strong, and that freedom depends on our strength. All of us who cherish and pray for that freedom must also support those who contribute to the strength that maintains our freedom."[30]

Can our allies do more?

For Democrats and moderate Republicans who have been critical of the Bush administration's unilateralist tendencies, there is a strong imperative to promise a foreign policy that would garner wider international support. Among the most tangible manifestations of such support would be greater burden sharing by major allies in military operations (greater, that is, than the typical levels in Iraq, where all other countries combined have been providing only about 15 percent as many troops as did the United States, or about 20,000[31]).

America's allies do carry out a great deal of peacekeeping under U.N. auspices, and most of the stabilization efforts in Bosnia and Kosovo. Their limited military means do not allow them to do a great deal more—especially in the most demanding military operations. Moreover, in addition to their collective presence in Iraq (almost 15,000 personnel), the NATO countries have recently had nearly 10,000 forces in Afghanistan, more than 20,000 in the Balkans, and modest numbers in other peace operations and military observer missions. Given their capabilities, these burdens, regrettably, are already rather significant.[32] Countries such as India, Pakistan, and Bangladesh provide large numbers of peacekeepers to U.N. missions, but they are less well suited to forcible operations of the type that might be needed in particularly dire situations and need to reorient their force structures to the extent that their own defense environments allow.

Few countries besides the United States are capable of projecting military force quickly beyond national borders today. By our estimates, about two-thirds of all deployable global military capacity resides in the U.S. armed forces—even more if one focuses on high-quality troops. Indeed, the United Kingdom, to some degree France and Australia, and to a lesser extent a few other Western countries such as Italy possess the only other militaries capable of any significant rapid intervention missions whatsoever. This situation could change over time so that demands on future American ground forces may be reduced as allied capabilities increase. But the added capability will probably be too slow in coming to help much with the current Iraq mission, or even to significantly affect U.S. force planning in the foreseeable future.[33]

Convincing allies to share more of the burden for interventions is not easy, even when the operations at hand are less contentious than the current Iraq mission. Financial resources limit many countries' efforts, and it is difficult to convince another democracy to rethink its budgetary priorities to accord with a global security agenda that its citizens may not share (or may prefer not to do their part to support).

All that said, however, Western countries can do better. By emulating Britain and Australia, as well as the U.S. Marine Corps, they can acquire significantly more deployable capacity without increasing budgets substantially. Reorienting defense priorities so as to buy enough dedicated strategic lift capability (ships and planes) as well as in-theater logistics support such as mobile hospitals, equipment-repair facilities, and old-fashioned trucks, can be very effective. The fact of the matter is that, today, America's European allies are spending about half of what the United States does on defense, yet they have less than one-fifth as much overall deployable capacity. So there is a great deal of room for improvement even in the absence of defense-budget increases, however desirable the latter might be in certain countries. Indeed, a prominent German think tank has recently made a similar argument, calling for European nations collectively to establish a goal of fielding 170,000 deployable forces.[34] These countries need to build on the useful but relatively small initiatives that NATO countries have promoted in the last few years, including an EU police capability and NATO Rapid Reaction forces, to double or triple their deployable capacities.

There are also a number of promising efforts to improve capacities outside of the Western world. Several merit greater U.S. support. Perhaps the most striking is in Africa. After the 1994 Rwanda genocide, the Clinton administration launched a program called the Africa Crisis Response Initiative (ACRI) to build African capacity to respond to such crises. The goal was to train and equip seven to ten interoperable battalions that, with airlift provided by others, could undertake complex humanitarian interventions effectively. More than 10,000 troops from Senegal, Uganda, Malawi, Mali, Ghana, Benin, Cote d'Ivoire, and Kenya have now been trained under this program and its successor, the African Contingency Operations and Training Assistance program. Later, the Clinton administration conducted Operation Focus Relief, a temporary but major program to prepare West African units for service in Sierra Leone. These programs marked a modest, but important, start. They have been marred by setbacks, to be sure, including huge losses due to AIDS and normal turnover in many of the units that have received training. But given the low price of the investment, they are programs worth continuing and expanding. In the late 1990s, the U.N. reviewed its peace-operations capacities and, in 2000, released its findings in the Brahimi Report, which stressed the urgent need for member states to make available to the U.N. rapidly deployable, trained and equipped forces.

During a February 2004 summit of the African Union, the European Union pledged $300 million toward the creation, training, and equipping of five regional, multinational standby brigades. At the G8 summit in June 2004 at Sea Island, Georgia, the major industrial nations agreed to train and equip up to 75,000 troops capable of peace-support operations by 2010, with a large fraction of them coming from Africa. The Bush administration has, to its credit, asked Congress for substantial sums approaching $100 million a year for the U.S. share of this effort.[35] But all of this will take time—as the world's experience in Darfur, Sudan, shows. Despite recent improvements to its capacities, the African Union was unable to stabilize that region with the 7,000 troops it managed to deploy there.

It makes sense to exhort allies to do more in overseas military missions and, in some cases, to provide funds and technical help to assist their efforts. Our allies will be most important, and most capable, in providing infantry forces, police, and the modest logistics tails needed to sustain them with fuel, food, medical care, ammunition, and other supplies in theater. Strategic transport, advanced communications systems, and the like are not needed by every country and can often be provided by a few states (including Russia and Ukraine in regard to transport). But the U.S. presence in peacekeeping and humanitarian missions will sometimes have to include U.S. infantry forces, especially in cases involving combat conditions and the need for rapid response.[36]

Can we cut back on "Cold War" weapons programs?
During much of the 1990s, the United States enjoyed a "procurement holiday" during which the Department of Defense did not buy very much equipment as it downsized the armed forces and benefited from its stocks of relatively new equipment purchased during the Reagan buildup. Procurement budgets were less than $50 billion a year throughout the mid–1990s; they were up to about $55 billion by 2000 and $60 billion by 2001 (at the end of the Clinton administration), but still well below any estimate of the steady-state requirement for equipping a force of 1.4 million active-duty troops.

Like all holidays, this procurement holiday had to end. As such, building on modest increases from the latter Clinton years, the Bush administration has been right to attempt to restore Pentagon procurement funding to a more historically typical share of the overall Department of Defense budget—about 25 percent, which would mean a procurement budget around $100 billion a year. However, despite the huge increase in the annual defense budget since 9/11 (the annual budget has gone from roughly $335 billion in 2001 to about $430 billion in 2006, not even counting the costs of war), the procurement budget has lagged. It has grown to about $85 billion. That is a healthy increase but still inadequate for equipping a force of 1.4 million active-duty troops.

The Congressional Budget Office (CBO) has estimated that the U.S. procurement budget under existing plans will have to average about $120 billion a year over the next two decades. It has further estimated that the overall defense budget will have to average $500 billion a year (in constant 2006 dollars) even in the absence of future combat, given those same plans. This very high price tag suggests a need for economizing wherever possible as the United States modernizes its military in future years. But it also suggests that future defense planners will do well to limit procurement budgets to between $90 billion and $100 billion a year, and to limit the overall defense budget to $475 billion or so.[37]

There are ways to do this without sacrificing important military-modernization efforts. While the armed forces must modernize in certain areas and ensure that weaponry remains safe and serviceable, the whole-sale rush to replace most major weapons platforms with systems that typically cost twice as much is neither necessary nor affordable. An alternative weapons-modernization strategy that utilizes the great potential offered by modern electronics and computers is possible. Such a strategy would certainly not entail canceling every major weapons system. F–22 and V–22 aircraft, advanced submarines, next-generation littoral combat ships, and the like would still play a role.[38] So would missile defenses and the Army's concept for a future combat system. But in general, such extremely expensive next-generation weapons platforms would be purchased selectively and in modest quantities.

The Bush administration shares responsibility for the Pentagon's current weapons-modernization plan with preceding administrations. In fact, the Bush II and Clinton procurement plans are quite similar. The only differences are Bush's cancellation of the Army's Crusader howitzer and Comanche helicopter and the Navy's lower-tier missile-defense system; the addition of a few new systems of generally modest scale; a major increase in funding for missile defense; and increased allocations for some so-called transformational programs. Because of these latter programs, among others, the Pentagon's research, development, testing, and evaluation (RDT&E) budget has increased faster than the procurement budget over the course of this decade, from roughly $40 billion a year in 2001 to $70 billion in 2006. (About $25 billion of the increase is for non–missile defense programs.)

Part of the Bush administration's rationale for such large increases in RDT&E funds is its belief, shared by much of the U.S. defense community, that a revolution in military affairs is under way. The "revolution" thesis holds that further advances in precision munitions, real-time data dissemination, and other modern technologies, if combined with appropriate war-fighting doctrines and organization, can transform warfare. The unprecedented pace of technological change, many observers maintain, will sharply alter the size and composition of our military forces—perhaps even allowing us to save money in the long run.[39]

This optimism needs tempering. Military technology is changing fast, but not necessarily faster than during the past half century. True believers in the "revolution" thesis invoke "Moore's law," which in 1965 predicted that the complexity of integrated circuits (measured in terms of the number of transistors on a semiconductor chip) would continue to be doubled every eighteen to twenty-four months. Moore's law may accurately describe the computer revolution, but believers in a similar revolution in military technology often arbitrarily extrapolate from it to predict equally rapid progress in entirely different realms of technology.[40] Such sweeping technological optimism is unwarranted.[41] Advances in electronics and computers do not necessarily imply comparably rapid changes in the basic functioning of tanks, ships, aircraft, rockets, explosives, and energy sources. Moreover, modernizing these types of major platforms is extremely expensive, so any hope that defense transformation will result in reduced budgets must be justified by careful and specific descriptions of the predicted transformation. Perhaps most significant of all, the transformation predicted by most believers in a military-technology "revolution" forecasts improvement in areas of warfare in which the United States is already very strong, but holds somewhat less promise for improvements in the technology required for the kinds of stabilization and counterinsurgency missions that are proving so difficult in Iraq and Afghanistan. Candidates for office should understand these limits of the defense revolution hypothesis.

Politicians on the campaign trail need to be wary about proposing major cutbacks to most types of weapons systems. Because presidents rarely make this sort of change once in office, campaign talk of proposed cancellations tends to breed political enemies without serving a much greater purpose. There are exceptions, of course, for weapons systems that are clearly wasteful or clearly focused on a military mission a candidate considers unwarranted, but such situations are relatively rare.

Still, candidates should talk about broad defense-planning principles and goals. President Bush's 1999 Citadel speech was, whatever its flaws and inaccuracies, a good model in this regard—as were some of President Clinton's defense speeches in 1992 (developed as they were with substantial help from the experienced Democratic chairs of the Armed Services committees on Capitol Hill, Les Aspin and Sam Nunn). In addition to placing broad emphasis on the twin pillars of people and modern electronics, Democrats and moderate Republicans should also emphasize the need for dependable and serviceable major vehicles. Candidates should avoid presuming that they can discern the nature of America's next major military battle and thus dismiss the need for certain kinds of weapons (such as advanced fighters or submarines) as relics of Cold War warfare. They should avoid talking about America's military industries and military services as part of a military-industrial complex that puts its own parochial interests above the nation's, for although there are greedy and narrowminded people in these sectors, they are the exceptions—and most of the weapons built by American defense industry have proven to be extraordinarily effective in recent combat. Criticism of military spending is appropriate, but it should be careful, specific, and somewhat restrained in tone.

There is a case for curbing, even significantly, a number of purchases of next-generation weapons systems. This could be done not to cut the defense budget but to change priorities somewhat—emphasizing electronics, sensors, precision munitions, and other such technologies, while hastening the replacement of aging equipment to ensure safety and reliability (even if this is sometimes done by purchasing equipment of similar vintage and cost to what is being replaced, rather than the next-generation variety). Such a more selective approach to modernization should not go too far, given the potential future threat of countries like China with advanced technology. And in fact it may not even be good politics to discuss frequently on the campaign trail. But wrestling with such alternative concepts of modernization and defense resource prioritization can help candidates understand the difficult tradeoffs involved in defense budget decisions while also providing some conceptual glue to their individual military proposals.

Although candidates may not wish to do so, it behooves us as analysts to try to translate some of these general principles into specific recommendations about individual weapons systems. Our goal is to illustrate the kind of thinking that has to go into developing a concrete defense plan as much as to advocate our particular proposal. Candidates need to be able to engage in these kinds of discussions, and demonstrate that they appreciate how defense tradeoffs must be considered and decisions must be made, without necessarily laying out a detailed plan for canceling or curtailing a host of military systems.

Missile defense is a good place to begin. The Bush II administration has increased funding for missile defense to some $9 billion a year. Although short-range or theater missile defense is clearly an important mission (as the Iraqi SCUD attacks during Operation Desert Storm in 1991 demonstrated), and national missile defense is potentially worthwhile (if the technology can be made workable), the Bush budget allots an excessive amount of money to missile defense. The $9 billion annual allocation is nearly double the funding level that the Bush administration inherited from the Clinton administration in 2001—which was itself almost as high as missile-defense funding in the Reagan or Bush I presidencies.[42]

As critics have noted, the missile-defense programs that have been recently deployed are far from mature. In the Alaska/California system, which is designed to shoot down intercontinental missiles from a country such as North Korea, a large, three-stage defensive rocket would ascend just above the atmosphere before releasing a small homing vehicle that would maneuver itself into the path of an incoming reentry vehicle that could carry a nuclear or biological weapon. The resulting high-speed collision would destroy the weapon. While "hit to kill" technology has shown some promise and produced some actual destructive intercepts on the test range, especially for shorter-range systems, a number of tests of the Alaska/California system have failed. And even those that have succeeded have involved surrogate components (e.g., a slower defensive rocket, not the actual three-stage version intended for deployment). The tests have also depended on artificial assistance given to sensors and computers to find and track the target warheads, since not all parts of the intended sensor network have yet been built.[43] As Lieutenant General Ron Kadish, director of the Pentagon's missile-defense efforts, put it, "The idea of fly before buy is very difficult for this system. This is fly as we buy."[44]

Since missile defense is not the country's top security priority, however, some sense of perspective is in order. Even as it continues to deploy an interim long-range missile-defense capability, improve shorter-range missile-defense systems, and work on technologies for better future systems, the United States should scale back its missile-defense plans. In broad terms, a level between that of the late Clinton years (when resources primarily funded a research-and-development program) and the current Bush level would be appropriate. That would allow for deployment of, perhaps, a two-tier strategic defense system featuring the Alaska/California midcourse system and one other defensive system. Such a system could be designed to intercept a number of warheads—but not more than a few dozen. Further improvements in theater missile defenses and ongoing research and development of improved technologies for strategic defense would be possible as well, albeit at a more gradual pace. The overall program would cost $7 billion to $8 billion a year.[45]

We will now move on to the main weapons programs of each military service, starting with the Air Force. Overall, Air Force equipment is generally still in good shape, especially by international standards, but it is aging rather fast. The Air Force's fighter fleets were purchased mostly in the 1970s and 1980s; refueling, transport, and combat-support aircraft are typically at least as old. The dilemma for the Air Force is that its modernization programs are generally so expensive that it will be quite hard to replace these aging systems fast enough—unless a more economical procurement strategy is devised that allows more planes to be purchased for a given sum of money. Under existing plans, the average age of fighter aircraft will be 20 years by 2012 (the average age today is 17 years), and airlift and tanker fleets will remain quite long in the tooth (with average ages remaining at 23 to 24 years and 38 to 40 years, respectively).[46] And those plans, given their expense, may slip, leading to even longer service lives.

The two main Air Force combat-weapons programs are the F/A–22 Raptor and Joint Strike Fighter programs. The first has entered production and is expected to turn out about three hundred stealthy aircraft. They were originally designed for air supremacy but, after the end of the Soviet threat and the correspondingly reduced need for a new state-of-the-art U.S. fighter, were given the additional mission of ground attack. The second is a huge program carried out in conjunction with the Navy and Marine Corps to produce more than 2,500 less expensive but still modern, stealthy, and costly ground-attack aircraft. The Air Force would purchase more than 1,500 of these planes, replacing its workhorse F–16 fleet with them over time.[47]

The need for two large-scale aircraft-modernization programs in such rapid succession is open to debate. First of all, American aircraft have conducted recent operations with stunningly few losses, raising questions about the need for whole fleets of stealthy airplanes. Notably, in roughly 20,000 sorties in Operation Iraqi Freedom in 2003, no aircraft were lost in air-to-air combat and only two fixed-wing aircraft (and five helicopters) were lost due to Iraqi ground fire.[48]

Second, the performance of existing aircraft in attack missions has continued to improve markedly due to the introduction of improved electronics and sensors. Better targeting and communications systems to direct weapons to their proper aimpoints quickly and lethally have also enhanced combat capabilities. Third, if done correctly, refurbishing or replacing existing aircraft with similar kinds of planes (notably, F–16s) would be substantially less expensive than buying new and stealthy aircraft. There are also clever ways to get more out of each existing plane, such as building smaller bombs so a greater number can be delivered per sortie (and perhaps putting air-ground munitions on F–15C air-superiority fighters).[49] Fourth, the increased performance of unmanned aerial vehicles raises doubts about the Joint Strike Fighter program in particular; planning to buy huge numbers of manned airplanes throughout the next decade may be technologically regressive. Unmanned combat aerial vehicles are technically feasible; in fact, development of them is progressing well.[50]

Given the mature state of the F/A–22 program as well as the F/A–22's new capabilities as an attack aircraft, and given the potential rise of a new and more technologically advanced threat (perhaps from China), there is a case for continuing with that program. Reports of a recent set of exercises in which Indian Air Force pilots flying aircraft built by Russia and France frequently defeated visiting U.S. F–15s in mock dogfights—admittedly with more planes on their side—add further credence to the argument.[51] Since more than $40 billion has been spent on the program and the purchase of more than sixty airplanes has been authorized, it makes sense to get something out of the effort.[52]

That said, there is no compelling case for the number of fighters called for in the current plan; a smaller fleet of 150 or so would provide as many air-superiority fighters as the U.S. Air Force has recently used in major regional wars. Cutting the F/A–22 program in half and buying or refurbishing F–15Cs to replace the extra Raptors that would have been built would save about $50 million an airframe, or some $7 billion over the course of the program, which would translate to an average savings of about $500 million a year for over a decade. Further, the F–15C refurbishing could be done fairly quickly, reducing the risk that the nation's combat air fleet will fairly suddenly develop serious problems and become difficult to keep operational.

Even more importantly, the Joint Strike Fighter program should be fundamentally revamped. As long as the main variants of the JSF continued to be developed, particularly the Marine and Air Force versions, the program could be implemented in such a way as to protect roles for key foreign partners such as the United Kingdom, Italy, Turkey, Israel, the Netherlands, Denmark, Norway, Canada, and Singapore. The JSF is a fairly rushed program experiencing some technical difficulties (such as excessive weight in the short takeoff and landing version)[53], so curbing production makes sense for that reason as well. In addition, the services are still producing F/A–18E/F Super Hornets (for the Navy) as well as the F/A–22, so substantial fighter modernization would continue even with a major cutback in the F–35 program.

Instead of purchasing more than 2,500 joint strike fighters, the military should instead buy about 1,000. The Air Force should buy a few hundred short-takeoff variants (now being designed exclusively for the Marine Corps) to hedge against future threats to its airfields, as Air Force leaders have recently suggested.[54] Then, the Air Force should refurbish or buy upgraded versions of current planes (e.g., the new F–16 Block 60 planes) as quickly as necessary to keep the core of its combat forces flight-worthy and safe. Over time, it should probably buy unmanned combat aerial vehicles as well. The net savings from this set of changes would be about $50 billion. Nearly half of those savings would be realized over the next ten years, making for an annual savings of about $2 billion (mostly for the Air Force) during the next decade.[55]

The Navy might consider getting out of the JSF program entirely to eliminate the need for a carrier-capable variant of the plane (now scheduled to be the third of the three types developed). Instead, it could purchase more F/A–18E/F Super Hornets (or refurbish existing F/A–18C/Ds) while awaiting improved unmanned-aerial-vehicle (UAV) technology. The JSF program is experiencing a number of developmental challenges, such as keeping weight within prescribed limits. Simplifying it by dropping the Navy variant, as well as downsizing it as suggested above, may have more appeal as time goes on.[56]

Another crucially important matter in defense policy is the U.S. nuclear-weapons arsenal. Despite the unthinkability of nuclear war, and the extreme incomprehensibility of a nuclear exchange involving more than a handful of weapons used against strictly military targets, America needs a strong deterrent. It does need the credible capacity to attack dozens or even hundreds of military facilities (in part to avoid having to target cities in the kind of apocalyptic scenarios that nuclear planners must analyze). And it also benefits from having a large enough arsenal that countries such as China do not feel tempted to try to reach nuclear parity with the United States, since that might embolden them in a crisis. But beyond these broad requirements, U.S. nuclear needs are flexible—and the U.S. nuclear forces retained since the Cold War greatly exceed these requirements. They are also more expensive than they need to be.

In the Moscow Treaty on Strategic Offensive Reductions of May 2002, the United States and Russia agreed to reduce their holdings of operational strategic warheads to between 1,700 and 2,200 (or to roughly one-third of existing levels) by 2012. The treaty does not require those reductions to happen quickly or in any particular way. But given the reduced importance of large strategic arsenals in the current world, and in the spirit of the treaty, the United States could choose to cut its nuclear forces to the appropriate levels quickly and in a manner designed to save money. Specifically, the United States could eliminate some Minuteman missiles and Trident submarines. That would mean going beyond its current plans to eliminate the country's arsenal of fifty MX missiles and convert four (of eighteen) Trident submarines and all eighty-one U.S. B–1 bombers to all-conventional roles. The Congressional Budget Office estimates that retiring two hundred Minuteman missiles and two more Trident submarines could result in savings of nearly $1 billion a year.

Indeed, the United States and Russia should aim for a follow-on to the Moscow Treaty, of similar simplicity and informality, that would reduce the total number of nuclear warheads for each country to between 1,000 and 1,500 (strategic plus tactical). That would preserve symbolic superpower status for the two countries and obviate the undesirable and complicating measure of bringing other nuclear powers into the process, while further marginalizing nuclear weapons in both U.S. and Russian security policies.[57] Enough warheads would remain to serve as a robust deterrent with a wide range of capabilities against different target sets, and further defense savings comparable to those estimated above could result.

The Army has come closest to following the exhortation of George W. Bush in his 1999 Citadel speech to "skip a generation" of weaponry and hasten the development of futuristic technologies. Consistent with that speech, the Army has canceled its Crusader artillery system, which was deemed too heavy to be quickly transportable, as well as the Comanche reconnaissance and light-attack helicopter, which continued to encounter delays. The latter cancellation was initiated by the Army itself, which elected to put saved funds into survivability improvements for existing helicopters.

In regard to future acquisition policy, the most notable program is the future-combat system. Part of the Army's future-combat system is replacement of major elements of the current heavy divisions, including replacement of existing battle tanks with next-generation concepts. The new vehicles are being designed to weigh much less than Abrams tanks, which means they will be more fuel-efficient and easier to deploy than the current model. Perhaps even more importantly, they will also depend more on information networking than heavy armor for survivability (i.e., their survival will depend largely on their avoiding being shot at or at countering any incoming weapons before they are struck). The new tanks are being designed to fit on C–130 aircraft; this suggests size and weight characteristics similar to the Stryker vehicle recently employed in Iraq.

Hardly limited to these next-generation tanks, the future-combat system comprises eighteen different types of systems, some intended to be manned and others unmanned. It is difficult to glean much from Army literature about the specific attributes of any of the elements.[58] The total cost of the future-combat system may reach into the $150 billion range.

The future-combat system represents worthy ambition, but it aims to go too far too fast. For one thing, it discounts the utility of heavy tanks. For all their downsides, they have performed impressively in modern wars, and they provide protection in settings such as the streets of post-Saddam Iraq that may continue to be of critical importance.[59] In addition, the modernization program is rushed. Technologically speaking, progress in armor and propulsion systems and other key components of modern military vehicles tends to be slower than the Army seems to assume.[60] Moreover, the Stryker program to build six medium-weight brigades is relatively new. It makes sense to learn more about its strengths and weaknesses before committing to the next modernization effort. Once the Stryker program has been tested more, in Iraq and elsewhere, and once the underlying technologies needed for the future-combat system have been more thoroughly investigated, the Army's next-generation weaponry will be more appropriate than it is now.[61]

Slowing the main objectives of the existing future-combat system by as much as another half decade seems reasonable. That would space successive generations of major Army weaponry about fifteen years apart—still a rapid pace of modernization. (The earlier generation of Abrams tanks, Bradley fighting vehicles, and other vehicles remains in generally reasonable shape; there is no need to rush to replace aging and unreliable weapons.) This would result in savings averaging at least $2 billion a year during the period of postponement.[62]

Consider one last example: the Marine Corps' V–22 tilt-rotor aircraft (a plane that then-Secretary of Defense Dick Cheney killed during the Bush I administration, only to see it revived by Congress and then the Clinton administration). This aircraft, known as the Osprey, has impressive new capabilities, but it also has its downsides. Its expected survivability in combat is estimated to be only about 10 to 20 percent better than a helicopter—and perhaps less than that, given restrictions that may have to be placed on its flight profile due to the aerodynamic dangers that have caused tragic accidents in recent years. Further, according to the director of the Pentagon's Operational Test and Evaluation office, flight procedures designed to avoid the risk of the dangerous vortex ring state that led to earlier crashes may be difficult to follow correctly in the face of hostile fire.[63] Overall, the V–22 may be as vulnerable to enemy fire and/or accident as are helicopters.[64] Even if the V–22 works, the Marines will still need helicopters to transport some of their heaviest equipment, meaning that the nature of amphibious assault operations will not change radically.[65] Viewing the V–22 as a technology-development program and a means of buying modest numbers of aircraft for special-operations raids and other niche missions demanding the V–22's speed and range would be a sounder course of action than the current approach. This would entail a modest purchase of just a few dozen V–22 aircraft, plus ample numbers of existing-technology helicopters (which, again, can be done as quickly as reliability and safety concerns dictate; this is a major advantage to a less costly and less ambitious modernization strategy). Accounting for the need to purchase new helicopters to provide a lift comparable to that of the V–22, net savings would total approximately $10 billion over the life of the program, or some $750 million a year.[66]

But, again, the main point of this analysis is not to suggest that any given candidate should argue for the addition of five hundred or one thousand joint strike fighters, or the cancellation of the Osprey plus a doubling of the Raptor program, or anything of the sort. Too many detailed military arguments would have to be considered for any presidential candidate, save the most experienced in defense, to be so specific (except on matters where a candidate's broad view of national strategy naturally leads to certain views on weaponry). But a candidate for president can, and indeed must, be able to demonstrate some familiarity with the kind of reasoning—and the types of weapons systems—we have explored to convince voters that she or he is a worthy commander in chief. A presidential candidate needs to indicate an overarching philosophy of defense modernization as well as an appreciation of the tradeoffs involved in defense-budget decisions. Moreover, such decisions happen early enough in each administration that any would-be president (or senator or member of the House) needs to hit the ground running on such issues. Learning some specifics in advance is absolutely critical, even if they are generally best left out of campaign platforms.

CREATING NEW DEFENSE STRUCTURES AND CAPABILITIES

This is not a time for radical overhaul of the nation's security institutions. Most of the main structures in the U.S. government for conducting foreign policy are appropriate for the challenges at hand; major restructuring such as creation of the Department of Homeland Security in President Bush's first term would likely cause more disruption than benefit. That said, there is a case for substantial change, at a somewhat smaller scale than that of complete departmental overhaul. Recent years have revealed the need for several types of capacities that do not currently exist in the government at anything like the requisite magnitude. They are the capabilities needed in disaster response or counterterrorism at home, as well as in stabilization missions abroad. All of these kinds of missions may well be necessary in the future.

There is also a need to rethink the way we employ the different tools of American foreign policy in complex crises. In short, the experiment of giving the Department of Defense primary control over the entire Iraq mission, including post-conflict stabilization and reconstruction, was a mistake. Much of the poor outcome of the Iraq mission resulted from the specific mistakes of Secretary Rumsfeld, which might not have been made by someone else. But part of the issue was structural; the Pentagon was given responsibility for tasks it was not naturally adept at performing, at a time when it was preoccupied with complex plans for invasion. This situation demonstrates the need for a much greater role for the State Department in particular in future missions.

The most familiar of our proposals is an enlargement of the nation's ground forces. Our other two main recommendations are 1) the creation of regional National Guard planning centers to improve responsiveness to domestic disasters (be they caused by natural or terrorist forces) by allowing governors to call quickly on the dependable resources of neighboring states during crises, and 2) the creation of State Department capacity for rapid response in stabilization missions to take some of the pressure off the uniformed military for reconstruction tasks. Together, these new capacities would cost about $10 billion a year, which means they would consume most of the savings proposed earlier in this chapter to provide much-needed capabilities for the nation.

But before getting to the solutions, it is important to hone in on the problems. In recent years, the U.S. defense structure has been shown to have two central problems. First, the government's poor response to Hurricane Katrina showed that the creation of the Department of Homeland Security did not improve FEMA and in fact probably weakened it. This happened after Republicans had won back the Senate in 2002 largely by promoting their party's role in the creation of the Department of Homeland Security and accusing Democrats of dragging their feet on the matter. Katrina also raised doubts about whether the nation's armed forces are properly organized to assist in domestic emergencies. In particular, the National Guard, organized as it is on a state-by-state basis, often provides insufficient resources to individual governors. Even if legally feasible, it is hard to make large-scale deployments happen quickly enough on large scale when major catastrophe strikes. Moreover, the prospect of federalizing the National Guard to counter this dilemma rarely appeals to anyone.

Second, the nation's difficult experience in Iraq has made many wonder if the U.S. military is large enough for the mission. We do not think that the military is falling apart, but we recognize that it is under enormous strain that poses a real threat to the sustainability of the all-volunteer force. In addition, the way the country is treating its uniformed personnel is not fair; they are being asked to return to Iraq far too frequently, with most major ground-force units on their second or third deployments. In the words of one retired four-star officer, "Never has the country asked so much of so few for so long." Simply as a matter of fairness, the next Congress and next president should endeavor to lighten the burden on current troops by, to the extent possible, increasing force levels by at least 50,000 active-duty personnel.

In addition, it appears that the non-military parts of government lack the flexibility and resources to do their part in such a complex stabilization and reconstruction operation. While the armed forces will always have to perform some reconstruction duties in the early, most dangerous phases of any post-invasion operation, they should be helped as much as possible by other arms of government. In Iraq, the involvement of non-military parts of the U.S. government has been patently lacking.

Before rushing to restructure the federal government in response to these and other problems, we need to bear several cautionary notes in mind. Restructuring large organizations is inherently difficult. It is commonly estimated that at least two-thirds of all mergers and acquisitions in the corporate world ultimately fail. This is hardly surprising; creating or remolding bureaucracies is difficult for those involved in the efforts and creates new lines of authority the limitations of which are typically revealed the first time they are employed in crisis conditions (as with the Department of Homeland Security and Katrina). People working in institutions undergoing restructuring have to worry not only about their jobs but also about new chains of internal command, the clout of their own units and offices in the revamped organization, and simple matters such as whom within the changing organization to contact for logistical support.

Democrats have been hurt by their reputation for seeing government as the main solution to the problems of the day. They never successfully rebutted Ronald Reagan's claim that government was itself the main problem. But Americans know better than to take the Old Gipper's line too seriously. Although they are skeptical of Washington, they also show great respect for the armed forces. The military is among the country's most trusted institutions. And George W. Bush, who probably styled himself after Reagan more than after his own father, was in the end the main promoter of the creation of the Department of Homeland Security. Moreover, the Katrina experience illustrated very clearly why we need certain types of governmental capabilities—even as it underscored the importance of the government's taking its job seriously and performing well.

None of our proposals for reshaping and reorganizing government are so radical as to be as potentially disruptive as the creation of the Department of Homeland Security. All would respond to specific needs in U.S. foreign policy, or weaknesses in the current government, that have been revealed by recent crises. They strike the right balance between decisive action and avoiding the temptation to view new government programs or organizations as panaceas.

In addition to enlarging its ground force, creating regional National Guard planning organizations, and creating State Department capacity for rapid response in stabilization and reconstruction missions, the United States should also expand the nation's special forces along the trajectory proposed by Secretary of Defense Rumsfeld in the 2006 Quadrennial Defense Review. This would allow not only greater commando-style capability, but also non-combat types of engagement. For example, it would strengthen the government's commitment and capabilities to train and equip African militaries for peace operations and relief missions. The latter idea, which was first introduced in the Clinton administration, was dramatically expanded by President George W. Bush as noted before.

Although this initiative would simply build upon what Bush and Rumsfeld have already been promoting, there are good reasons for politicians to keep pushing it. First, it is a good idea given the challenges we face today. Second, it will hardly be complete by the time President Bush leaves office. Third, it will require strong congressional support, meaning that leaders outside the White House will have to share with Bush and Rumsfeld some sense of ownership of the idea. Fourth, the nation's citizens welcome some degree of continuity in policy from time to time. Promoting an idea advanced by Bush and Rumsfeld could therefore be not only good policy but also good politics. It could soften the tone in the nation's political discourse on at least some issues (without necessarily doing so on others!).

Expand the Ground Forces by at Least 50,000

The United States Army and Marine Corps should together increase their ranks by at least 50,000 active-duty personnel, largely to hedge against the possibility that the Iraq mission will continue at a substantial scale longer than many hope or expect. This would be a modest-scale initiative. The total combined size of the active Army and Marine Corps today is more than 650,000, so this would represent an increase of less than 10 percent. It would be a change much smaller in magnitude than the elimination of 300,000 troops after the Cold War. Indeed, this point rebuts those who say that we must not increase the size of the Army and Marine Corps today because we will then be stuck with an excessively large, and expensive, ground force even after it is no longer necessary. The simple solution to that problem will be to downsize, smoothly and non-disruptively, over several years' time—as we have done before.

As noted earlier, a larger increase would have been appropriate earlier, shortly after it became clear in 2003 that the Iraq mission would be difficult and long, but, unfortunately, it is probably too late for that now. However, a more modest initiative is still warranted, largely because the war in Iraq is not yet anywhere near over, so the force will continue to be strained for some time to come. Given the difficulties of the contemporary recruiting environment, expanding the force is not simply a matter of adding money to the defense budget, but also a matter of reaching out to people who would not otherwise be likely to serve. In addition to structuring recruiting incentives correctly, and generously, national political leaders can also help in this effort by consistently calling on young individuals to consider a career—or at least a tour of duty—in the nation's armed forces. Democratic politicians, and Democratic parents, historically have not often done this, but the nation's armed forces need help from candidates of both parties today.[67]

Beyond Iraq, other missions requiring substantial numbers of U.S. ground forces could arise. It is unlikely that any U.S. president would enter into such a mission lightly, especially during or in the immediate aftermath of the Iraq war. But, to paraphrase Lenin, some of these scenarios could have an interest in Americans even if Americans have no particular interest in them. One possible scenario is another war on the Korean peninsula—be it one that arises over a further provocation from North Korea (e.g., expansion of its nuclear arsenal) or one provoked by a collapse of that country. A possible war against Iran, perhaps sparked by the nuclear crisis there, could also require large-scale ground operations.

There are many other possible scenarios. In general, 9/11 showed that the United States has at least some national-security interest in many, if not most, places where states may fail, since such locations can wind up providing sanctuary or resources to movements such as al Qaeda. Other scenarios could create even greater and more direct risk. For instance, there is a chance that someday nuclear-armed Pakistan could teeter on the brink of dissolution. Consider what such a scenario could entail. The combination of Islamic extremists and nuclear weapons in that country is extremely worrisome; were parts of Pakistan's nuclear arsenal ever to fall into the wrong hands, al Qaeda could conceivably gain access to a nuclear device. The possible results are terrifying.[68]

Auguring against the Pakistani-collapse scenario is that country's relatively pro-Western and secular officer corps.[69] But Pakistan's intelligence services, which played a key role in the creation of the Taliban and have condoned if not abetted Islamic extremists in Kashmir, are less dependable. And the country as a whole is sufficiently infiltrated by fundamentalist groups—as the assassination attempts against President Musharraf as well as other evidence make clear—that the terrifying scenario of civil chaos cannot be dismissed.[70]

Were it to occur, it is unclear what the United States and like-minded states would or should do. It is very unlikely that "surgical strikes" could be conducted to destroy the nuclear weapons before extremists could make a grab at them. It is doubtful that the United States would know their location and at least as doubtful that any Pakistani government would countenance such a move, even under duress.

If a surgical strike, series of surgical strikes, or commando-style raids were not possible, the only option might be to try to stabilize the situation before the weapons could be taken by extremists and transferred to terrorists. The United States and other outside powers might, for example, respond to a request by the Pakistani government to help restore order. But given the embarrassment associated with requesting this kind of outside help, such a request might not be made until it was almost too late, which would complicate the task of helping Pakistan to restore order before nuclear arsenals could be threatened. Hence, such an operation would be extremely challenging—but there might be no alternative to attempting it. The international community, if it could act fast enough, might help defeat an insurrection. Or it might help protect Pakistan's borders, making it hard to sneak nuclear weapons out of the country, while providing technical support to the Pakistani armed forces as they tried to put down the insurrection. Given the enormous stakes, the United States would have to do anything it could to prevent nuclear weapons from getting into the wrong hands.

Should stabilization efforts be required, the scale of the undertaking could be breathtaking. Pakistan is a very large country. Its population is just over 160 million, or approximately six times larger than Iraq's. Its land area is roughly twice that of Iraq; its perimeter is about 50 percent longer. Stabilizing a country of this size could easily require several times as many troops as required by the Iraq mission. Americans would not and could not provide such a force entirely by themselves (nor could the United States single-handedly deploy such a force quickly enough to prevent chaos under scenarios of complete collapse). However, some fraction of Pakistan's security forces could well remain intact, able, and willing to help defend the country. Pakistan's military comprises 550,000 army troops, 70,000 uniformed personnel in the air force and navy, another 510,000 reservists, and almost 300,000 gendarmes and interior-ministry troops.[71] If some substantial fraction of the military dissolved or even supported extremist militias while the rest stayed loyal to the government, the international community might deploy 100,000 to 200,000 troops to help ensure a quick restoration of order. Given the need for rapid response, the U.S. share of this total would probably be large, especially at first. And the mission could clearly endure for months or years.

Such scenarios—involving Iran, North Korea, Pakistan, or another country—do not themselves warrant an expansion of the U.S. ground forces. But considered in conjunction with the Iraq operation and other ongoing missions, they are enough to justify some modest expansion in the U.S. Army and Marine Corps for the foreseeable future. The figure of 50,000 additional troops is not magical; it represents a balance between what would be enough to at least modestly relieve the strain on current ground forces in Iraq and Afghanistan and what is doable in this recruiting environment. Clearly, if the Iraq mission endures at a larger scale than expected for a number of years, an increase of 50,000 might prove to be inadequate, and an additional increase might be necessary.

But expanding the ground forces by about 25,000 a year for two years is already an ambitious target today.

The country will have to be creative and assertive in figuring out how to increase the strength of the all-volunteer force. Presidential rhetoric can make a difference, and a concerted and consistent call to serve is warranted.[72] But the military will also have to consider relaxing some of its rules. While the quality of personnel should not be reduced, it may be necessary to recruit more individuals with high-school equivalency degrees rather than diplomas, to change age restrictions on who may enlist, to create somewhat shorter tours of duty for certain military jobs, and to expand educational allowances and options for individuals who have served.[73]

Some experts would not only enlarge U.S. ground forces, but also revamp their basic structure. For example, analysts have argued for a dedicated, separate force devoted to stabilization missions and other complex interventions.

There is an obvious appeal to creating dedicated peacekeeping units, given how frequently the United States deploys troops to peace operations and stabilization missions. Regular combat troops do not always relish such tasks and are not fully trained for them. Specialized units could be properly structured to include the appropriate contingents of civil-affairs personnel, military police, and psychological-operations experts.

However, there are downsides to this idea if taken too far. Most importantly, in many peace operations, it is necessary to deter renewed conflict. Or it is necessary—as in Iraq, not to mention Somalia and Afghanistan— to prevail in a counterinsurgency campaign. Combat units are best at these jobs, as they are trained to win battles and as they inspire respect and fear in those who would challenge them.[74] In addition, in large operations (most notably Iraq but also Bosnia in the early years), the missions are too large in scale (and, typically, too long in duration) for a small number of specialized units to handle on their own. Even if such units existed, they would require considerable help from general-purpose formations.

Create Regional National Guard Planning Offices and a Dedicated Response Brigade

The United States also needs new regional National Guard planning offices. They would allow governors to depend upon and expeditiously draw on the resources of neighboring states in times of emergency more easily, quickly, and efficiently. They would further help the National Guard organize and plan for disaster or terrorism response more effectively in conjunction with Northern Command, FEMA, and the states. They could also provide the planning capacity to ensure that key technical matters—such as the need for interoperable communications systems usable by the Guard, first responders, and others—get the attention, resources, and follow-through they require.

This approach represents an alternative to the unpalatable choice between resource-constrained state-based disaster response or distant, Washington-run disaster response. Neither is the best first option. The alternative we propose would address problems evident in the Hurricane Katrina response, as documented in a bipartisan Congressional investigation: that states could not easily communicate with each other during the emergency, that regional National Guard teams would have been helpful but were not available, that Northern Command had never helped create specific requirements or capabilities for the National Guard for disaster and terrorism response, that the active and reserve parts of the military did not have good chains of command for communication or for sharing equipment with each other, and that training for such crises had not been sufficiently challenging.[75] The urgent need to do better is reflected in the Bush administration's own assessment of what went wrong with Katrina, including the remarkable fact that during "the first two days of Katrina response operations, USNORTHCOM did not have situational awareness of what forces the National Guard had on the ground."[76]

Some have proposed that the United States radically rethink its approach to the structure of the military. For example, they advocate relieving the National Guard of its overseas military responsibilities and making it a domestic protection force.

However, having the reserve component of the U.S. military involved in overseas combat missions is central to the post-Vietnam notion that the country should only go to war when its citizenry is broadly involved in the decision to do so and in the conflict itself. Because the active-duty military makes up a much smaller percentage of the total national population than in past decades, and because it is concentrated in certain geographic areas, this goal is best accomplished by continuing to use National Guard and Reserve units. Moreover, changing this approach would be extremely expensive, since reserve-component forces on average cost about half as much as active-duty units of comparable size and capability (and somewhat less than half for ground forces, the sector of the military most relevant for this discussion).[77]

Further, Guardsmen and Guardswomen reservists are poorly positioned to become the nation's primary line of defense against threats to the homeland. Most would arrive too slowly to the site of any attack to be nearly as useful as firefighters, police, and health-care workers. Whether an attack involved a chemical or biological agent, a radiological weapon, a collapsed building, or even a nuclear detonation, most victims with serious injuries would have to be treated before most reservists could be activated. And most security for the site would have to be provided by police, who could be on the scene quickly, rather than by reserve infantry units, which might take twelve to twenty-four hours to mobilize. It is important to have a certain number of such infantry units, and related forces, dispersed around the country and ready for deployment in the event of an attack. But their tasks would likely consist of maintaining public order and, perhaps later in the operation, cleaning up a chemical or biological agent—not preventing terrorism or carrying out immediate consequence management.

For these reasons, our proposal to create regional National Guard planning centers would not entail expanding or changing the National Guard's operational roles. Thus, it would not require that most of the National Guard receive training, equipment, or mission assignments radically different from those which it currently receives.

But the National Guard does need two things beyond its existing homeland security–related special capacities (e.g., nuclear-biological-chemical response teams). First, it should create a dedicated brigade for domestic response with a wide suite of capabilities. This brigade would be available to any governor who makes an official declaration of disaster (subject, perhaps, to a presidential veto in the event of competing demands for the same assets). It would be able to supplement any given state's organic capabilities, quite possibly creating an aggregate capability that would suffice for most crises. It would have a battalion on call at all times to enhance rapid response in the minutes and hours after an incident, natural or terrorist, occurred. And it would become a center of excellence for disaster-response missions that could help develop domestic disaster-response doctrine and instruct the rest of the nation's military units about proper procedures should they be called upon to participate as well.[78] (The brigade might, alternatively, be deployed as three self-reliant battalion-sized formations in three parts of the country.)

Second, the National Guard needs new coordination structures to allow smoother and faster mechanisms for sharing assets among states.

Mechanisms already exist to allow states to share assets more readily than they could in the past. But we need to go further, empowering governors with the knowledge that they will, in an emergency, be able to draw on assets from neighboring states without encountering long delays. To accomplish this, the National Guard might create several regional planning centers—Southeast, Northeast, Midwest, Plains States, Mountain States, West Coast. Any governor within one of these regions would be presumed to have guaranteed access to National Guard units from any other state in the region, unless the governor of that other state explicitly and formally objected—assuming that the state making the request for forces was prepared to foot the bill for their activation, at least until reimbursed by the federal government.

Create a State Department Response Force

Although it would not be a DoD force, a deployable response corps within the Department of State would be enormously useful for missions like those in Iraq and Afghanistan. Today, too many tasks fall by default on the armed forces, adding strain to their jobs and sometimes resulting in requests that they do things for which they are not optimally trained. As former CENTCOM commander General Tony Zinni has put it, in regard to U.S. management of various hot spots around the world, all three post–Cold War U.S. presidencies have failed "to develop tools other than military force for managing the crisis" at hand.[79]

In addition, while the Iraq experience will surely again chasten Americans about the desirability of embarking on major stabilization and counterinsurgency missions, there may be instances in which the country has little choice but to do so, as noted above. The National Intelligence Council predicts a continuation of the kind of ethnic and civil conflict that can lead to failed states; it also predicts a long-term problem with Islamic radicalism.[80] The combination of these two circumstances is especially dangerous, since terrorists can use failed states to establish sanctuaries and training camps or to gain resources.[81]

All of these facts demonstrate the need for the creation of additional governmental capacities to handle complex contingencies such as those recently undertaken in Iraq, Afghanistan, the Balkans, and elsewhere, as a Center for Strategic and International Studies study group has argued. The main tasks of such a capability, in short, are rebuilding a country's government and economic system—challenges that are daunting, critical, and very different from the challenges of fighting wars. Hence, they are not tasks that fall within DoD's optimal purview. (In our experience, most war fighters would agree with this argument.) There are also several things that such a civilian capability should *not* attempt to do. Specifically,

- major elements of it it should not be deployed while intensive combat is under way, though some advance civilian planners should be;
- it should not of course create a capacity of many thousands of permanent government employees who would have nothing to do but train and plan during the potentially long periods between major deployments (no one is proposing this at present, but in theory it could be contemplated);
- it should not compete with DoD, but rather coordinate closely with the Pentagon;
- and it should work as a joint staff, not as lots of small offices strewn throughout the government, as a dispersed structure would ensure that the agency was feeble and bureaucratically neglected in peacetime, and incapable of acting cohesively in the initial stages of any deployment.

The State Department's new Office of Reconstruction and Stabilization is a step in the right direction. Its mission is to manage crises and provide capacities on the civilian side to complement DoD's efforts. To be exact, "the office will lead, coordinate, and institutionalize U.S. civilian capacity to prevent or prepare for post-conflict situations, and to help stabilize and reconstruct societies in transition from conflict or civil strife so they can reach a sustainable path toward peace, democracy, and a market economy."[82] The 2006 budget provides the possibility of DoD's shifting $100 million of its own money to that new office in the State Department should a contingency arise in which such a transfer was appropriate. But the office is rather skeletal in size, with an annual budget about $20 million in 2006 and only about 65 employees. It can begin to conduct some useful planning but is hardly an operational capacity at that size. Even adding in the capabilities of the Agency for International Development's Office of Transition Initiatives (also within the State Department), the government remains woefully unprepared for the types of tasks that could soon be required of it. OTI has only about seventy-five employees dispersed over twenty-five countries.[83] The Office of Foreign Disaster Assistance has only about two hundred staff members, including field employees spread around the world.[84]

What the government needs is a quickly deployable capability large enough to coordinate an effort in a country the size of Iraq or Afghanistan or even Congo (a country with a population of, say, 25 million to 50 million). It need not and should not have all the capacity in house; a reservist capability of individuals who periodically train for post-conflict missions could provide much of the necessary personpower. As the CSIS study group has argued, such capabilities could also be woven into the broader national-security system through a quadrennial national-security review, rotations of personnel, and interagency exercises.[85] But the full-time deployable capability should be large enough to provide serious direction and oversight not only in the capital of a country but also in its various provinces. To attract excellent people and reduce the risks that such a capability would be relegated to the distant reaches of the Department of State bureaucracy, its importance might be underscored, as Tom Brokaw has suggested, by describing its employees as the Diplomatic Special Forces.[86] As the Defense Department's Special Inspector General for Iraq Reconstruction has concluded, moreover, such a capability should be organized under a single point of authority to ensure coherence and clarity of command. The State Department is the natural home for this capability.[87]

The missions of this deployable civilian force would of course be quite broad. The Office of the Coordinator for Reconstruction and Stabilization identified five types of efforts that the civilian force would at least have to initiate, or help provide the foundation for: providing security, building governance, providing humanitarian assistance, stabilizing and developing the economy, and ensuring justice and reconciliation. Within each, anywhere from six to seventeen key areas of concentration are specified, making for a total of fifty specific objectives.[88]

One way of estimating the appropriate size of an organization that could accomplish these objectives is to examine the precedent of the provincial reconstruction teams, particularly in Afghanistan but also in Iraq. They typically contain sixty or more personnel per team, with fifteen to twenty teams in a mid-sized country of the type that should form the template for planning.[89] That suggests an organization of roughly 1,000 people, plus supporting players and leaders in the capital, for a total capability of 1,500 or so.

Whatever ballpark estimate is right for a given situation, however, the above assumes just one mission at a time, and also considers only the personnel deployed at a given moment. There has been no consideration

given to the necessary rotation base. Going on the basic, familiar bench-
mark from military planning that personnel should spend twice as much
time at home as they do on their missions (to recover, to prepare, and to
maintain close contact with their families), the above figures might be
multiplied by three. As for how many simultaneous missions might be
contemplated, it would be ideal to have enough capacity for two at a time.
Historically, more than that have sometimes been undertaken, but the
United States need not play an equally major role in each. In addition, allowing for the possibility of two missions in countries similar to Iraq or
Afghanistan provides some capacity to handle a single much larger country if need be—such as Congo.[90]

In all, a total government response capacity of about 10,000 deployable
civilians would be desirable. While that is certainly a major capability by
comparison with existing capabilities and the overall size of the State Department (with its 7,500 foreign service officers), it is nonetheless substantially less than the core elements of one Army division and less than
1 percent of DoD's total uniformed strength. Given that the purpose here
is to take a substantial fraction of DoD's burden off the military's shoul-
ders in future missions, and that DoD often devotes tens of thousands of
troops to a given mission of this type, it would be surprising if the scale of
the needed initiative was not in the range of many thousands of individuals. Several hundred of them should be on the full-time federal payroll.

As another indication of why the numbers are so large, consider that in
the original Iraq mission plan, an assessment by the Coalition Provisional
Authority suggested deploying 6,500 police advisers alone, until the proposal was recognized to be far beyond the capacities of the international
community. Alas, that is precisely the kind of capability that Iraq may
have most needed in the early months after the invasion.[91]

That is not to say that initial efforts must be so large. The 2004 Lugar-
Biden Initiative, also sponsored by Senator Hagel, envisioned 250 full-
time U.S. government employees and five hundred reservists.[92] That
would amount to a substantial increase over existing capability and would
itself be a useful step in the right direction. But we would advocate a substantially greater initial effort, especially in the size of the reservist force.

The total costs of the above-listed set of activities have been estimated
at about $150 million a year, including costs for staff, reservist salaries, re-
tainer contracts for contractors, and training and exercises to bring all the
pieces together. On top of that, roughly $200 million a year might be
made available in contingency funds to start operations, with additional

initiatives that would break down certain budgetary firewalls and allow flexibility in the use of such funds.

Commensurate with the ultimate scale of this capability and the importance of the tasks at hand, the coordinator for this job should have the rank of undersecretary of state, as recently recommended by Sandy Berger, Brent Scowcroft, and a Council on Foreign Relations task force. That would not only ensure access to the secretary of state and president, but it would also give the coordinator sufficient bureaucratic clout to hold his or her own in dealings with DoD and other parts of the government.[93]

Managing the military is critical for any national-level U.S. politician. The Constitution gives the executive unusually strong powers in this domain; the state of the world makes the associated issues even more important than usual; and the problem that Democrats have had, politically and substantively, with this institution in the recent past cries out for a new approach and better effort for them in particular.

Although it is always easier to argue in the abstract than to accomplish in real life, Democrats and Republicans must find a middle ground between the domineering approach of Secretary Rumsfeld and the sometimes timid role played by civilians during the Clinton administration. Rumsfeld is a tragic figure. A very talented man of great energy, charm, and natural optimism, he nonetheless overplayed his hand and overruled the military too often on what will probably turn out to be the most momentous set of decisions of his tenure at the Pentagon in regard to post-Saddam Iraq. But it would be a mistake for Democrats to adopt an "anything but Rumsfeld" approach to managing the military. Rumsfeld's willingness to challenge the uniformed services has generally been healthy, and offers important lessons for his would-be successors as well as other top national-security officials and future presidents.

Defense-budget decisions also pose huge challenges for future leaders. But if there is an initial guideline that Democrats and moderate Republicans might bear in mind, it is that the system is not in need of major overhaul. There is a role for scrutinizing the details of major weapons systems and the like, to be sure—though generally not on the campaign trail. But the basic framework of America's defense forces have changed little in recent administrations, largely because they make sense for the uncertain and challenging world in which they must operate.

All that said, some substantial changes in America's national-security capabilities are in order. We highlight three, significant in scale yet not radical by historical standards: an increase of at least 50,000 in the nation's active-duty ground forces; creation of a State Department reconstruction and stabilization capacity that can grow to 10,000 strong (including reserves and contractors) at times of crisis; and, in the National Guard, a new domestic-disaster-response brigade and regional coordination system for organizing forces in the event of a domestic emergency.

These latter initiatives, modest in scale and cost yet potentially quite significant in the capabilities they would create, are the type of "third way" thinking popularized by President Clinton that Americans seem to appreciate. It is politically advantageous to make targeted policy interventions that create maximum effect for modest cost.[94] There is also enough consensus on the need for a larger Army and Marine Corps among many defense observers that a proposal to expand the nation's ground forces, in addition to being good policy, is safe politics—provided a candidate can begin to explain how the necessary recruiting can be accomplished. Similarly, while the State Department response force is a bit of a newer idea, the Pentagon and the Bush administration have both advocated such a concept—they and others in government simply have not yet been able to make it happen in a significant way. In other words, the ideas advanced in this chapter are large enough to be important, yet time-tested enough not to be politically dangerous. They are also all fairly straightforward to explain to the American people. They should be part of any agenda for national-security action in the coming elections.

CHAPTER 4

HOMELAND SECURITY

Taking It to the Next Level

A CRITICAL ISSUE IN any national-security agenda for the United States is how to protect America against the most immediate and direct threat to U.S. security—the possibility that future attacks like those of September 11, 2001, will kill large numbers of American citizens here in the homeland. If the nation's enemies are able to obtain weapons of mass destruction, particularly nuclear weapons or advanced biological agents, the toll could easily be ten or even one hundred times greater than that of 9/11. Politically, the issue of counterterrorism and homeland security is of manifest importance. As noted in chapter one, the Bush administration achieved a greater advantage over Democrats in general and Senator John Kerry in particular on this issue than on any other in the 2004 presidential race.

Addressing the threat of radical-jihadist terrorism requires a broad-based approach. We begin with the "hard power" issue of homeland security. However, a much more extensive strategy on such matters is required—as Secretary of Defense Rumsfeld himself noted when he lamented in 2003 and again in 2004 that the United States could not be sure that it was killing or arresting current al Qaeda members faster than the next generation of them was being created. We will turn to the broader, long-term issues associated with countering radical jihadism, a subject on which the current administration's record is fairly weak, in Chapter 5.

Homeland security is a matter on which the Bush legacy is mixed. There have been major gaps in its work to date, leaving a long agenda for the next administration. And even on those areas where it has taken action, the Bush administration made at least one glaring mistake. After trumpeting its desire to create a new department of homeland security and using the position against Democrats in the 2002 midterm elections, retaking the Senate in the process, it then failed badly in its employment of FEMA (by then inside of the new department) at the time of Hurricane Katrina in 2005. Again, a defensible theoretical idea was very poorly implemented. Again, the Bush administration's competence in protecting the homeland was called into serious doubt, countering any notion that Republicans have an innate advantage in the broad realm of protecting Americans against various threats (although this threat was a natural disaster, the same mechanisms would have been employed after a terrorist strike).

That said, the arguments of critics of the current administration are often too harsh and sweeping. It is misleading to suggest that the Bush administration has been categorically weak on what might be termed the hard-power aspects of the homeland-security agenda—improving the country's defenses against further attacks. Those who would challenge the Bush legacy and chart a different path for the country need to develop a clearer sense of what has been achieved, and of what must still be done. Of course, more important than politics are America's security and the well-being of its citizens—and these things depend on a clear-headed assessment and sound policy agenda from political leaders.

The war on terror has been a hot subject in American politics at least since President Bush broadened the scope of his definition of the effort to include the doctrine of military preemption and the overthrow of the Saddam Hussein regime. In fact, it was controversial even before that. Bush's State of the Union speech of January 29, 2002—also known as the "axis of evil" speech—signaled a broader scope for the war on terror than that originally described by the president in his address to another joint session of Congress the previous September 20, just nine days after the September 11 attacks.[1] The debate over the creation of a Department of Homeland Security was central in the Congressional midterm elections of 2002, in which President Bush campaigned more actively than presidents typically do at such points in the political cycle. Bush had originally opposed the idea of a new department, which was initially Senator Joseph Lieberman's idea. But after accepting the notion in the spring of 2002 and proposing a bill to create it that year, the president argued that Democrats were placing their political interests in defending unions ahead of their obligations to help defend the American people. Democrats countered that protecting workers remains a critically important goal for the nation, and that a federal workforce deprived of traditional rights and protections by the Bush administration's proposal for a much different type of federal personnel policy within the new department might suffer weaker morale and as a result perform suboptimally in trying to protect the country. But Bush's argument seemed to resonate with voters; Republican candidates won several tight races and took back the Senate.

Democrats have responded by arguing that the Bush administration has tolerated glaring gaps in the nation's protection against terrorism here at home even as it has prosecuted wars abroad with vigor. For example, they point to the very slow integration of terrorist watch lists during Bush's first term, and to the administration's weak efforts to help states and localities improve their counterterrorism capabilities.

The president has weathered sharp critiques in part because his critics have been less than skillful. Democrats have arguably often raised the wrong issues or done so in the wrong way—on both policy and political grounds. In the 2004 presidential race, for example, Senator Kerry and President Bush competed to see who could more quickly and convincingly align himself with the recommendations of the 9/11 Commission on matters such as the need for reform and restructuring of America's intelligence community. Kerry often criticized Bush for delaying action in these areas. But many of the key changes to the U.S. intelligence community that were most needed to break down stovepipes in the system had already been fixed prior to the release of the 9/11 Commission's report. Critics of the Bush administration from both parties have also argued that the PATRIOT Act does not give proper due to the civil liberties of American citizens, and that detention policies at Guantanamo Bay and prison policies at Abu Ghraib have hurt America's reputation for fairness and created even more hatred of this country that has helped al Qaeda with its recruiting worldwide. These criticisms of U.S. policies at Guantanamo Bay and Abu Ghraib have generally been appropriate and fair. But the PATRIOT Act, which updated surveillance methods for the era of computers and cell phones, broke down barriers to the sharing of intelligence across agencies, and strengthened standards for ensuring the authenticity of documents such as passports, was far better legislation than critics often allowed. By so strongly condemning it, many Democrats set themselves up for a Bush-administration counterattack.

Finally, Democrats and other critics of the Bush administration have often purported that the administration did not do enough to train and equip first responders around the country to deal with possible attacks. In some ways that charge is correct, but it would have been expensive folly to invest tens of billions of dollars in protective gear and rudimentary training for all of the nation's first responders, as sometimes proposed. A more targeted set of investments—focused on the most likely terror targets in the country geographically, as well as on the types of technologies and training that provide the most capability per dollar—makes a good deal more sense.[2]

We will argue in this chapter for several specific policy initiatives on homeland security, and somewhat greater spending by the federal government as well as the private sector, but not for a kitchen-sink approach to the problem or any radical increase in resources. In dealing with this huge set of challenges, clear priorities and a clear conceptual framework for guiding investments are essential. Otherwise, costs can be exorbitant, and less important tasks may distract attention from more important ones.

To preview our main arguments, we will advocate new initiatives to encourage the private sector to protect itself more effectively, especially in areas such as the chemical industry and high-rise buildings; to develop a more comprehensive system for cargo security on airplanes, in shipping containers entering the country, and in trucks and trains carrying toxic materials domestically; to create national standards for driver's licenses with biometric indicators (not photos) and to encourage improvement of the biometric indicators used on U.S. passports; to encourage more large-city police departments to build dedicated counterterrorism cells, as New York has done; and to develop a quick-manufacture capacity for vaccines and antidotes to new pathogens that the nation does not now possess.

Before developing the logic behind these prescriptions, however, it is first important to assess where we stand in the war on terrorism. The situation is exceedingly complex, and not easily amenable to simplistic political sloganeering.

A STATUS REPORT ON PROTECTING THE HOMELAND

In developing their policies and positions on counterterrorism strategy for the coming years, candidates need to begin with a clear sense of the facts. While much is still undone, the fact is that much has been accomplished in the last five years. Increased safety has been achieved largely via offensive operations abroad: the military overthrow of the Taliban and associated attacks against al Qaeda, as well as the intelligence and covert operations conducted by the United States in conjunction with key allies such as Pakistan and Saudi Arabia.

Homeland-security spending has increased by at least 300 percent, to more than $40 billion a year; the initiative is hardly "on life support," as some critics have charged. U.S. intelligence spending is now reportedly up to $44 billion a year, as much as $10 billion more than estimated levels from the 1990s, with nearly 100,000 individuals working for American intelligence agencies.[3] There is more debate in the analytic process, and a clearer emphasis in finished reports on the uncertainties of various types of assessments (to avoid the mistakes not only of 9/11, but also of the Iraqi WMD experience).[4] Terrorist watch lists are now integrated; domestic and foreign intelligence operations no longer have strong "firewalls" between them, and that change was made quickly.

The PATRIOT Act, whatever its problems in insufficiently protecting civil liberties, or its possible over-exuberance in allowing subpoenas of library records and the like, on balance has been good legislation. Democrats and other critics of the Bush administration need to acknowledge that updating wiretap authority for the era of the Internet, allowing roving wiretaps not fixed to one phone or location, breaking down barriers between the FBI and the CIA, making banks report suspicious money transfers, requiring visa-waiver countries to have biometric indicators on their passports, prohibiting possession of dangerous biological materials in the absence of good research or medicinal reasons for such possession, and similar measures were overdue and prudent.[5] There is room for debate about specific provisions of the PATRIOT Act, but it is neither sound policy nor sound politics to rail against it categorically as critics have sometimes done.

Similarly, in the debate over domestic eavesdropping, Democrats and many Republicans have been right to expect President Bush not to disobey the law (or push it all the way to the breaking point). Asserting greater executive privilege should not extend to flouting existing legislation or claiming to find incredible loopholes within it. But Democrats should recognize that obtaining warrants in a timely manner for all eavesdropping, even from a court set up to do so quickly and secretly, is neither practical nor prudent, as argued convincingly by law professors and judges with experience in the field such as Philip Bobbitt and Richard Posner.[6]

On Guantanamo, critics have again been largely right to criticize as un-American and counterproductive the willingness of the Bush administration to hold detainees indefinitely without charges or any type of due process. This has been a huge policy mistake of the United States, and as the Supreme Court confirmed in a major decision in June of 2006, a number of specific aspects of the policy have been in contravention of American law. It reflects some partially correct observations—that terrorists are not like soldiers, that introducing the cases of detainees into normal U.S. criminal courts is not practical given the kinds of classified information, including sources and methods on how we monitor possible terrorists, that would then have to be discussed openly. On the whole, however, the Bush administration's treatment of terrorist detainees has caused far more damage to the United States than any of the policy's authors seem to appreciate—and far more damage than can be easily or quickly repaired.

Yet critics must be careful. Tone matters, and critics of the Bush administration will not succeed if they sound as if they fear a hypothetical executive threat to civil liberties more than they fear another al Qaeda attack, or if they suggest that the country is now safe enough that we can place every last hypothetical civil-liberties concern ahead of confronting al Qaeda. In this light, a recent quote by a senior Democratic political strategist, reflective of a good deal of ongoing thinking, strikes us as wrongheaded. In regard to the eavesdropping issue, he stated early in 2006 that "I don't think the national-security attack works this time . . . we have a politically weakened president whose poll numbers are down and whose credibility is under increased scrutiny."[7] This is exactly the wrong kind of political conclusion to reach for anyone wishing to win an election.

Guantanamo has been a major mistake. A smarter policy would recognize the need for special legal procedures for suspected terrorists but create a legal firewall inside the government between those charged with arresting and holding terrorists, on the one hand, and those determining their fate, on the other. In particular, the administration should have moved far more quickly to ask Congress for legislation that would create an independent authority inside the executive branch with the binding power to release detainees it deemed no longer a threat, and that would set up a regularized hearing process to assess the status of detainees promptly and fairly. But it is also perfectly clear that trying terrorist cases in normal criminal courts would have been unworkable in cases where evidence against suspects was either classified in nature or not quite conclusive enough to prove guilt by legal standards (yet far too convincing to allow hugely dangerous terrorists back on the world's streets).

The United States now processes and shares information about specific individuals suspected of ties to terrorism much more efficiently throughout the federal government than it did before 9/11. It does so through increased integration of databases, which enables more effective offensive operations abroad and homeland-security operations within American borders (admittedly, that process took longer than it should have after 9/11), and greater collaboration between the FBI and the intelligence community, which began to occur shortly after 9/11. These initial efforts have now been reinforced by the passage of the Intelligence Reform and Terrorism Prevention Act of 2004, which restructured the intelligence community and created the position of director of national intelligence.

The share of FBI resources devoted to counterterrorism has doubled, and the number of CIA/FBI personnel working on investigations of terrorist financing alone has increased from less than a dozen to more than three hundred, since September 2001.[8] International cooperation in sharing information on suspected terrorists has improved. Many close allies, such as France and Britain, have been helpful for many years, but intelligence sharing on known al Qaeda threats has also become reasonably good with states such as Pakistan and Saudi Arabia—in part because some of these states now take the jihadist threat to their own interests more seriously than they used to.

Air travel is also much safer today than before 9/11. The United States now screens all passenger luggage, requires hardened cockpit doors on all large American commercial aircraft, deploys thousands of air marshals on commercial carriers, and allows armed pilots on commercial and cargo flights.

Suspicious ships entering U.S. waters are now screened more frequently, and containers coming into the United States are two to three times more likely to be inspected than they were before 9/11. Hundreds of millions of doses of antibiotics and enough smallpox vaccine for every man, woman, and child in the United States have been stockpiled.[9] Oversight rules have been tightened on labs working with biological materials (including rules relating to background checks on lab employees).[10] Terrorism insurance is backstopped by a new federal program that was renewed in 2005.

Well-known bridges and tunnels are protected by police and National Guard forces during terrorism alerts. Nuclear-reactor sites have better perimeter protection than before 9/11.[11] Federal agencies are required to have security programs for their information-technology networks. Many private firms have backed up their headquarters computers and their data banks so that operations and information systems could survive the catastrophic loss of a main site.[12]

What all of these efforts amount to, in short, is this: We have prepared fairly well to fight the last war—that is, to stop the kinds of attacks that the United States has already experienced. Importantly, the United States has also gotten much better at trying to prevent attacks by tracking suspected terrorists more assertively. Since prevention should be seen as the most crucial stage of the homeland-security effort (more important, for example, than hardening most individual targets), this is real progress.

The United States cannot be complacent, however. We have done much less than we should have in the way of detailed preparation to thwart other kinds of plausible strikes. It made sense to move quickly to prevent al Qaeda, with its longstanding interest in airplanes, from easily repeating the 9/11 attacks. But it is high time to do a more comprehensive and forward-looking job of protecting the American people.

Al Qaeda may not be as capable as before of performing "spectacular" attacks in coming years. It is, however, certainly still capable of using explosives and small arms, with considerable lethality.[13] There have not been more attacks within the United States. But according to an October 2005 speech by President Bush, the United States has disrupted three attempted al Qaeda strikes inside the United States, and intercepted at least five plots to case targets or infiltrate terrorists into this country.[14] There were serious worries that al Qaeda would use truck bombs to destroy key financial institutions in New York, Newark, and Washington, D.C., in 2004.[15] The "shoe bomber," Richard Reid, attempted to destroy an airplane headed to the United States in December 2001. U.S. intelligence reports in early 2005 suggested the possibility of attacks using private aircraft or helicopters. Interviews with suspected members of Al Qaeda and confiscated documents suggest other possible attacks ranging from blowing up gas stations to poisoning water supplies to using crop dusters to spread biological weapons to detonating radioactive dirty bombs.[16]

The years 2002, 2003, and 2004 were among the most lethal in the history of global terrorism, with attacks afflicting a wide swath of countries from Spain to Morocco to Tunisia to Saudi Arabia to Pakistan to Indonesia—and, of course, Iraq.[17] The pattern continued in 2005, a year during which the number of global terrorist attacks again grew relative to the year before (though new counting methods and limits upon the public release of data make it somewhat difficult to compare precisely from year to year).[18] The July 7 London attacks that year should have vividly reminded Western-ers in general of their continued vulnerability.[19] According to Hillary Peck of the RAND Corporation, even though fewer Americans were killed, global fatalities from terrorist action exceeded the 2001 total of 4,555 in both 2004 and 2005 (the death toll exceeded 5,000 in each of those latter two years).[20]

Al Qaeda has clearly been weakened at the top since 9/11. That said, it remains extremely dangerous, and not just because bin Laden and al-Za-wahiri remain at large.[21] Al Qaeda is now less of a vertical organization than an ideology or a method used by a collection of loosely affiliated local groups that share similar goals. They also watch and learn from each other, through television, the Internet, and extended family connections and other social networks.[22] Former CIA Director George Tenet put it succinctly in 2004: "Successive blows to al Qaeda's central leadership have transformed the organization into a loose collection of regional net-works that operate more autonomously."[23]

There are benefits to dispersing al Qaeda in this way; the near-term risk of sophisticated catastrophic attacks has probably declined as a result. But the risk of smaller and sometimes quite deadly strikes clearly has not—and the possibility of further catastrophic attacks may well increase again in the future. To underscore the enduring risks, a U.N. study in early 2005 argued that al Qaeda continues to have easy access to financial resources and bomb-making materials.[24] The plot to bomb airliners headed from the U.K. to the U.S. that British intelligence rolled up in August 2006 was a stark reminder of enduring dangers as well.

Great benefits were gained by depriving al Qaeda of its sanctuary in Afghanistan in Operation Enduring Freedom. Al Qaeda has learned to reconstitute itself with a less formal and more virtual and horizontal net-work, however. It could also avoid terrorist watch lists with some effec-tiveness, for example by using new recruits—including women, non-Arabs, and European passport holders—to conduct future attacks against Western countries.[25] The United States is fortunate not to have, as far as we know, many al Qaeda cells presently on its soil, as several European countries do. It is not a foregone conclusion that things will stay this way, however.[26] For all these reasons, it is hard to disagree with former CIA Director Porter Goss, who told Congress in February 2005, "It may be only a matter of time before al Qaeda or another group attempts to use chemical, biological, radiological, and nuclear weapons."[27]

The Iraq war, whatever its other merits, has probably not alleviated the global terrorism problem. Indeed, it may have worsened it, by aiding al Qaeda's recruiting efforts and providing jihadists a focal point to practice their crafts and establish new networks. To quote Goss again, "Islamic extremists are exploiting the Iraqi conflict to recruit new anti-U.S. jihadists. These jihadists who survive will leave Iraq experienced and focused on acts of urban terrorism."[28] The National Intelligence Council reached a similar conclusion in its 2004 report, *Mapping the Global Future*.[29]

THE AGENDA FOR THE NEXT PRESIDENT

Of course, it is not possible to defend a large, open, advanced society from all possible types of terrorism. The United States contains more than half a million bridges, nearly five hundred skyscrapers, nearly 200,000 miles of natural-gas pipelines, more than 2,800 power plants—the list of critical infrastructure alone is far too long to expect that everything could be protected, to say nothing of subways, restaurants, movie theaters, schools, and malls.[30] Certain special measures, such as providing extremely tight security around the nation's 104 nuclear power plants, clearly cannot be extended to all possible targets.[31]

But by focusing on the worst possible attacks, the United States can establish priorities and make further progress in protecting the country. Several guidelines should inform both future work in this area and politicians' efforts to speak to the American people about the broad principles that should guide next steps in enhancing homeland security.

First, while it was correct to focus initially on preventing al Qaeda from carrying out attacks similar to those of 9/11, we have prepared a bit too exclusively to fight "the last war." Heeding the counsel of the 9/11 Commission, we now need to stretch our imaginations a bit to identify other key national vulnerabilities, such as possible attacks on chemical plants or skyscrapers or the air-circulation systems of stadiums.

Second, we should focus on prevention—that is, on obtaining good intelligence on terrorists and impeding their movements, their financial transactions, and their communications—rather than focusing on point defense of the nation's key assets or on mitigating the consequences of successful attacks (the latter tasks are important, but are not as important as preventive efforts).

Third, since we cannot protect everything, we should worry most about possible terrorist strikes that would cause large numbers of casualties. Only slightly less critically, we should focus intensively on preventing attacks that might cause only a relatively small number of casualties, but huge economic ripple effects, such as the possibility of smuggling weapons or other dangerous materials into the United States through shipping containers.

Consider another example of the latter type of scenario. If a shoulder-launched surface-to-air (SAM) missile took down an airplane, the number of casualties might be relatively modest—dozens or hundreds. It would be a tragedy for those involved, to be sure, but in and of itself would not be debilitating to the nation. The effects of such an attack on the nation's air travel could be devastating, however. They also could endure much longer than those of September 11, 2001, since it would take a good deal of time to figure out a workable response to avoid future SAM attacks. Another possibility is the use of a radiological weapon that uses conventional explosives to disperse radioactive material in an urban area. Such an attack would not kill many people, but it would likely cause mass panic. It would also probably require a very costly and time-consuming cleanup—as well as implementation of disruptive security measures throughout the country.[32]

There are also general areas of homeland security where important progress has occurred in some ways but where key shortcomings remain. Consider America's vulnerability to biological attacks. Although antibiotic stocks for addressing any anthrax attack are now fairly robust, means of quickly delivering the antibiotics are not.[33] Long-term worries about biological attacks remain acute, since there could be many types of infectious agents for which antidotes and vaccines prove unavailable (or nonexistent) when they are most needed.

As for air travel, most passengers are still not screened for explosives, cargo carried on commercial jets is usually not inspected, and private planes face minimal security scrutiny.[34] Moreover, although many security improvements have been made on U.S. carriers, fewer have been made on many foreign carriers that transport large numbers of Americans to and from the United States.

More generally, the U.S. private sector has done very little to protect itself.[35] From chemical plants to trucks carrying hazardous shipments to skyscrapers, vulnerabilities are often acute and not very different from how they presented themselves prior to 2001.[36] Owners of private infrastructure know that the chances of any one facility they own being attacked are miniscule, so they are not apt to incur added costs—and concede to shareholders and neighbors that their facilities might be vulnerable—on their own volition. Yet viewed from a national perspective, this means that certain systemic vulnerabilities remain unaddressed.

The creation of the Department of Homeland Security has not automatically led to better protection against threats, as the hapless response to Hurricane Katrina revealed. Many capable and dedicated individuals are serving within DHS. However, reorganizations can distract attention from efforts to identify remaining key American vulnerabilities and then mitigate them. Carrying out a major governmental overhaul during what is essentially a time of war is a risky proposition. It is also not the way the country has typically responded to national crises. The Department of Defense was not created during World War II, but afterwards. The Goldwater-Nichols Pentagon reorganization in 1986 was carried out during a time of relative international peace. Now that reorganization has occurred, we do not favor removing FEMA from DHS; it can be made successful within that larger bureaucracy with good management. But creation of a new department was clearly no panacea.

Congress has improved its ability to address homeland-security issues by creating dedicated authorization committees and appropriations subcommittees in both houses. Yet it has not gone far enough. These dedicated committees and subcommittees must share jurisdiction with many other committees and subcommittees that insist on a share of the decisionmaking power.[37] This approach leaves homeland security matters vulnerable to Congressional parochialism among the individual committees and subcommittees about the particular dimensions of homeland security they address. It can also reinforce the tendency of members of Congress to allocate precious homeland-security dollars to their districts rather than to districts where they might do more good.[38] Congress should ensure that homeland-security committees and subcommittees generally have exclusive jurisdiction over funding within the homeland-security realm.

In sum, then, much has been done in homeland security, and much remains to be done. The FEMA experience in Hurricane Katrina was very poor, but otherwise the Bush legacy on homeland security is mixed and not overwhelmingly strong or weak. That message, with that balanced tone, may be unappealing to politicians seeking to excoriate the Bush administration's record, but it is a fair reflection of reality. In tone and temperament, it also conveys a seriousness of purpose that Americans may appreciate more than the wanton partisanship of recent years. A candidate offering specific critiques not only comes across as more affable than one offering general criticism, but also sends a message that he or she is seeking concrete, specific improvements in policy rather than opportunities for partisan attacks the likes of which will be of little use once he or she is in office.

In addition to the recommendations we made in Chapter 3 on government reorganization for the National Guard, we would suggest emphasis on several areas of homeland security, some of which are detailed further below.[39] The organizing philosophy should be to protect against attacks with potentially catastrophic impact on the country, in human or economic or political terms. In the interest of cost-effectiveness, possible action should focus on prevention of attacks rather than site defense of potential targets or consequence mitigation after attacks have occurred. But a blend of all approaches will be needed. Our recommendations are as follows:

- create incentives for the private sector to protect itself more effectively, especially in areas such as the chemical industry and high-rise buildings
- develop a better and much more rigorous security system for container cargo coming into the country
- greatly expand screening of cargo on airplanes
- create national standards for driver's licenses with biometric indicators (not photos) and encourage improvement of the biometric indicators used on U.S. passports
- encourage more large-city police departments to build dedicated counterterrorism cells, as New York has done; among its other benefits this would help improve coordination between federal homeland security efforts and those of states and localities
- encourage cities and other localities that have not already done so to make targeted investments in certain technologies, such as mobile interoperable command centers, that can ensure quick and efficient responsiveness to any attacks (or other large-scale disasters) at reasonable cost
- create a Google-like search capacity across different police and intelligence databases for correlations of suspicious behavior
- develop a quick-manufacture capacity for vaccines and antidotes to new pathogens that the United States does not now possess.[40]

It is always sound to begin a discussion of a new homeland-security agenda by focusing on intelligence—the front lines in the program, and the most important type of homeland-security effort since an ounce of prevention is worth a pound of cure (or consequence management). Since there is too much to protect in this country, the only way to make homeland security successful is to stop most terrorists before they can even position themselves to attempt an attack.

One key area of needed improvement in this domain is coordination between the federal government and state and local governments. Today, the FBI runs the Joint Terrorism Task Forces (JTTFs) in major cities. Although the JTTFs' effectiveness in helping state and local police forces is improving, it is very small compared with police forces. That means its ground presence cannot match theirs. In addition, while changes have occurred within the JTTF, the FBI has been slow to change its traditional focus on solving criminal cases. An approach recommended recently by a team of Brookings scholars would use federal funds to expand local police intelligence and counterterrorism units in America's larger cities.[41] Today, only New York takes police intelligence and counterterrorism seriously. The use of federal funds to recruit an additional 10,000 police officers for this purpose would cost around $1 billion a year. It could be financed through the very urban area security initiative grants that in fact were cut back for New York City in 2006 by the Department of Homeland Security. (DHS did so on the grounds that other cities supposedly needed assistance more, and that salaries and other such recurring costs should not be financed by Washington—a reasoning that seems illogical given the nature of homeland security work and the importance of preventive intelligence operations.) Alternatively, a new program could be created.

Other steps are needed too. Notably, despite the opposition of a number of states, federal standards for driver's licenses must be mandated. Further, U.S. security agencies should create "data czars" to protect information and also to facilitate its timely exchange when appropriate.

As Brookings scholar Jeremy Shapiro and Dean James Steinberg of the LBJ School of Public Policy have recently argued, the transatlantic homeland security-agenda requires further work as well. An assistance and extradition treaty was signed between the United States and the European Union in June 2003. But there is still a need for measures on both sides of the Atlantic that allow the admission of intelligence information as evidence in court while protecting against its disclosure.[42]

There are also some areas where existing European efforts at home-land security exceed those of the United States. In particular, as Michael d'Arcy of King's College in London has argued, the U.S. choice of using only a facial image as the biometric indicator in its passports is unwise. Photographs are inherently unreliable. The United States should follow the EU in incorporating fingerprints data, and, ideally, nations on both sides of the Atlantic will move to using iris data in time.[43]

Foreign airlines should also be expected to meet tighter security stan-dards in short order. This problem is of particular concern in regard to airlines based outside the European Union. Deployments of hardened aircraft doors and air marshals are imperative. They are also overdue.

Considerable progress has been made in the US-VISIT program, which requires most people entering the United States to submit finger-prints and a digital photograph. These biometrics can then be checked against the Department of Homeland Security's IDENT database and the records of visa holders. The United States should also speed up ef-forts to track the exits of visa holders. This is important in preventing peo-ple who have managed to get into the country on a visa from overstaying their legally allowed stays and possibly conducting terror attacks.

There are also still major problems at the U.S. borders, which remain porous despite improvements. The PATRIOT Act increased the number of patrol agents at the U.S.-Canadian border to 1,000, but more are needed, as evidenced by the continued high flow of people across the border. It is difficult to know in advance how many more will be enough, but it is likely that at least five hundred to 1,000 more would be useful. (In this light, the Bush administration's decision to use National Guard troops at the border as a temporary complement to DHS personnel has a reasonable logic behind it.) Better equipment for surveillance and mo-bility is also required, and can complement the added personnel, obviat-ing the need for unrealistically large increases in staffing. And whatever the problems at the U.S.-Canadian border, problems are of course much worse at the U.S.-Mexican border, where thousands of illegal immigrants cross each day. The United States and its neighbors should move to a regime in which all people who cross the border at checkpoints, includ-ing passengers in cars, are individually screened. This is not standard practice today.

Those who have traveled by plane from certain U.S. airports in recent months may have undergone the straightforward process of explosives "sniffing." This should become standard practice at all U.S. airports as quickly as possible. A national trace-detector network would cost about $250 million. Just as importantly, this country needs a comprehensive means of either screening cargo carried on airplanes or hardening aircraft cargo holds. And private aircraft are still insufficiently monitored. To prevent plane-based suicide attacks, there should be greater screening of private-aircraft pilots by the federal government.

The threat to aircraft from surface-to-air missiles is real. Unfortunately, the technology to counter them is not yet ready for deployment. A sustained and serious research-and-development program is appropriate and might be expanded, but on this issue, available technology does not yet offer a good enough option to warrant the effort and expense of deployment, as argued convincingly by Michael d'Arcy. After a shoot-down of a civilian aircraft, however, that assessment could quickly change.

The container trade is another area of major potential vulnerability. As with many of the issues considered above, perfect solutions are elusive, and brute-force methods of providing comprehensive security could be very expensive. But there are still practical steps that could be taken to substantially improve American security. From 2001 to 2004, the number of cargo inspectors in the United States grew by 40 percent and the number of inspections by 60 percent. Even so, only 6 percent of seaborne cargo containers are inspected today. To have a good chance of inspecting any suspicious container that is not being shipped by a company and port with strong security records, it would be safer, according to the statements of experts in informal conversations, to aim for inspecting 10 to 15 percent of all traffic. Over the long term, a new type of system might provide positive confidence in virtually all containers—and such a system is now in use in Hong Kong.[44]

As for state and local governments, in addition to committing to the greater prevention efforts noted above, they do need the right kinds of improved consequence-management capabilities. For example, a major city could purchase several dozen mobile interoperable communications systems, at a cost of perhaps $1 million each, to facilitate communication among first responders. The idea is that not every police radio needs to have the capacity to talk with every fire or rescue radio, but interfaces are needed that can facilitate the cross-communications that are required at the scene of any given incident. Huge additional expenditures are not needed, but targeted additional investments make sense in such cases. Technologies are available, and procedures have been tested (through some first-responder communities as well as the military's Joint Forces

Command and Northern Command), to make these interlinkages work. But procurement practices need to be standardized and concrete plans need to be devised and implemented.

Since 9/11, as noted, key parts of the private sector have done relatively little to protect themselves. And Washington needs to spur them to do so. The role of the government is not to regulate onerous security standards everywhere, but to catalyze the private sector to protect itself. As suggested by Peter Orszag, an appealing approach would make use of the nation's insurance system, coupled with some minimal regulation of safety standards. By this concept, terrorism coverage would be mandatory on all commercial policies above some minimum threshold (e.g., several million dollars). The government would play the role of a financial backstop, as indeed it already does, given the renewal of the Terrorism Risk Insurance Act in 2005—but its role would be modified such that it would cover only extreme, catastrophic losses. A graduated rate structure in the insurance market, rather than government regulation, would then encourage best security practices at reasonable cost.

We also recommend some specific private-sector initiatives. Chemical and nuclear plants are potential targets for low-tech attacks with massive consequences. The U.S. chemical industry still has no legal framework guiding its security measures (which so far have been taken voluntarily). In this case, direct regulation is appropriate. Legislation to rectify the present lack of regulation, including requirements for periodic safety assessments and common-sense solutions, should be a priority. There are also numerous cases where dangerous chemicals should be routed around large cities, and where substitutes for them should be sought, as with chlorine for purifying water.

Nuclear power plants are now relatively well protected. However, areas where low-grade waste is stored are often not. This increases the likelihood of a radiological attack, and so the level of security in these areas must be improved.

Large buildings should have better security provisions too. Again, common sense, the use of the market, and a degree of patience can make such measures affordable. For example, when built or renovated, buildings should be fitted with air-filtration and -circulation systems that would minimize the permeation of chemical or biological agents. The most important and practicable step is to ensure that air intakes are above street level, not easily accessed, and monitored. Other steps can be taken to protect buildings against bombs and infrastructure attacks, and these should be reflected in new building codes. These could include elevators that descend to the nearest floor in the event of a power outage, the construction of important buildings at a distance from roadways, design codes for prominent buildings that would impede the progressive collapse of the structures should an explosion or other compromise occur in one part of the building, the use of shatterproof glass in large buildings' lower floors, and controlled access for entry and for parking.

The next president and future leaders in Congress will need to pursue an important homeland-security agenda. Some key vulnerable sites such as chemical plants are unprotected. So are most skyscrapers. Police forces in most cities have scant capacity to conduct counterterrorism work and depend excessively on a small national FBI capacity. Container shipping remains very lightly monitored; much air travel remains unsafe; international collaboration on homeland security has not progressed very far beyond the sharing of names on terrorist watch lists. The progress we have seen to date has been significant, and the country has become much more secure. Yet a great deal remains to be done.

The Bush administration's legacy on homeland security is likely to be mixed, with some areas of achievement and some areas of unfinished business. Future candidates should acknowledge the areas in which the Bush administration has made progress while offering well-reasoned critiques of the remaining gaps and shortcomings in the overall Bush approach.

CHAPTER 5

WINNING THE
"LONG WAR"

U NDER THE BUSH administration, America's progress in winning the long-term war on terror has been mediocre. While we have
been killing terrorists abroad and reinforcing cockpit doors at home, we
have not made progress in reducing the next generation of radical jihadists. In fact, indicators suggest that the radical-jihadist diaspora may
have grown in size since 9/11. Our reformist allies are not prevailing in
the struggle for hearts and minds between reformers and violent reac-
tionaries within the Islamic world.

. Given the seriousness of the problem at hand, and the newness of the
types of responses required to address it, no single presidency could be expected to strike a decisive blow against global violent jihadism. However, the
image of American unilateralism and arrogance that the Bush administration
has often projected to the world has complicated our efforts to prevail in this
titanic struggle. Moreover, despite its good initiatives toward the Islamic
world on matters such as trade, the Bush administration has not seized the
historic moment to develop a wide-ranging policy for addressing the full
breadth of the challenge. Most importantly of all, it has done little to help the
Islamic world strengthen and moderate itself.

As a result of all these limitations to the current administration's policies,
the next president will face an acute, enduring threat from radical, violent
Islam. As the National Intelligence Council put it bluntly in 2004, "The key
factors that spawned international terrorism show no signs of abating over
the next fifteen years."[1] That means that, while al Qaeda may not have the
cohesive leadership or sanctuary in Afghanistan that it once did, and while

the United States homeland may now be better protected than it was before, the long-term struggle to defeat terrorism at its roots remains.

Some Democrats and moderate Republicans might worry that any talk
of defeating terror at its roots will sound weak and play into the stereo-
type that progressives want to understand and coddle terrorists rather
than confront and kill them. Some of Senator Kerry's political advisers reportedly told him something like this in 2004, in discouraging him from
developing an agenda to win the long war during the campaign.

The current generation of al Qaeda and related violent jihadists need
to be destroyed, to be sure, and moderates and progressives should say
so. But we absolutely need a strategy to prevent the next generation
from forming.

No lesser hawk than Secretary of Defense Donald Rumsfeld agrees.
Although he was responsible for misguided policies at Guantanamo Bay
and elsewhere that hurt America's image and hindered the long-term
war on terrorism, he was right about the need for a strategy to win that
war. In his famous memo of October 2003, Rumsfeld wondered if the
next generation of terrorists was being recruited and trained faster than
the current generation was being arrested or killed. He also asked com-
batant commanders to consider whether the United States needed an
integrated and sweeping strategy "to stop the next generation of terrorists," noting that winning in Iraq and Afghanistan would require "a long,
hard slog."[2]

This observation seems even truer today than when Rumsfeld wrote
his memo. Al Qaeda as a strong, vertical organization has been weakened. But it has also metastasized into many local groups that form a
broad radical-jihadist movement showing no signs of weakening. And
extremist ideological groups such as Hizb ut-Tahrir are vigorously and
actively advancing the ideologies that help inspire radical-jihadist violence in dozens of countries.[3]

The Bush administration's 2006 national-security strategy makes similar points about the need for a long-term strategy, arguing that "in the
short run, the fight involves using military force and other instruments of
national power to kill or capture the terrorists; deny them safe haven or
control of any nation; prevent them from gaining access to WMD; and
cut off their sources of support. In the long run, winning the war on terror means winning the battle of ideas, for it is ideas that can turn the dis-
enchanted into murderers willing to kill innocent victims."[4]

President Bush came up with a partial answer to this challenge in his second inaugural address, with its focus on the promotion of democracy. It was a good speech as far as it went. While hardly a panacea, and hardly a radical notion in the history of American foreign policy, promoting democracy should be part of America's long-term counterterrorism policy. Democracy is consistent with not only American values but universal human aspirations. Promoting democracy is consistent with Americans' longstanding view that values should help share their nation's foreign policy, and with other countries' historical tendency to look to the United States for leadership and inspiration. An emphasis on democracy, human rights, and values helped win the Cold War; it has also inspired democracy movements over the years from East Asia to Latin America to Eastern Europe, to the benefit of the vast majority of peoples in those regions. By contrast, where America has placed less value on democracy over the years, largely in its dealings with many countries of the broader Middle East, it has built relationships on sand—as demonstrated most vividly in the U.S. estrangement from Iran after the fall of the Shah and the actions of 15 Saudi hijackers on September 11, 2001. Democracy promotion is a sound pillar for American foreign policy. What is needed is not to discard Bush's framework, but to apply it sagely—and to complement it with other policies.

A broader policy framework would feature elements of foreign-assistance programs, better diplomacy, and similar "soft" programs. By implication, this approach would also raise the profile of the secretary of state in the long-term war on terror, since most such activities are under that official's jurisdiction. These programs may not seem to have much to do with hard power. But they do. Employing hard power well usually requires elements of soft power in the mix. Defeating an enemy requires a comprehensive approach when the enemy is entrenched in many countries and capable of regenerating its ranks through propagation of a popular, if brutal, ideology. So while Democrats and moderate Republicans should probably begin their discussions of counterterrorism policy by talking about military power and homeland defenses, they should also recognize that their fellow citizens are savvy enough to know that a long-term strategy to defeat terrorism in all its aspects is smart, not woolly-headed.

In addition, many of the key initiatives we propose below can be accurately described as tough-minded policies. For example, efforts to foster greater study of Islam and Arabic in the United States will produce more Americans who understand and empathize with Muslims, to be sure. But they will also produce more capable intelligence analysts and war fighters to deal with any future problems in the Islamic world.

The core of the strategy we develop below, however, focuses on helping Islamic societies strengthen their own developmental paths. The single most important element in this type of program should be a major global initiative to help improve education throughout the developing world—not an initiative led exclusively by the United States, but one led by the community of donor nations in general, and not an initiative directed exclusively toward Islamic countries, but one directed toward the developing countries as a group. This type of approach, built on the logic of the United Nations' Millennium Development Goals, would not be vulnerable to charges of American imperialism and the damage to U.S.-Islam relations such charges could cause, yet it would directly address the counterterrorism agenda.

Taken together, the various proposals presented in this chapter might cost the United States about $5 billion a year—a substantial figure, but roughly equal to one month's military expenditures in Iraq. Given the stakes, the price is hardly excessive.

TRENDS IN THE ISLAMIC WORLD AND IN U.S.-ISLAM RELATIONS

To gauge progress in the long-term war on terrorism, it is important to assess two key dynamics. The first is the health of individual Islamic societies in terms of quality of education, economic opportunity, political discourse, gender equality, and civil society. Scholars have been right to point out that individual poverty and/or lack of education do not correlate strongly with proclivity to carry out terrorism. But as Susan Rice has compellingly argued, most terrorists nonetheless are spawned in societies, or pockets of countries, where extremism flourishes and educational and economic opportunities are weak.[5] That means the basic health of societies is a critical determinant of progress in the long-term war on terrorism.

A second indicator of trends in the counterterrorism agenda is the state of Islamic-world relationships with the West in general and the United States in particular. If America is hated more, and vilified more, it seems likely to be attacked more.

Of course, in a world with 1.2 billion Muslims and dozens of Muslim-majority states, assessing the state of Islam is a complex undertaking. But it can be beneficial nonetheless to try to take stock and note trends. Although it is an imperfect method, the easiest way to do this is to focus primarily on the bellwethers of the Islamic world—its largest and most influential states.

A convenient categorization of Islamic or largely Islamic countries might first divide them into two main groups: those falling within the U.S. military's Central Command area of responsibility and those falling within its Pacific Command's purview. We do not mean to suggest that America's primary approach for dealing with this part of the world should be military; quite the contrary, in fact. Military areas of responsibility simply happen to describe the Islamic world in categories that prove useful in this discussion. It so happens that CENTCOM's area of responsibility—Pakistan and the greater Middle East—combined with parts of Northern Africa covered by the U.S. European Command, will be the site of the primary challenges in the near future. The Pacific Command (PACOM) zone, which covers India and points eastward, including Bangladesh, Thailand, Malaysia, and Indonesia, is of secondary concern because the general situation in these places is better.

A third zone, much smaller geographically and in terms of Muslim population, is Europe. It is important, to be sure, and the fact that radical jihadists are fairly numerous within Europe places further importance on some of the homeland-security measures we discussed in Chapter 4 (e.g., improved use of biometrics on passports). But otherwise, as important as this issue may be, the presence of radical jihadists within Europe is largely a question for Europeans to address, and a less central determinant of the general state of the Islamic world.

Trends in the Pacific Command Region

Most trends are at least generally favorable within the PACOM zone. India is booming economically and, despite serious Islamic-Hindu problems in the 1990s, enjoying better inter-religious relations of late. Its basic human indicators—literacy, GDP growth per capita, child mortality—are all moving clearly in the right direction. Its politics, while highly contentious at times, are solidly democratic, offering outlets for those desiring change. And as for the second issue raised above—perceptions of the United States as an indicator of trends in the counterterrorism effort—India's relations with the United States have never been better.[6]

Bangladesh has seen some cases of terrorism recently, but in general has seen nothing like the violent Islamic fundamentalism seen in Pakistan to the west. There is no issue like Kashmir or Afghanistan to give the government of Bangladesh incentive to stoke fundamentalist rage.

GDP growth is less strong than in India, trends in human-development indicators are somewhat less impressive, and overpopulation is a big problem. But the country has nonetheless made progress in basic health and education indicators and GDP growth. It also has fairly good relations with the United States.[7]

Indonesia, the world's most populous Muslim country, is a complex case. It has been a major home to Jemaah Islamiah (JI), a close affiliate of al Qaeda. It has also been the site of several serious terrorist strikes, including the Bali bombing of 2002. Corruption remains a major problem, and the army remains too heavily involved in internal security. But the society is strong in many ways after decades of gradual economic improvement. There has been recent progress toward a peace accord in Aceh. And the tsunami-relief efforts of 2004 have helped America improve its standing in that key nation.[8]

Thailand, which has a substantial Muslim population, experienced political tumult in early 2006 due to the actions of a prime minister widely seen as corrupt. But in the aftermath of that crisis, Thai politics are likely to stabilize. The country has been growing strongly for quite a while, and there has been no jihadist element to indigenous terrorism problems.

Malaysia is more strongly Muslim than Thailand, and its territory and citizens have had somewhat greater roles at times in the global radical-jihadist movement. But Malaysia is doing well economically and otherwise, so the appeal of radical thinking is limited in that country.

The Philippines have their problems, but the linkages between these problems and global terrorism are for the most part quite limited given its small Islamic population.

Trends in the Central Command Region

Things are worse, and not headed in as auspicious a direction, in the greater Middle East. Starting in Pakistan and moving westward, the major countries in this zone face larger internal challenges than do those in the PACOM zone—and the United States often has more severe difficulties in getting along with them.

Only a few countries in Central Command's area of responsibility can be said to be doing well and enjoying good relations with America—Jordan, Morocco, Qatar, Bahrain, Kuwait, and the UAE. (And of these, several need to make much more serious efforts to democratize.) Turkey has been anti-American of late, largely in response to the situation of the Kurds in Iraq, but even so, it is not a major cauldron for radical jihadism.

Within the broader Middle East region, al Qaeda and related groups continue to have large numbers of followers bent on using violence at home or abroad. There is an uncomfortably high risk of a catastrophic event in this region—such as a coup in Saudi Arabia or Pakistan.

Pakistan displays gradually improving GDP per capita and some positive movement on human-development indicators such as health and literacy rates. In addition, the country's ruling elite remains solidly pragmatist and generally pro-Western. Pakistan has been central in the war on terrorism, killing or capturing more than six hundred suspected operatives from al Qaeda and related groups in the last five years.

Nonetheless, on balance the picture in regard to Pakistan is bleak. That country has been described as a time bomb waiting to explode, and such an assessment may not, alas, be far off base. Birth rates remain high, poverty is endemic in much of the country, economic progress is slow, and regions in the south and west are only partially controlled by the government. The Musharraf government has failed to return the country from military to civilian rule to date. It has also done little to strengthen the political-party system so that civilian rule might be solidly established in the medium to long term. Anti-Americanism, while widespread, may have declined in recent years, as anger about the Iraq invasion has faded slightly from its 2003 peak, and as U.S. earthquake-relief efforts in 2005 and 2006 have helped America's image. But the improvements are not yet substantial. Although the best-known terrorist groups operating in Kashmir have been outlawed, elements in both the Pakistani army and the intelligence services are still believed to support them. Most concerning of all, of course, is the fact that this unstable country has nuclear weapons.[9]

Iran remains the number-one state sponsor of terrorism in the world, especially due to its close association with and sponsorship of Hezbollah. Iran's primary focus has been on attacking Israel, but it has shown a willingness to attack others—including American military personnel at Khobar Towers in Saudi Arabia in 1996, Jewish sites in Argentina in 1992 and 1994, and 241 American and fifty-eight French peacekeepers in Lebanon in 1983.[10]

Iraq remains an unfinished project likely to produce nothing more than a costly passable outcome—a country that will likely be the Arab world's largest democracy, but also its most violent and unstable state, for years to come. We do not mean to deny the strategic benefits of unseating Saddam, only to clearly take stock of the very substantial costs of that mission—and the fact that, the Bush administration's greatest hopes notwithstanding, it is difficult to envision that Iraq will be a model many Middle East countries will wish to emulate.

Egypt's presidential elections in 2005 were not a serious exercise in democracy. The country's huge population and weak economy provide the raw materials for support for terrorism. That said, some trends in health, education, and income mitigate what is on the whole a less than inspirational story.[11]

A similar conclusion must be reached about Saudi Arabia. Of course, Saudi Arabia is far wealthier than Egypt, but it is even more seriously afflicted by violent Islamic extremism—and by a nondemocratic ruling elite. The U.S. government has been heartened by Saudi Arabia's initial clampdowns on terrorism in the wake of 9/11 and violent jihadist attacks on Saudi soil in 2003. The Saudi government killed most of the country's top terrorists, disseminated antiterrorism messages through public media, and froze hundreds of thousands of bank accounts suspected of being linked to terrorism-related activities. But structural political reform remains necessary and is being attempted only very slowly, if at all.[12]

Lebanon may have taken a modest step forward after the departure of Syrian troops in 2005. However, all that changed in July of 2006. Its politics will likely remain highly unstable and vulnerable to sectarian strife for a very long time.

Equally distressing, the surprise victory of Hamas in 2006 elections in the Palestinian Authority, which gave the group outright control of the parliament and the prime ministership, constitutes a major setback for the Palestine-Israel peace process and for the momentum of the Bush administration's democracy-promotion agenda.

The Hamas victory is a huge setback for President Bush and the United States, and it shows that a more sophisticated, patient doctrine is needed. Democracy promotion should never be equated with simple support for elections—which can translate into a tyranny of the majority. It is essential to build respect for minority and individual rights as well as for nonviolence. As Martin Indyk, former assistant secretary of State for the Near East and former U.S. ambassador to Israel, put it, "democracy cannot be the antidote to terror if the terrorists use democracy to gain advantages against us, and yet that is what is happening."[13] Promoting democracy, in the end, means asking people who hold absolute or near-absolute power to take steps that may diminish their power or create risks that may lead to their losing it altogether. As such, it requires extremely adept diplomacy, patience, and a subtle touch (to avoid discrediting re-formers in a region where association with the United States is often seen as more bad than good). It also requires firm and principled use of carrots and sticks, an arena in which the Bush administration has been better suited. But in countries where immediate alternatives to current regimes are nonexistent or unacceptable to American interests, and where stark economic or military punishment is not practical, patience and soft power must be married with principle and hard power if the United States is to be effective.

Other Trends of Note

Certain parts of Northern Africa remain of great concern in the broad struggle against terrorism. Somalia is still lawless, and the combination of that fact and its geographic proximity to Arab states with strong al Qaeda links makes it a plausible haven for jihadists. Parts of the Sahel extending to northern Nigeria are also weakly governed, home to radicalized popu-lations, or otherwise appealing to the global terrorist movement.

America's public standing in the Middle East remains at a low point. A slew of public-opinion polling, from Pew and Zogby and others, shows that America's favorability rankings in the region are now typically 20 to 40 percent. We must take steps to reverse this trend. There has been some progress since the low point of 2003, with U.S. favorability typi-cally increasing by 10 percentage points or more, but the numbers are still poor. (For example, according to Pew, U.S. popularity in Indonesia in 2000 was 75 percent, declining to 15 percent in 2003 but rebounding to 38 percent in 2005 and slipping somewhat to 30 percent in 2006. In Turkey, the trend was actually worse; the respective figures were 52, 15, 23, and 12 percent. In Pakistan, the figures for 2000, 2003, 2005, and 2006 were 23, 13, 23, and 27. For Lebanon and Jordan, 2000 data from Pew is not available, but the respective figures for 2003 and 2005 were 27 percent and 42 percent in Lebanon, and 1 percent and 21 percent in Jordan (with the Jordan figure slipping to 15 percent in 2006) Another reason for hopefulness is that younger people in some Middle Eastern countries are more pro-American than older adults. All that said, there is still a long way to go.[14] And the above numbers pre-date the Lebanon crisis of 2006.

What about the strength of violent jihadist international networks? There is good news here as well as bad. As noted, al Qaeda has been weakened and put on the run. The movement also lacks a compelling strategic vision, and this may limit its appeal over time. Al Qaeda's tendency to turn on its own—attacking the governments of many Islamic countries, and their broad interests, as well as the West—has already limited its appeal.[15] But these judgments must be seen as provisional. Also, even if they are correct, they should not be wholly reassuring. Osama bin Laden remains popular in the Middle East. Al Qaeda and related movements do not appear to have diminished in overall membership and may well have grown. Total numbers of attacks globally remain very high by historical standards; incredibly, global terrorism has caused more annual fatalities in recent years than it did in 2001, as noted before.

THE AGENDA FOR THE NEXT PRESIDENT

The language of official Bush-administration policy is generally convincing in its call for a broad strategy focused on the "long war" and involving all elements of national power. What has often been lacking is policy initiatives that go beyond rhetoric.

The Bush administration has come up with a few useful programs. For example, the Middle East Partnership Initiative, designed to foster development of democratic institutions and better governance, is a good idea. But even with MEPI, there have been problems, such as the failure of the U.S. government to convince Arab governments to come to the June 2004 G8 summit in Sea Island, Georgia, where the related Broader Middle East and North Africa Initiative was unveiled.

Political Reform and Democracy Promotion

Direct support for political reform within the Islamic world is critical, as President Bush has recognized. The idea that the West could continue to buy Saudi oil and provide for the Kingdom's security while ignoring its internal practices has been invalidated—by Saudi support for the Taliban in the past, by Saudi funding of extremist mosques and madrassas, and by the fact that fifteen of the nineteen September 11 hijackers originated from that country.

Despite the arguments of some critics, it was therefore appropriate for the president to promote democracy as the broad, unifying, and idealistic theme of his second inaugural address. It may have given a boost to reformers in places such as Lebanon in ensuing months.[16] Moreover, the president's encouragement of democracy is consistent with the Clinton administration's strategy of "engagement and enlargement," which sought to solidify the zone of democratic peace in Europe and elsewhere using tools such as NATO enlargement and Madeleine Albright's idea for a community of democracies. And although President Bush's speech did not immediately win converts around the world, and his idea for a G8 Broader Middle East Initiative met with skeptical reactions in June 2004, the Middle East Partnership Initiative has apparently become more popular throughout much of the Arab world—as indicated, for example, by the numbers of groups applying for MEPI grants.[17]

But the Bush vision has been flawed. To begin, it has not been sufficiently conditional. In fact, while democracy promotion has often been the bumper sticker used by American presidents of both parties to describe part of their foreign-policy platforms, in fact the United States does not believe in just any kind of democracy. We do not support the tyranny of the majority. We also do not support elections that usher in governments that then terminate the future democratic process in their own countries, and essentially allow themselves to be voted into positions of autocracy. The United States supports constitutional democracy with protection for individuals and minorities. It also supports democracies that try to resolve their differences with other countries peacefully.

In the specific case of the Middle East, where Islamist parties are clearly both popular among citizens and often inimical to core U.S. interests, simple majority rule can lead to oppression of losers, violence against other countries in the region, support for terrorism, and the possibility of "one person, one vote, one time" (i.e., singular democratic elections followed by constitutional changes that work against future exercises in democracy). Where political reform has worked acceptably well, as in the cases of Turkey and, to lesser extents, Lebanon and Jordan, it has been in situations where Islamists were forced to moderate their agendas by relatively strong political systems involving significant forces besides a single, oppressive ruling party.[18] That is not to say that Islam must be kept out of politics to create true democracy; most Muslims would insist on having their religion influence their political views to an extent.[19] But genuine, peaceful political competition with protections for minorities and for electoral losers is of paramount importance.

If the United States and other outside actors are to be successful in promoting reform, they will have to support elections even if that means bringing to power more anti-Western elements at times.[20] But elections should not, as noted, amount to tyranny of the majority. Groups that win elections but then impose draconian measures on their populations, use violence against their people or their neighbors, reverse the democratic changes that allowed them to come to power, or support terrorism need not be generously aided if and when they do win.[21] Moreover, the United States need not push equally hard for immediate elections in all places; in some cases, a more gradual route to democracy may be most sound.

Fortunately, the United States and other outside powers have help in this matter—from those Arab reformers who have even more of a stake in the problem than we do, and who can help sketch out the bounds of the feasible and desirable. Some groups have already organized conferences and issued declarations of principles or roadmaps for reform, as with the Arab NGO Beirut Summit Letter of March 2004, the Alexandria Charter of that same month (written by 150 prominent Arab intellectuals), and a similar effort by one hundred prominent individuals resulting in the Doha Declaration of June 2004. The thrust of these efforts is a clear and impassioned push for more democracy and more rule of law, with an acknowledgment of the difficulties of moving directly to national elections in many countries.[22]

The United States should be willing to push Arab governments toward reform at key moments, but it should also have healthy doses of patience in its overall approach. Washington can reduce diplomatic contacts when setbacks occur, as with Egypt's recent sham presidential elections. It can make support for membership of key Arab states in the World Trade Organization contingent on at least some steps toward political reform. Congress and the president can consider reducing aid to those repressive Arab regimes (again, Egypt may be the most important potential case) that do not develop a reasonable reform strategy.[23] In all such efforts, however, patience will be essential, since a push for immediate elections would be futile or even counterproductive in most cases—as Hamas's victory shows.

Educational Reform in Islamic Countries

Another limitation of the Bush vision of democracy promotion has been a lack of appreciation of the fact that, by themselves, efforts to seek more elections cannot effectively rebuild societies. A healthy democracy requires a robust civil society that produces good candidates with serious platforms, and a citizenry aware of the challenges and tradeoffs that are inevitable in governing. Developing a healthy democracy requires programs that are expensive, multifaceted, and long term in nature.

The Bush administration has made several small steps in helping a number of Mideast states strengthen their economies and their societies. Most notable, perhaps, has been the promotion of free-trade pacts with Bahrain, Jordan, Morocco, Oman, and the United Arab Emirates. But much more is required. For one thing, the concept of free-trade pacts with Middle East countries should be broadened to become a larger initiative that would include Egypt, Bangladesh, Pakistan, Afghanistan, and Indonesia. Through the lifting of textile quotas and other measures, this initiative could increase employment and expand income in these states by $40 billion a year, according to economist Edward Gresser—hardly a panacea, but the kind of direct support for the working poor that can greatly help the economic health of the region.[24]

In addition, policy should go beyond existing ideas to complement the top-level push for political reform and free-trade pacts with stronger human talent and capacity.[25] Rather than rely on a top-down approach, we should also work from the bottom up and build stronger societies and economies where possible.[26]

In this regard, educational reform is a critical challenge and opportunity. And there is a major role for outside donors, including the United States and a group of moderate but credible Muslims, to play in overseeing and guiding curriculum reform. We must support educational reform in the Islamic world wherever countries are prepared to put aid resources to good use in creating schools—public or private—with more nuanced curricula and a smaller role for firebrand clerics. A number of experts have pointed out that better education (or higher income) hardly guarantees less terrorism—after all, many of the 9/11 hijackers had studied in their home countries and in the United States at an advanced level. But it is also true that societies lacking strong educational systems and thus the solid underpinnings of vibrant economies tend not to be healthy societies. As a result, cynicism and extremism are more likely to take root. At an individual level, better education and more money do not prevent terrorism. But the regions of the world that are busy educating their children, developing their economies, and otherwise building up their societies are generally not the cauldrons of Islamic extremism today.

Pakistan, Yemen, Indonesia, and other relatively poor Islamic countries could benefit greatly from more aid for education. Pakistan alone has more than 160 million people, including more than 50 million of school age, yet it devotes a miserly share of its government budget to education and, consequently, fails its people in this area. Almost 60 percent of the population gets no schooling; 15 percent gets only one to six years of school. The problem, of course, is much broader than Pakistan. After sub-Saharan Africa, Southern Asia and Western Asia are the world's worst-performing regions in terms of providing universal primary education for their children.[27]

U.S. aid to Pakistan has increased greatly, to over $300 million a year, since 9/11. But only a few tens of millions are devoted to education.[28] The World Bank does not do a great deal itself; annual educational aid to the entire South Asia region has averaged about $300 million a year since 2000 (including loans and grants), and educational aid to the Middle East has averaged just slightly more than $100 million a year.[29] As the 9/11 Commission and subsequent 9/11 Public Discourse Project have pointed out, the United States has initiated no major effort to improve education in Pakistan or other Muslim countries, and broader international efforts remain weak as well.[30]

Many of the Islamic countries at issue do not meet the president's criteria to qualify for his major foreign-assistance initiative—Millennium Challenge Account (MCA) funds. Indeed, among Arab states, in 2005 only Morocco met the income criteria as well as the good-governance criteria required to qualify for these funds.[31] One could make the case that helping these nations is urgent enough on national-security grounds to require a separate, new, and bold effort such as the education initiative proposed here, even for countries that do not fully meet MCA guidelines. This is not to say that money should be thrown at the problem. However, more resources would be appropriate for some countries and some usages.[32]

Although the United States does provide more than $5 billion a year to the Arab world in aid, most of that goes to a small number of key partners—Egypt, Jordan, and the Palestinian Authority prior to Hamas's 2006 election victory. America's major initiative toward the region since 9/11, the Middle East Partnership Initiative, has been funded at only about $100 million a year for the combined purposes of improving civil society, governmental performance, *and* economic entrepreneurship.[33]

Within the broad context of educational reform, the United States should promote several specific efforts as well. One is improved science education in the Islamic world.[34] Other targeted efforts could include journalism fellowships at American media organizations, policy institutions, and journalism schools.[35]

An education initiative of this type would effectively constitute one piece of the U.N.'s broad Millennium Development Goals initiative for

2015. The MDG initiative lays out ambitious goals not only in education, but also in health care, income growth, and other important aspects of global development. Supporting the full agenda of the MDG would cost the United States some $20 billion a year, and all donors combined about $65 billion.[36] Such an increase seems unrealistic, especially as part of a U.S. presidential-campaign platform. But a robust global education initiative makes sense even if other aspects of a full MDG agenda are scaled back or pursued more gradually, since it also could serve a key role as a counterterrorism strategy. Such a program would require an increase in America's aid levels of several billion dollars a year, and would constitute the bulk of the costs of all programs proposed in this chapter.[37]

Providing aid for such educational projects is a delicate political matter and must be handled carefully. Aid given generously and sincerely can greatly help America's image while it helps the recipient nation. This occurred in a different way in Pakistan after the earthquake-relief effort of 2005, a year in which America's popularity rose among that country's population to about 45 percent while Osama bin Laden's popularity was declining into the mid–30s.[38]

But to accomplish this, the United States must avoid giving the impression that the educational initiative is a naked attempt to defeat terrorism or purchase better public relations. These are legitimate goals, but they should not be promoted as the *only* important objectives of this initiative. As such, the effort should be pursued multilaterally, and its target should be not only Islamic countries but developing states in general. President Bush missed an opportunity to take this approach in 2005 when, at the Scotland G8 summit, he disagreed with British Prime Minister Tony Blair over the desirability of drastically increasing foreign-aid levels in general.[39] The president was right that the proposed increase— $50 billion a year from the United States alone, if it were to donate 0.7 percent of its GDP as suggested—would be too much and wasteful. But rather than simply oppose the idea, he should have sought a scaled-back version of it that he could support.

The United States and other donors would also be well advised to heed the advice of reformers within the Islamic world in devising their education initiatives. For example, the well-known *Arab Human Development Report 2002*, written by Arab intellectuals, noted both the considerable progress of Arab countries in recent decades in educational realms as well as their remaining challenges. Female literacy has increased greatly, some governments spend more on education than do their counterparts in other regions of the developing world, and adult literacy has improved as well. But the quality of schools needs work, research and development as well as information-technology resources are in need of expansion, and freer political debate is needed—not only for the good of the region's politics but also for the broader intellectual development of its citizenries.[40]

Sophistication and nuance are also needed in addressing the problem of madrassas. These religious schools are often better, or at least less dangerous, than critics argue, and also have an important historical and contemporary role in serving populations often not reached by the public educational system or social safety net. In addition, while they do sometimes teach radicalism, it is only fair to note that most terrorists have not come from the madrassas. Even if one includes Saudi public schools in the mix, given their propensity to teach fundamentalism the way madrassas often do, fewer than half of the terrorists in scholar and former foreign-service officer Marc Sageman's well-respected database come from such schools. As such, ideas such as India's program to offer funding for madrassas to add teachers in the sciences and other topics of modern relevance may be a better type of approach than generally futile efforts to regulate the madrassas rigorously or shut them down altogether.[41]

Educational Initiatives in the United States

The United States should also develop initiatives to help the American public better understand Islam and Muslim peoples. These programs could breed greater U.S. respect and appreciation for this great civilization and great religion. Acquainting more Americans with the Islamic world, Islamic history, the Koran, and the Arabic language could also help us win the war on terrorism in a more concrete way by addressing our nation's dearth of sophisticated, Arabic-speaking diplomats, soldiers, and intelligence experts.

This initiative could have many aspects. One would surely be expansion of foreign-language and cultural-awareness programs in secondary and college education, as well as in professional military and governmental training. In this regard, President Bush's proposed initiative for 2007 to spend $114 million more on federal support for foreign-language instruction is laudable, if overdue.[42] In many parts of the United States today, while the popularity of various foreign-language courses is evolving, it is Chinese more than Arabic that is captivating the attention of students and educators.[43] As such, it may be difficult to promote and sustain more intense focus on Arabic; to address this, presidential candidates should talk about Arabic-language learning supportively and frequently.

In addition, the State Department should, as Robert Satloff has suggested, aim for a higher level of fluency among its foreign-service officers serving throughout the Islamic world. Current levels of recommended proficiency (technically known as 3.0 on the official rating scale) are adequate for conversation but not for making convincing TV and radio appearances or public speeches.[44] As of 2003, only about fifty-five American diplomats were truly fluent in Arabic and able to meet the latter standard of excellence. One means of increasing this number may be to allow American diplomats to spend most of their career in one region (in this case, the Arabic-speaking world) so they can develop more language proficiency as well as historical knowledge and cultural sensitivity.[45]

Another aspect of this initiative could be the launch of joint speaker and writer programs. Such programs could send more Americans abroad; they could also bring more speakers, writers, and journalists from the Islamic world to engage with the U.S. public. The idea should be to help both groups better understand the opinions, aspirations, and grievances of the other.

The Mideast Peace Process

No broad policy toward the Islamic world can be complete without guiding principles for addressing the ongoing need for a Mideast peace process and a resolution to the Palestinian challenge.[46] As Shibley Telhami has argued, if 9/11 is the "prism of pain" through which Americans tend to view their relations with much of the Islamic world, the plight of the Palestinians is Muslims' prism of pain through which they understand and assess the United States.[47] Alas, as of the summer of 2006, the plight of many Lebanese may now reinforce the problem.

Of course, pursuing a Mideast peace process has been complicated historically by many factors. Most recently, it has been enormously complicated by Hamas's electoral victory of 2006. Neither Israel nor the United States can negotiate with, let alone deal very actively with, a Palestinian Authority controlled by a group that has not renounced terrorism and that officially still denies Israel's right to exist (there is some hope that this latter matter is in flux within Hamas, but it is too soon to be sure).

The Bush administration made a mistake in supporting the idea of Palestinian elections involving an unreformed Hamas. It should have encouraged Palestinian friends to demand that Hamas either renounce

violence, accept Israel's right to exist, and disarm—or (at a minimum) create a separate political organization like Northern Ireland's Sinn Féin that
would be made up of individuals not actively involved in Hamas. Again,
America's support for democracy should not be support for tyranny of the
majority against the minority, or for groups that would use their power to
attack their neighbors, as Hamas's own charter implies it might.

What is done is done. Through the first few months it was in office,
Hamas was respecting a ceasefire. Under such circumstances, outside
donors can fund nongovernmental organizations within Palestine, and
work to the extent possible through Palestinian Authority president Abu
Mazen to route assistance to the Palestinian people. Such efforts will
surely result in a reduced flow of resources compared with the recent
past, but would be far preferable to a cutoff. It would also be appropriate
for Israel to consider giving the Palestinian Authority money from cus-
toms and border-collection activities that is rightfully Palestinian, as long
as the truce continues. Alternatively, as Tamara Wittes and Martin Indyk
have argued, these and other funds could be placed in trust funds to be
made available to the Palestinian people once Hamas meets the basic requirements outlined above.[48]

More fundamentally, the United States must clearly send two messages—that it is absolutely and irreversibly committed to Israel's security,
and that it is absolutely committed to the pursuit of an independent
Palestinian state and to security and well-being for the Palestinian people. The Bush administration has been much better at conveying the first
message than the second.

Beyond this dual message, things get trickier, especially regarding Israeli settlements in the West Bank. For American political candidates,
this is a delicate question, given the need to be strong against terrorism
coupled with the moral imperative to be supportive of Israel. The United
States should understand Israel's stance on matters such as construction
of the security barrier, which is an unfortunate but reasonable exercise of
sovereignty by a state repeatedly attacked by its neighbors, as well as aggressive Israeli action against terrorists. The United States cannot, however, condone illegal and illegitimate Israeli confiscation of land that according to the U.N. is Palestinian.[49] The settlements should generally be
removed in the end, and Palestinians should have access to an East
Jerusalem that they can call their capital if they wish. Democrats have
sometimes had as hard a time clearly stating this fact as has the Bush administration. Candidates need the backbone to articulate a message some

Israelis and American Jews will not like—even as they underscore America's unwavering commitment to Israeli security.

Indeed, on the latter point, there is no reason that Israel's security partnership with the United States need stay as informal as it has been. The partnership could be made more official by bilateral treaty. Any such move should, however, require Israel to return the overwhelming majority of the West Bank to Palestinians, and to compensate the Palestinians fairly and equitably for any small amounts of land that are not returned.

Summits and Exchanges

Although summits and exchanges are more naturally part of the realm of diplomacy than that of hard power, high-level diplomacy can play a role in the long-term war on terrorism. Former president Clinton provided an example of how effective such exchanges can be in a very well-received speech he gave to a set of American and Muslim world leaders in Qatar in January 2004.[50] Clinton expressed admiration for Islam's culture and history. He noted its common roots with Christianity and Judaism. He acknowledged the West's tendency to be ignorant of the many aspects and characteristics and countries of the Islamic world—while at the same time challenging the common misperception among Muslims that the United States is indifferent to their well-being and always opposed to their interests.

Of course, greater interaction between Western and Islamic societies should not depend exclusively or even primarily on the speeches of current or former officials. University, think tank, and other collaborations, some of them televised, can make a contribution as well. Government funding, delivered through an independent organization, may be useful for some such efforts, but many—if not most—should be unofficial, unabridged, and uncensored. Debate should be as prevalent as agreement, and it should cover a range of issues from religious doctrine to historical grievances and legacies to the role of women in society to the media to foreign-policy issues. Indeed, following the recommendations of the Djerejian Report, a 2003 task-force study focused on public diplomacy toward the Islamic world, a center for U.S.-Arab/Muslim studies and dialogue might be created for this purpose. It could serve as the focal point for many such events in the United States, as well as for ongoing scholarship, research, writing, and exchanges.[51] In addition to a physical center, the United States and other donors should also establish a Middle East foundation to support these and other exchange activities.[52]

Further, the United States should follow former CIA director Robert Gates' suggestion to ensure that more Muslim students can study in the United States, and that other legitimate visitors can come to this country without undue hassle, delay, or limitations. This policy would necessitate more resources for various visa and immigration services and the creation of expedited procedures for student visas. The case can be made not only that the Bush administration has undermined long-term security by turning away young cultural ambassadors when we need them more than ever, but also that the inefficient visa policies have hurt U.S. higher education and the international business of U.S. firms. In the years 2003, 2004, and 2005, the number of young people from the Middle East coming to the United States to study declined by 9 percent, 10 percent, and 2 percent, respectively.[53]

Beyond the matter of formal education, the United States and other Western countries should endeavor to make their ideas and their resources available to more Muslims. Innovative uses of new technology, such as inexpensive, accessible Internet centers sponsored by the United States State Department, could be more effective than the cultural centers of old. A candidate for president could also propose cultural-exchange programs such as more sister-city partnerships and initiatives to bring the private sector into outreach toward poor Islamic regions. Several other worthy ideas were also put forth in the Djerejian Report. They include translating more English-language books into Arabic, expanding English-language instruction in the Islamic world, creating American-studies centers at universities in the Arab and Islamic worlds, and creating more "American Corners" with access to American cultural and political information and related matters at a multitude of locations to re-create some of the benefits of the cultural centers of old.[54]

CONCLUSION

The Bush administration's official doctrine on how to win the long-term war on terrorism has been partially correct. For example, the Quadrennial Defense Review of February 2006, in a section titled "Fighting the Long War," provides a very clear proposition about the nature of the campaign the United States has been waging: "Since 2001, the U.S. military has been continuously at war, but fighting a conflict that is markedly different from wars of the past. The enemies we face are not nation-states but rather dispersed non-state networks. In many cases, actions must occur on many continents in countries with which the United States is not at war. Unlike the image many have of war, this struggle cannot be won by military force alone, or even principally. And it is a struggle that may last for some years to come."[55] The call to use all elements of national power in the war against al Qaeda and like-minded radical terrorists echoes President Bush's earlier national strategy for combating terrorism as well as the 9/11 Commission's report, but is even more blunt in stating that military tools may be less important than other instruments.[56] And the continued focus on confronting jihadist terrorism is appropriate, given the likely durability of the threat, as expressed by the National Intelligence Council and others.

Whatever the soundness of our concepts, however, global terrorism is still rampant, hatred of the United States is still prevalent, and the next generation of violent jihadists is continuing to be motivated, recruited, and trained across much of the Islamic world. To date, alas, Bush-administration rhetoric and doctrine have been stronger than U.S. action.

This situation can be changed. Most of the world's Muslims have interests that are generally compatible with those of the United States. Majorities of Muslims in most places have had favorable feelings toward the United States, or at least toward Americans, even fairly recently, and have complained more about American policy on issues such as support for Israel and the invasion of Iraq than about the United States itself.[57] In addition, however it may be perceived today, and however its own fundamentalists may wish to portray it, Islam has a strong history of supporting the rule of law, women's rights, and just government. It is not true that Islam and the West must clash over issues such as democracy or the rights of women; many strong traditions in Islam and the Koran are entirely consistent with the core values of equality and individual rights that Americans hold dear.[58] The Islamic world, with its 1.2 billion people, is a very diverse place, with large numbers of followers in countries such as Indonesia, India, Pakistan, and Bangladesh who are neither Arab nor radical. Even within the Arab world, while many have mixed feelings about the Western world, the allure of fundamentalism and terrorism is confined to a very small fraction of the population.[59]

Just as Muslims do not generally dislike what the West stands for, Americans have not historically displayed categorical animosity toward the Islamic faith or Muslim peoples. In fact, in recent military interventions, Americans have more often than not tried to help Muslims—in Lebanon in 1983, Kuwait in 1991, Somalia in 1993, Bosnia in 1995,

Kosovo in 1999, Afghanistan in 2001, and Iraq in 2003. They have often had strategic motivations as well, and have often had limited success, but they have nonetheless generally been at least somewhat effective in promoting the well-being of the peoples in question. However, it must be noted that many Americans are increasingly fearful of Islamic extremism, and this fear has led to a temporary increase in negative perceptions of Islam in general.[60] This is regrettable. Any presidential candidate needs to remind Americans of the need to make a distinction, just as George W. Bush has, between Islamic radicalism and the core tenets of the Muslim faith.

But we need to face squarely the fact that what happens within Arab and other Islamic societies is now of direct consequence to us. We also need to realize that what is now a growing tension in the relationship between the West and Islam could become a fundamental divide, complicating America's ability to work with many governments in Islamic countries and helping radical jihadists recruit many more followers in the years ahead. The long-term war on terrorism has been largely a problem for the Department of Defense, small offices with limited resources at the State Department, and the U.S. Trade Representative during the Bush administration. It is time to bring to bear a wider range of the tools of American national power and influence and to do so with much greater focus and effort.

CHAPTER 6

THE REAL TRIPLE THREAT

Energy and Security, Global Climate Change, and Terrorist Financing

THE NEXT AMERICAN president will have the opportunity to be the "energy president," seizing on a confluence of domestic factors, technological opportunities, strategic vulnerabilities resulting from current energy policy, and global environmental considerations to transform the way our society produces and consumes energy.

While the opportunity is real, so are the challenges. Increasing Americans' usage of energy-efficient vehicles, including hybrid and flex-fuel varieties, and creating a new U.S. energy portfolio, with biomass fuels leading the way, will be complicated. It will require a broad set of policy initiatives, largely in the form of tax incentives and rebates for consumers as well as producers, that will be hard to master and very difficult to describe in short political speeches. While new technologies and fuels will be economical once introduced (especially given oil price levels of 2005 and 2006), the initial annual costs could be $15 billion to $25 billion a year. Since a new president will have to make progress in curtailing the enormous federal budget deficit, as we have mentioned elsewhere in this book, a new energy program should be funded with a dedicated source, if possible. Optimally, that would involve some type of windfall-profit tax on American oil companies—and although that may sound like a political cinch, it will require consensus building and careful framing to avoid vilifying an industry that the United States still badly needs.

In other words, while any president can (and will) introduce targeted energy proposals and incentives here and there, a major national program of energy transformation will be difficult and demanding. Getting it right will not be easy; proving to the public that one has gotten it right will be even harder. It is a classic situation in which Americans will need to engage in serious and substantive political debate. It is a prime example of why the country needs a revived two-party debate on core matters of national security.

President George W. Bush spent five years promoting an energy policy that did little more than argue for drilling for oil on Alaska's north slope while ignoring the case for improved gas-mileage standards, other conservation programs, and a broad range of new energy sources. However, even he changed his tune somewhat in 2006, emphasizing the need for a new energy economy that includes much greater use of biomass and nuclear power in his State of the Union speech. But Democrats and moderate Republicans are better placed to handle this issue than are most conservatives, because they are less afraid of using the gentle hand of carefully devised government incentives to complement Adam Smith's hidden hand of the market. And that gentle, but firm, hand is needed now.

The energy issue is well positioned to benefit from a major government initiative. Those who would oppose that kind of initiative on free-market grounds should remember that there is no free market in oil today to begin with. Oil is heavily favored by government policy. Assistance for alternative fuels would largely amount to leveling off the playing field. Moreover, the aid should not have to be permanent, since alternative energy sources are becoming cost-effective. What is most needed from government is help in the process of transitioning to a more diversified U.S. energy portfolio.

Energy and American national security have been closely linked for decades. Ever since the fall of the Shah of Iran in 1979, and the Soviet invasion of nearby Afghanistan shortly thereafter, the U.S. military has focused intently on the Middle East. And since the end of the Cold War, that region has been viewed as one of two main possible locations of large-scale military activity for the United States (northeast Asia being the other). With Operation Desert Storm in 1991, and Operation Iraqi Freedom from 2003 through the present, the long-imagined possibility of large-scale U.S. military action in the Middle East has become reality.

In the age of radical jihadism, energy security and national security are now linked in another crucial way that has radically reshaped the politics of energy policy since the Carter years. All of the 9/11 hijackers came from states in the Middle East. The September 11, 2001, attacks thus threw into doubt the basic bargain the United States at least tacitly maintained with Saudi Arabia for decades—that we would tolerate its oppressive internal politics, self-indulgent royal family, and refusal to recognize Israel in exchange for cheap oil. This was a Faustian bargain, never America's proudest accomplishment, but it proved also to be strategically wrongheaded when fifteen of the nineteen September 11 hijackers turned out to be from Saudi Arabia and when radical madrassas and mosques from Afghanistan to Pakistan to the Arabian peninsula turned out to be funded largely by wealthy Saudi Wahhabis.

These facts have made Americans more willing than they have been in the past to contemplate an assertive energy policy that would lessen our dependence on the Persian Gulf region. In simple economic terms, high oil prices resultant from conflict, Hurricane Katrina, and rising global demand have increased the appeal of alternative sources of energy. So has the specter of global warming, an increasingly real threat, as not only most scientists but also most Americans now recognize.

There is also a positive case for rethinking the substance and the politics of energy security. Technology has greatly improved since the 1970s. No longer must an effective alternative-energy policy emphasize, as Jimmy Carter did, the need to wear sweaters in the winter and set the thermostat at 78 degrees in the summer. While conservation still has a very important place in energy policy, a new policy must focus on alternative sources of supply. America is not and will not soon be in a position to eliminate all dependence on foreign oil. It will be even less able to eliminate the oil import dependence of many of its closest friends, allies, and economic partners; the world economy will continue to depend on a global oil market. But the United States can dramatically reduce its dependence, increase its ability to ride out political shocks in the oil-producing regions of the world (most of which correlate with unstable or undemocratic regimes, as Senator Richard Lugar pointed out in a March 2006 speech at the Brookings Institution), and improve its leverage over dangerous regimes like Iran's that cannot now be easily sanctioned because the world needs their oil so badly.

The global-warming issue has also contributed to the new politics of energy security. This is a very important argument for changing America's energy portfolio. Indeed, in the broadest perspective, it may even be the most important reason, given the potential for dramatic consequences from rapid global warming. In the spirit of this book's main thesis, however, we would suggest that the political case for a new energy security begin with the more straightforward arguments about mitigating our nation's dependence on volatile parts of the world—and reducing the cash flows to countries that have not always put that cash to constructive use. The global-warming argument can then be introduced as a powerful reinforcing rationale for major change in how we produce and consume energy.

The scientific consensus on global warming is now strong—and harrowing in its implications. In simple factual terms, oceans could rise twenty feet or more (if most of the Greenland ice sheet melts), Europe could become ten degrees colder as the Gulf Stream is weakened, and low-lying countries such as Bangladesh could lose much if not most of their territory to the sea (as could Florida and other lower-lying American states). Global weather could also continue to become more volatile and dangerous, featuring stronger hurricanes (due to rising water temperatures), longer and deeper droughts, and major displacement of large numbers of species from traditional habitats. Most of these things have already begun to happen and have been linked at least in part to global warming; for example, in the last thirty-five years, the frequency of Category 4 and 5 hurricanes appears to have doubled.[1]

These developments are serious enough in and of themselves, and they could also have important foreign-policy consequences for the United States. As a country containing only 5 percent of the world's population but consuming 25 percent of its fuel, and refusing to sign the Kyoto Treaty or seriously pursue any alternative to it, the United States could be blamed by many others for these consequences. Under such circumstances, the transatlantic tensions over Iraq policy could seem like a minor tiff as Britain became a quasi-arctic land and central Europe began to resemble Siberia. Our purported mistreatment of certain groups of Muslims in the past could seem like small potatoes compared with our culpability for the consequences of rapidly rising sea levels throughout coastal South and Southeast Asia.

Because of these changed environmental and security landscapes, the new politics of energy security are much more appealing than those of the malaise days of the late 1970s, in the sense that we must change our ways and large numbers of Americans now realize it. Whoever succeeds George W. Bush will have huge opportunities to become the country's first real "energy president." And there is a very practical agenda that a candidate could propose on the campaign trail, then pursue while in office, to make this happen.

To date, the changed politics of energy security have led to a bit more support for research and development on alternative fuels and more-efficient cars, as President Bush espoused in his 2006 State of the Union address. There is logic to this; for example, cellulosic ethanol in particular (that is, ethanol made not from corn but from certain woods and grasses) is not yet proven to be competitive in price with gasoline. But increased use of it is a much more appealing notion overall than reliance on corn ethanol; it yields far more energy than it consumes in production, and large amounts of it can be made without diverting existing agricultural farmland to non-food uses.

Still, on balance the Bush energy agenda is much too meek and traditionalist. In tone, it is anachronistic—push research into new technologies while placing the primary thrust of policy effort on increasing production of oil (in places such as Alaska and the continental shelf). There is a serious case for more domestic oil production, to be sure, but the United States should not postpone serious promotion of new energy technologies any longer. Moreover, much of the proposed increase in funding for ethanol comes at the expense of certain other types of research into conservation and renewables.

The next American president will be in a position to push many new technologies to widespread use. To be sure, natural market forces will do some of this—particularly if oil prices stay high due to tight global supplies, natural disasters, or other causes. And the market should be allowed to do as much as possible on its own.

But the next U.S. president will be in a position to use government to hasten a process that economic and national-security fundamentals demand. The goal should be to reach a "tipping point" where technologies such as ethanol pumps and hybrid as well as flex-fuel cars are so widely available that costs go down and convenience goes way up. Candidates should talk about such plans in detail in the coming months and years. Simple language about cellulosic ethanol and hybrid or flex-fuel vehicles will no longer be enough to earn attention and credibility on the subject. Candidates should address the following matters in some detail:

- how we get to an energy-efficient economy (especially in terms of government's role in using subsidies, tax credits, and occasional regulations to hasten adoption of new technologies)
- how much of our oil demands can realistically be satisfied with alternative fuels and alternative vehicle technologies

- how much farmland, if any, will be needed for the harvesting of alternative fuels
- how greater use of ethanol should affect broader trade and agricultural policy in the United States
- which other energy-saving measures can reduce our need for imported oil in particular

The issues are numerous and complex—but the good news is that Americans can easily understand a good deal about energy policy because it affects their daily lives so greatly, and because debates over energy have been occurring for more than a quarter century.

AMERICA'S DANGEROUS OIL DEPENDENCE

Much of the problem with current American oil dependence can be seen by examining current U.S. relationships with Saudi Arabia and Iran. Particularly after jihadist attacks on their own soil in 2003, the Saudis clamped down on some types of egregious practices they had previously tolerated. But the 9/11 Public Discourse Project reported in December 2005 that reforms in Saudi Arabia have been of limited significance to date (the project's participants gave the Saudis a grade of D on their progress).[2] Beyond that, moreover, the United States has not truly reassessed its basic bargain with Saudi Arabia or its basic posture toward the Persian Gulf. It has continued to assume, and accept, that it will depend on that country and the broader region for oil. In fact, it is on a trajectory to increase its dependence in the years to come, as the tables below suggest. The broad message here is that the United States needs to recognize that its heavy energy dependence on a few key volatile regions of the world will not resolve itself naturally with time. In fact, the situation is likely to get worse.

This reality of extreme dependence, fostered by the absence of a serious U.S. energy policy, is problematic for a number of reasons—even beyond the crucially important issue of global warming. The flow of petrodollars continues to put huge funds into the hands of rich princes (some of them still sympathetic to Osama bin Laden). Our dependence also makes us vulnerable in both economic and military terms, as we must worry acutely about the stability of the Middle East, which holds two-thirds of declared global oil reserves. (Saudi Arabia holds a quarter of the global total itself.)[3]

TABLE 6.1 Key Nations with Proven Oil Reserves (2004)

Country	Thousand Million Barrels	Share of World Total
Saudi Arabia	262.7	22.1%
Iran	132.5	11.1%
Iraq	115.0	9.7%
Kuwait	99.0	8.3%
UAE	97.8	8.2%
Venezuela	77.2	6.5%
Russia	72.3	6.1%
Kazakhstan	39.6	3.3%
Libya	39.1	3.3%
Nigeria	35.3	3.0%
United States	29.4	2.5%
China	17.1	1.4%
Canada	16.8	1.4%
Qatar	15.2	1.3%
Mexico	14.8	1.2%
Other	124.9	10.5%
Total	1,188.6	100%

SOURCE: Putting Energy in the Spotlight: BP Statistical Review of World Energy, 2005, page 4–19.

NOTE: The figure for Canadian oil reserves includes an official estimate of Canadian oil sands "under active development."

Trends in global and U.S. energy use are also worrisome. China and India will each double their energy use between 2000 and 2020. (This fact and others make Senator Hillary Clinton's idea of expanding the size of the U.S. strategic petroleum reserve, and encouraging India and China to create their own substantial stocks, a good idea.[4]) The world on the whole will increase energy use by about 50 percent by 2025, with nearly 40 percent of the total being provided by oil, almost 25 percent by natural gas, more than 20 percent from coal, 8 percent from renewables, and 6 percent from nuclear-power plants.[5] The United States continues to increase its need for foreign oil, both in terms of numbers of barrels per year and as a fraction of total petroleum use. While the United States has become much more energy-efficient per unit of GDP, it has stopped making major improvement in areas such as automobile fuel economy. And while coal remains abundant in the United States, even natural gas is

TABLE 6.2 Key Oil Producing Nations (2004)

Country	Million of Barrels/Day	Share of World Total
Saudi Arabia	10.584	13.1%
Russia	9.285	11.9%
United States	7.241	8.5%
Iran	4.081	5.2%
Mexico	3.824	4.9%
China	3.490	4.5%
Norway	3.188	3.9%
Canada	3.085	3.8%
Venezuela	2.980	** 4.0%
UAE	2.667	3.3%
Nigeria	2.508	3.2%
Kuwait	2.424	3.1%
United Kingdom	2.029	2.5%
Iraq	2.027	** 2.6%
Other	20.847	25.5%
Total	80.260	100%

SOURCE: Putting Energy in the Spotlight: BP Statistical Review of World Energy, 2005, page 4–19.

TABLE 6.3 Key Oil Consuming Nations (2004)

Country	Million of Barrels/Day	Share of World Total
United States	20.517	24.9%
China	6.684	8.2%
Japan	5.288	6.4%
Germany	2.625	3.3%
Russia	2.574	** 3.4%
India	2.555	3.2%
South Korea	2.280	2.8%
Canada	2.206	2.6%
France	1.975	2.5%
Mexico	1.896	2.3%
Italy	1.871	** 2.4%
Other	30.286	38.0%
Total	80.757	100%

SOURCE: Putting Energy in the Spotlight: BP Statistical Review of World Energy, 2005, page 4–19.

becoming less readily available. All signs point towards greater, not lesser, energy problems in the years ahead.[6]

The latest demonstration of this problem concerns Iran, and in particular the world's efforts to deal with its nuclear program—advertised as an energy activity, but surely providing Iran with much-desired means of developing a nuclear-weapons arsenal as well. As Iran shows no signs of agreeing to proposals that would help it acquire nuclear power without gaining access to bomb materials, the world faces a dilemma. Absent military strikes, with all their downsides, the only measures that might be proportionate to Iran's offenses—and that might stand a chance of changing that country's behavior—would likely involve sweeping oil sanctions that the international community has no interest in imposing.[7]

Unfortunately, the world has steadily lost its spare production capacity over recent decades. In early 2006, the world had about 1 million barrels a day of spare production capacity, down from 7 million as recently as 2002.[8] Given the tightness of global oil markets, and Iran's substantial share of total world production (about 4 million barrels a day, or 5 percent of the global total of some 85 million barrels a day), such sanctions could drive the price of oil toward $100 a barrel or more.[9] As such, in its efforts to pressure Iran, the world is talking about little more than the usual litany of limited sanctions—on travel that Iranian leaders tend not to undertake anyway, on pistachios and rugs that account for only small parts of the nation's economy, and so on.

What to do? While there is a strong case for accepting the economic pain associated with sweeping sanctions, not even the Bush administration seems eager to pursue this option, and other countries will almost surely demur. In short, the world needs to develop an energy cushion that will allow it, if not now then over time, to consider sanctions against a country such as Iran, which so flagrantly defies the international community. To put it more positively, we need to de-link our energy security from the unpredictable and often dangerous behavior of extremist regimes.

Such an energy cushion would also be very important in the event of exogenous shocks beyond our control. For example, if political instability in Saudi Arabia temporarily put that country's energy production at risk, or shut down part of that production, the extreme dependence of the world economy on Gulf oil might lead the United States to feel the need to intervene quickly and unilaterally to restore order and oil production. After all, along with the United States and Russia, Saudi Arabia is one of the world's big three oil producers (see table), and is the largest oil exporter. It also has by far the world's largest estimated oil reserves (260 billion barrels, or nearly a quarter of the world total).[10] A sustained cutoff of Saudi oil production would wreak havoc with the world economy. Even the limited type of terrorist attack on Saudi oil attempted in early 2006 near Abqaiq, if it had succeeded, could have taken about 5 million barrels a day off the market for a stretch. This is similar in scale to what sanctions on Iran (or an Iranian refusal to export) could do.[11]

A coup in Saudi Arabia would raise other worries, some even worse. They would include the harrowing possibility of Saudi pursuit of nuclear weapons. An intensified funneling of Saudi funds to al Qaeda and radical madrassas in countries such as Pakistan would also likely result. In the event of a Saudi coup or major disruption to Saudi oil production, it would be difficult for the world not to respond assertively given current global-oil-market conditions. Although it is not a scenario we must face now, and not a scenario that political candidates should ever discuss hypothetically, it is nonetheless true that under the types of circumstances imagined here the military option might be increasingly hard to avoid. For example, if the new regime refused over a long period to pump oil, or, worse yet, if it began destroying the oil infrastructure and damaging the oil wells on its territory—perhaps out of a fundamentalist commitment to a return to the lifestyle of the first millennium—forcible intervention might be appropriate. Since virtually all Saudi oil is in the eastern coastal zones or in Saudi territorial waters in the Persian Gulf, any military mission to protect and operate the oil wells would be geographically specific and finite.[12] The United States and its partners might then put the proceeds from oil sales into escrow for a future Saudi government that was prepared to make good use of them.

But the simple act of thinking through such a scenario underscores how undesirable it would be—even if, mechanically and militarily, it would be feasible. Even though it would be serving other countries' interests as well as its own with such an action (since other industrial countries typically import an even higher fraction of their fuel from the Gulf), the United States would take the hit for putting "infidel" forces on Islam's holiest turf.

For all these reasons, the United States needs to find ways to lessen its dependence on any one oil supplier—especially while the problems inherent in depending heavily on undemocratic or unstable suppliers are likely to get worse, not better. In regard to Iran, we need the ability to impose sanctions if necessary (such capacity might also someday be needed for dealing with Venezuela or some other important oil producer). In regard to Saudi Arabia, we need enough of an energy cushion that rapid and largely unilateral military intervention would not be required in the event of turbulent events in the kingdom. It would be far preferable to permit the Saudis time to sort out any such problem on their own—or even to be able to boycott their oil for a stretch (in the event of a coup by a radical element). Even if such measures did not succeed and military intervention ultimately became necessary, the United States would benefit from having enough time to develop an international coalition acting under U.N. Security Council auspices before deploying large forces to the region.

At present, the United States is taking a foolish and unnecessary gamble by continuing to rely so heavily on every drop of oil pumped around the world that the global economy would verge on recession—and the 82nd Airborne might have to be deployed—the minute any major source was threatened.[13]

ENDING AMERICA'S ADDICTION TO FOREIGN OIL

Some politicians, sobered by 9/11 and the role of many Saudis in funding radical jihadists, are now calling for complete energy independence for the United States within twenty years. They sometimes point to estimates that the United States spends up to $100 billion a year on the military defense of oil-producing regions in the Persian Gulf—as well as more than $25 billion a month for overall oil imports.[14]

The idea of complete energy independence is appealing, but it is almost surely unrealistic, and may even be undesirable. Frankly, we have an interest in sending oil money to countries from Nigeria to Iraq to Saudi Arabia; if they use such revenue well, it can help build their economies and stabilize their politics. What we must avoid is undue, complete dependence (which might be better termed addiction), which leaves us no real room for policy maneuvering or for dealing with the unexpected. This addiction does not seem to be healthy for the big oil-producing states, either, as it can lead to distorted economies and huge excesses of cash that discourage the formation of normal work ethics.[15]

The more practical option is to diversify our liquid energy supply, which is the main cause of our excessive dependence on foreign suppliers. With his 2006 State of the Union initiative, President Bush became the latest in a long line of presidents to propose a significant new energy policy. To his credit, he zeroed in on the right alternative fuel, cellulosic ethanol, but he did not convey much sense of urgency to the initiative or propose an integrated energy policy.

The Iran crisis should clarify our understanding of how to think about such an alternative policy. We do not need to make the global oil trade obsolete. We do need enough energy independence that when people such as the mullahs in Iran pursue the nuclear bomb while supporting state terrorism and denying Israel's right to exist, we can muster the verve to stand up to them with enough leverage to have a chance of prevailing.

The first and probably most important key to this is the increased use of biofuels. It is time for the United States to do what Brazil did a generation ago and commit to providing up to half our liquid fuel from ethanol. It can now be produced from waste wood and other such agricultural products. (Corn ethanol can help, but it is cellulosic ethanol made from these other products that has the most promise for its ability to make use of marginal farmland and a wide range of plants and trees.[16]) Breakthroughs in bioengineering over the last decade have made this possible. It can be done without significantly crimping available farmland. And it can ultimately help transform the nature of the global agricultural business by reducing the rationale for the traditional subsidies we pay our farmers for food crops (and thereby providing farmers in developing countries more market opportunities, since excess production of foodstuffs in the United States would eventually decline as farmers put more effort into fuel crops).

At present, the cost of cellulosic ethanol fuel cannot easily be estimated because there are no working commercial plants. But it is expected to be competitive within several years, given current gasoline prices.[17] Indeed, depending on how one factors in the implicit cost of defending Persian Gulf oil militarily, cellulosic ethanol may even be competitive with gasoline today.

Even though Congress has been pushing gradually in this direction of late, and even though sentiment in favor of such an idea is growing, not enough will happen without a concerted and bold policy initiative. President Bush's proposal to increase spending on clean-energy research by 22 percent in 2007 (relative to a baseline level of just under $2 billion a year) is rather meek given the more ambitious rhetoric surrounding his announcement of the plan.[18] It is also too timid given the state of available technologies. The 2006 congressional campaign and, even more, the 2008 presidential race will provide excellent opportunities to debate much more ambitious ideas.

There is no reason that such a debate need be limited to Democrats, of course. As a group, they do have one ideological advantage over conservative Republicans—their typical willingness to use government initiatives to spur needed change (as opposed to conservative Republicans' tendency to rely almost totally on the free market to do so). But moderate Republicans may well be willing to use the visible hand of the federal government, rather than just the hidden hand of the market, to spur a new energy economy that, once established, should be competitive with existing energy markets and self-sustaining. Indeed, in one of the best energy speeches by any politician to date, his March 2006 Brookings address, Senator Richard Lugar made a number of suggestions in this spirit. There is a strong national-security argument for using government policy more actively in this way. Moreover, today's energy economy is hardly a free market. The United States in effect subsidizes oil enormously, mostly through the large military expenditures required every year to ensure protection of Persian Gulf supplies. The United States further advantages oil and other carbon-based fuels by not charging their consumers for their contributions to global warming. To the extent that global warming can have large, if admittedly very uncertain, costs that society and government will have to contend with, those whose energy use contributes to global warming should pay for the consequences. To ignore such costs may seem the free-market solution, but in reality it gives oil an unfair advantage.

This is not an anti-oil screed; we do not believe it necessary or practical to wean the U.S. economy from petroleum, or even petroleum imports, in the foreseeable future. Nor is it a call for subsidies that would permanently prop up inherently uneconomical alternative fuels. Rather, the goal is to level the playing field that other energy sources share with oil, and to catalyze wide adoption of an alternative-energy economy that, once established, will be viable.

Gasoline taxes are one way to bring about such an outcome, but they are politically explosive. Targeted subsidies or tax breaks—for cars that can use ethanol as well as gas, for pumping stations that offer both types of fuels, for production of appropriate agricultural products by farmers, for construction of ethanol and biodiesel production facilities—may be a smarter way to go. They are already in use for hybrid cars, typically to the tune of $2,000 to $3,000 a car in the form of tax credits.[19] There is no reason to limit the use of such financial instruments to that technology. Tax credits can be expensive, in the ballpark of $10 billion a year. But much of the money would go to American farmers and innovators, rather than Mideast oligarchs. And it would help give us the means to stand up to the latter when their political behavior becomes egregious.

Beyond vehicle subsidies, it is important for federal policy to ensure that enough fuel is produced and then made conveniently available. The latter is fairly straightforward to conceptualize, though it will take concerted effort to achieve. In the early going, before the country reaches a "tipping point" on the popularity of flex-fuel cars, service stations can be encouraged to add ethanol pumps through tax subsidies. They could even be given tax credits, allowing a large fraction of the total cost of installing a pump to be paid by Washington. The credits could be designed to phase out within a couple of years, increasing the incentives for prompt action.

An integrated policy framework to encourage ethanol production and use would take several years to achieve major results. As such, the timing should work well for the likely path of technology. As noted, cellulosic ethanol plants today are not yet in operation and may not be totally competitive right away. Based on the state of technology, the government might commit to a certain subsidization—in terms of cents per gallon—for production of ethanol, tied to the notion that Washington will ensure that the industry is profitable for the first few years of its large-scale operations. Subsidies would be phased out over time as cellulosic ethanol production technology improves. (Corn ethanol made in the United States probably has the potential to replace only 10 percent of the nation's gasoline.)[20]

To be sure, a broader national energy policy requires much more than a biofuels initiative. Political leaders seeking to make good policy, but also effective politics, out of this issue must go beyond any single solution to understand the technical and economic realities of many types of energy sources as well as many energy-efficiency measures that can reduce demand (e.g., improved appliances, a straightforward area for initiatives where U.S. efforts lag badly behind those of countries such as Japan).[21] At the same time, to communicate effectively with the American people, and to educate them, politicians must simplify their messages. There are far too many types of technologies at issue and far too many numbers, facts, and figures to toss around for political leaders simply to arm themselves with competing factoids and anecdotes about new energy ideas.

Ethanol, Better Cars, and Beyond

We propose an energy-policy framework that focuses on petroleum, that finds a simple and memorable way to talk about the magnitude of our current dependency, and that sets concrete targets for diversifying supply (and, in some cases, reducing demand). The latter targets should focus primarily on greater use of biofuels and more efficiency in consumption of energy, with a particular focus on vehicles. Making this happen without major disruption to the market or large cost to the government would require one additional key idea—creation of an official energy and economics regulatory commission that would be empowered by the Congress and the president to determine proper levels of subsidization for purchasers of vehicles, farmers cultivating biofuel feedstocks, and producers of ethanol.

Focus on the Petroleum Problem

Petroleum accounts for more than two-thirds of America's foreign energy imports as measured in energy content (see table). It is also the most difficult energy source to replace with non-petroleum options at present. And it provides some 95 percent of the total transportation fuel supply in the United States today.[22]

Emphasizing petroleum's role in fueling transportation should not mean ignoring other aspects of the broad energy issue. Oil is used extensively for heating and industrial operations, for example, so moving toward alternative fuels for such purposes or more efficient oil-burning facilities makes sense where possible.[23]

But America's overseas energy dependence is dominated by the petroleum issue. Moreover, while technology is improving all the time, the main candidates for providing electricity over the long term still require more research and development. While modern coal-burning plants are already a major improvement over older varieties, truly clean coal technologies are relatively young, with a major ten-year demonstration plant having just been initiated in 2003. Relatedly, research must continue into how to sequester carbon dioxide from coal plants for this type of energy source not to cause major climactic consequences.[24] Nuclear-power plants can probably be made safe and proliferation-resistant, at least against criminal or terrorist activity (at least in the United States and other stable societies). But they continue to raise the fundamental and ongoing challenge of waste disposal, a problem that has hardly yet been solved. On balance nuclear power probably does have a larger future in

TABLE 6.4

US Primary Energy Consumption by Source, 2004

Petroleum	39.8 (percent of total US consumption)
Transportation	67 (percent of petroleum towards transportation)
Industrial	24
Residential and Commercial	6
Electric Power	3
Natural Gas	23.0
Transportation	3
Industrial	38
Residential and Commercial	35
Electric Power	24
Coal	22.5
Industrial	10
Residential and Commercial	<1
Electric Power	90
Renewable Energy	6.1
Transportation	5
Industrial	27
Residential and Commercial	8
Electric Power	59
Nuclear Electric Power	8.2
Electric Power	100

US Primary Energy Consumption by Sector, 2004

Transportation	27.7 (percentage of total US consumption)
Petroleum	96 (percentage of transportation from petroleum)
Natural Gas	3
Renewable Energy	1
Industrial	22.1
Petroleum	43
Natural Gas	39
Coal	10
Renewable Energy	8
Residential and Commercial	11.1
Petroleum	21
Natural Gas	73
Coal	1
Renewable Energy	5

(continues)

TABLE 6.4 *(continued)*

Electric Power	38.9
Petroleum	3
Natural Gas	14
Coal	52
Renewable Energy	9
Nuclear Electric Power	21

SOURCE: Energy Information Administration, Annual Energy Review 2004, Tables 1.3 and 2.1b–2.1f.

NOTE ON US ENERGY CONSUMPTION CHARTS: The petroleum category excludes 0.3 quadrillion Btu of ethanol, which is included in renewable energy. Renewable energy includes conventional hydroelectric power, wood, waste, alcohol, geothermal, solar and wind. Coal includes coal coke net imports. Industrial includes industrial combined-heat-and-power (CHP) and industrial electricity-only plants. Commercial includes commercial CHP and commercial electricity-only plants. Electric power includes electricity-only and CHP plants whose primary business is to sell electricity or electricity and heat to the public.

America's (and the world's) energy portfolio, but important questions need to be addressed first. Solar energy and wind power are improving rapidly and contributing much more to national and global energy needs. That said, their capacity to be a source of large-scale electricity production is limited in most parts of the country.[25] A candidate to become America's "energy president" should certainly not ignore the above technologies. At a minimum, much larger increases in aggregate energy research budgets would be appropriate. The candidate could also pledge to develop new energy initiatives later in his or her first term based in part on the results of the research. By contrast, not only is the need to deploy alternative liquid-fuel technologies acute, but the technological opportunity for doing so is already at hand, and the case for doing so promptly is already very strong.

Simplify the Numbers—Millions of Barrels of Oil a Day

When dealing with a topic as complex as energy, political candidates need to simplify the discussion—not only to help voters grapple with the issues, but also to help themselves keep track of the fundamentals. For oil, millions of per barrels per day is the natural unit of measure.

Today's U.S. demand for oil is about 22 million barrels per day; 12 million of those barrels are imported. (Of the imports, about a quarter come from the Persian Gulf, a quarter from other OPEC producers such as

Venezuela and Nigeria, and the other half from non-OPEC countries ranging from Canada and Mexico to Britain, Norway, the Caribbean nations, Colombia, and Angola.[26]) Demand is expected to grow to 28 million barrels a day by 2025 if nothing is done in the meantime, and the number of barrels imported will grow to 20 million barrels a day.

Aim for a New Energy Economy by 2025— and Start Action Now

To show seriousness, but also to show realism, political candidates should lay out ambitious yet attainable goals for diversifying America's energy supply in the coming years. The year 2025 is a good target date. By that point, as noted, U.S. demand is projected to have grown to at least 28 million barrels per day, and imports to slightly more than 20 million. A major new policy initiative could greatly reduce this national thirst.

After a good decade of becoming more efficient in the use of energy starting in the mid–1970s, our national effort has seriously wavered. What can we do about that 28 million figure and, even more importantly, the projected 20 million barrels a day of imported oil? And what can be done within the global economy to reduce dependence on any given supplier?

Although it is implausible to avoid a fairly strong level of dependence on Saudi oil, the goal should be to prevent it from growing above its current total of more than 10 percent of global supply. With other volatile producers, the goal should be to reduce dependence to less than what we face today in regard to Iran. Even if a future market became as tight as today's, with little spare capacity available, the global economy's vulnerability to a cutoff in one place would be less serious than it is now. Ideally, no politically unstable country would supply more than 2 to 3 percent of the total. That way, not only would more energy money stay at home, but any major disruption to one country's supply could more easily be addressed through a combination of tapping the U.S. strategic petroleum reserve and tolerating some modest price increases.

A number of policies can help, in theory, at least eventually. Greater use of renewable energy sources such as wind, hydroelectric, and solar power can in theory be used to create hydrogen, which could then power alternative types of cars (notably those with fuel cells).[27] More nuclear power can do the same thing, provided that the spent-fuel problem can be dealt with effectively (in terms of environmental concerns as well as proliferation risks).[28] Advanced coal technologies can be utilized on a large scale.[29]

All of these electricity sources can be used to fuel plug-in hybrid cars through the electricity grid—and such vehicles, which are totally practical now, should receive favorable tax treatment.[30] Battery technology may require some improvement to make such plug-in cars widely desirable, but it is already quite close, and providing subsidies soon is warranted.[31] In addition, certain types of agricultural and food waste can be used to make biodiesel fuel. Some combination of these methods has the potential to totally replace oil as an energy source sometime later this century.[32]

But as the authors of *Winning the Oil Endgame* so lucidly argue, the core elements of an affordable and near-term alternative-energy policy can be grouped into three main, understandable categories—conservation, biofuels, and more efficient use of natural gas. To be sure, there is a case for other energy technologies too, and a case for expanded research-and-development programs like the one President Bush called for (in a recent report, the National Commission on Energy Policy itself recommended an increase of DoE's research-and-development activities to just over $3 billion a year).[33] But there is also a case for prompt and focused action in these three categories of energy opportunity.

The first need not reduce quality of life; it does not chiefly concern carpooling and thermostat adjustments, but greater emphasis on efficient cars, appliances, and buildings. The second would profit from the biofuels revolution of the last decade and build as well on the Brazil model so convincingly put into effect over the last quarter century. The third would allow natural gas to provide an even higher percentage of heating-fuel requirements. Of course, the benefits go well beyond diversification of our liquid fuel supply to a more robust electricity production and heating capacity as well—with fewer greenhouse emissions.

In the absence of action in these areas, the demand for imported oil is likely to double by 2025. But with focused action on conservation, biofuels, and the use of natural gas, it could be cut in half. Projected total demand would be reduced by about 8 million barrels a day, to just over 20 million barrels a day. Biofuels would replace another 5 million barrels a day; the improved natural-gas economy would reduce the total by yet another 2 million barrels a day. That would leave a total need of about 13 million barrels a day of oil. As projected domestic oil production could provide 8 million, imports would be down to 5 million barrels a day rather than up to 20 million.[34] The two big contributors to this improved fuel picture, reduction of

demand and increased use of biofuels, deserve fuller consideration here—
and on the political campaign trail.

Reducing Demand by 8 Million Barrels a Day   On the issue of reducing
demand, there are a host of areas where progress is possible, some major
and some very specific and narrow—ranging from incentives or state regulations for more efficient household appliances to better tire fuel economy to less idling of trucks and schoolbuses.[35] A bill introduced in Congress in 2005 (H.R. 4409) promoted many such worthy ideas. But for a
political campaign, and for convincing Americans in a simple and clear
way that big progress is feasible, it is most important to focus on the areas
where very large-scale savings are possible.

The hybrid-car phenomenon of the last few years in the United States
shows what is possible when affordable new fuel-efficient technology is
juxtaposed with a price shock. Hybrids have perhaps reached a "tipping
point"—they are well known, highly valued, and often favored through
local regulations (e.g., those allowing individual hybrid drivers to use
high-occupancy-vehicle lanes during rush hour). The hybrid phenomenon has been encouraged in part through government incentives, showing that this is possible economically as well as politically in the contemporary American environment.

Big next steps are now needed that go beyond exclusive focus on what
powers a given vehicle. An important starting point should be again raising mile-per-gallon standards for automotive fleets, which can be done
without reductions in safety or performance if done gradually—even
without major changes in technology.

We should also aim much bigger than such incremental change. To
reduce overall fuel demand further, new types of ultra-light (yet equally
safe) car-manufacturing technologies can be promoted. For instance,
carbon composites are ultra-light and stronger than metal, in part because they absorb collision energy more uniformly throughout their
structure (as evidenced by the number of race-car drivers who have survived high-speed crashes in such vehicles). They can reduce fuel use by
two-thirds by comparison with current cars, and they can be used in
large vehicles.[36]

But there are major investment costs associated with building the factories necessary for such production. The American car industry needs
some signal from the government that it will help absorb these costs. One
simple way would be to promise a national tax deduction or tax credit for

anyone buying carbon-composite vehicles, with the amount of the deduction designed to cover the added costs that Detroit and other automotive production centers would incur in the early years of building these new types of cars.

Of course, calibrating the proper sizes of subsidies and incentives cannot be done from the campaign trail or the White House. There are complex economics at play here. A candidate for office needs to set up a mechanism for gaining optimal professional advice from technologists and economists about what types of incentives are needed, and of what magnitude, to accelerate the transition toward much wider use of ethanol as well as other technologies such as hybrid cars. Specifically, we recommend creation of an official energy-security economics board, with members appointed by the president as well as the congressional leadership. It would be authorized to determine, on an annual basis, relevant subsidies for the production and consumption of energy. (It would perhaps be subject to a total fiscal cap of $15 billion to $25 billion a year, with an agency such as the Congressional Budget Office charged with making official estimates of the expected cost of the recommended subsidies and credits). A five-year sunset clause would ensure that neither this commission nor the general notion of energy subsidies and incentives became permanent.

Using Biofuels to Replace 5 Million Barrels a Day of Oil   In addition to promoting more-efficient cars, we can change their fuel. There are some efforts already under way to do this. Specifically, U.S. energy legislation passed in 2005 mandates a doubling of ethanol use by 2012. (This legislation also shows that the politics of energy are beginning to change; a Republican-led Congress used explicit government regulation to affect the nation's fuel supplies in a manner that would have been very difficult on ideological grounds in previous eras.) But as ethanol currently represents only about 2 percent of U.S. demand for liquid fuels, this is a very modest goal.[37]

There has been a technological revolution in biofuels. This is true less of the nature of the crops grown for such purposes—sugarcane in Brazil, primarily switchgrass and such trees as poplar and willow in temperate climates like that of the United States—than of the genetically engineered bacteria and enzymes used to break them down. Without displacing ongoing food-production activities or creating new irrigation systems in more arid states, the equivalent of nearly 5 million barrels a day of oil could be produced without any enduring subsidy and without assuming a high price of oil. (Indeed, most of the studies conducted to show what is now possible in biofuels were done in the early years of this decade when oil cost $30 a barrel, half the current figure as of this writing.) Some have questioned this optimistic target, doubting whether enough land is available and arable to reach it. But again, the calculations here presume that no domestic food production would be displaced and no substantial amount of ethanol would be imported. Such assumptions may be too pessimistic when estimating the potential for future ethanol production. On balance, the goal of reaching the ethanol equivalent of 5 million barrels of oil a day seems reasonable.[38]

Historically, corn ethanol has not been a major net energy producer. But efficiencies are increasing substantially and there is reason to think that improved yields combined with improved farming methods will soon allow corn ethanol to produce roughly twice the energy required to make it. Moreover, with corn use otherwise largely flat in the United States, new feed stocks for cattle becoming available, and yields per acre increasing continuously, there is reason to think that corn ethanol might provide five times as much of the nation's energy within a decade—without displacing food production.[39]

Studies generally agree that cellulosic ethanol contains about five times as much usable energy content as is required to produce it.[40] Initial data from pilot plants suggests the possibility of producing it on a commercial scale at well under $2 a gallon. If that is indeed feasible, cellulosic ethanol could become an even more important source of energy than corn ethanol with only a limited amount of additional government intervention.

What must be done to make all this happen, apart from relying on the market to encourage Americans to buy alternative-fuel cars? Many different approaches are feasible. But basically, consumers and producers each need incentives. Consumers need to be convinced to buy vehicles that use fuel that is somewhat more costly than gasoline at present, that is not yet widely available, and that contains somewhat less energy content per gallon than gasoline. Producers need incentives to make the investments in fields, machinery, and factories to produce fuel that may not yet be fully competitive with gasoline—and that may even become temporarily less competitive in the future, depending on the price of a barrel of oil.

A candidate presenting these ideas should make two important points. First, incentives to producers and consumers need not be huge and need not be permanent. Cellulosic ethanol's day is coming. The technology is improving, and costs are coming down—even as oil prices remain high and the indirect costs of our oil economy (in the form of military expenditures and foreign-policy commitments) remain onerous. Second, professionals would help determine the size of the economic incentives.

But a candidate needs to indicate where initial incentives might be directed and roughly how large they would be. This would give the public a sense that the candidate knows the relevant technology issues and help convince voters to provide the candidate with the mandate that would be required to make such policy happen.

The simplest system of consumer incentives would extend the same types of tax incentives to flex-fuel cars that have been employed with hybrids of late. Government tax credits in the range of hundreds of dollars per vehicle for flex-fuel or ethanol-burning vehicles should be sufficient in this case. The flex-fuel cars should be able to burn a high percentage of ethanol fuel.

Generalizing this idea to plug-in hybrids and ethanol-fueled cars, however, subsidies would be expensive because the additional costs per car are high. If 5 million cars eligible for the rebate were sold a year, the cost might approach $10 billion. (The Rocky Mountain Institute places such a concept at the center of its proposed national strategy, though it actually favors revenue-neutral "feebates," as used in Canada and elsewhere, by which purchasers of less-efficient vehicles must pay a greater tax that can then fund rebates to those buying optimal vehicles.)[41] William Ford of Ford Motor Company has advocated a government deal with Detroit by which the federal government would subsidize some of Detroit's costs (perhaps paying the automakers' pension costs, as David Sandalow of the Brookings Institution has suggested) in return for a commitment by automakers to retool their production lines.[42] This approach might be used instead of, or in addition to, consumer tax incentives. The recent proposal of the Senate Democratic Caucus to require that, by 2010, 25 percent of new vehicles sold in the United States be flex-fuel, rising to 50 percent by 2020, is also a worthy proposal.[43] It may wind up being somewhat redundant with major tax incentives, but the imperative of shifting our national fuel portfolio is great enough that some risk and some potential duplication of effort are acceptable.

The role of government would not stop at vehicles, however. This matter is far more complicated than the tax treatment of hybrids; a new fuel economy needs to be galvanized into being. Several things need to be done—farmers need to grow and collect biofuel crops, factories need to turn them into ethanol, that fuel needs to be distributed, and fuel stations need to sell it.

Some aspects of this are being addressed already. The 2005 energy bill already partially subsidizes the installation of ethanol pumps through tax breaks (there are fewer than 1,000 in the United States at present).[44] As Senator Richard Lugar first suggested, if tax breaks do not suffice, the government might also consider mandates—just as it could mandate that cars be produced with flex-fuel engines by some date in the near future.[45] The Center for American Progress has offered similar suggestions in a recent report.[46]

Farmers should be incentivized to look for ways in which they can generate biomass feed for cellulosic ethanol plants. They need to be encouraged not only to grow crops suitable for biomass but also to collect waste, such as rice residue and wheat straw, that they already grow.[47] A guaranteed market—that is, price supports that ensure that any suitable crop will be purchased at a price exceeding the cost of its growth—should be provided in the early years. Similar price supports would ensure that refineries make money. (Construction of new refineries could also be encouraged through loan guarantees.[48]) Again, this should only have to be a temporary policy tool. After a few years, subsidies can be phased out altogether, or at least made commensurate with government subsidies for growing other kinds of crops.

Price supports for domestic ethanol would have the further advantage of ensuring that any imported ethanol would not depress prices to the point where American farmers lost interest in the new venture. Brazil produces sugarcane ethanol quite inexpensively; at present, the United States levies a tax of 54 cents per gallon on its fuel as a result. Setting this rate appropriately, and lowering it over time, would be another task of the energy-security economics board (which would also consider whether Brazil was destroying rain forest to produce the ethanol before lowering rates).[49] It would be important that the reduction in the tariff not happen in such a way as to discourage greater production of ethanol in the United States, meaning that the reduction would probably best happen gradually and as part of a broader ethanol strategy ensuring sufficient incentives for domestic producers.

Over the long term, farm subsidies could be focused *primarily* on energy crops, at least in geographic regions where farmers have that option available to them. This would provide a way of supporting the American family farm while allowing reductions in the types of existing food crop subsidies that distort global markets and cause problems in global trade talks. This issue need not be raised in the short term. Doing it right would require detailed regional analysis of American agriculture to be sure that farmers throughout the country enjoyed good market opportunities for crops that could be grown locally. But despite this caveat, the potential benefit for American trade policy, and for helping farmers in developing countries (who often cannot compete with exported American food that enjoys production subsidies), is another reason to be excited about ethanol.

The next American president should be our first energy president. The national-security argument for a leader to step into this role is overwhelming. The environmental argument to do so is overwhelming. The potential benefit to American farmers, and general effects on the international trade system, are highly positive. The technological opportunities are extremely appealing and mark a sharp break from recent decades.

It is not easy to get this issue right, however. A candidate needs to understand a fair amount about the economics of energy and the technology of cellulosic ethanol and other alternative sources, as well as vehicles and other machinery that consume fuel. It will take some money, and some government involvement, to succeed. It will also take enough mastery of the subject to convey the basic choices we face to American voters in language that is accessible and in policy proposals that, whatever their wonky details, are concrete and simple in their main elements. The politics of energy security offer huge opportunities to candidates who can master the subject—and the new opportunities offer huge benefits to the nation and indeed the world.

Through the right use of the bully pulpit, targeted tax breaks, and, occasionally, other mechanisms, whoever succeeds George W. Bush can do much to move the United States toward the attainable goal of getting half of its transportation fuel from ethanol by 2025. In the process, American oil imports can be cut to perhaps less than half of what they are now—and only a fourth of what they would likely be in the absence of a major policy move.

Using government policy to make the transition to much greater use of ethanol would be only a temporary measure. Once some of these steps began to create a market momentum in favor of ethanol-burning or flex-fuel cars, government could step aside. Since the fundamentals—not to mention national-security arguments, as well as global-warming consider-ations—increasingly favor these fuels, Washington's role should be simply to jump-start the process.[50]

Depending on how it was done, and most specifically on how the question of tax credits versus rebates versus "feebates" was resolved, annual costs for this energy-transition strategy could range from roughly $15 billion to $25 billion a year for a decade. As Senator Hillary Clinton has suggested, much of this could be paid for—at least during years of high oil prices—with a windfall-profit tax on oil economies, which earned $113 billion in profits in 2005.[51] In any event, the range of $15 billion to $25 billion a year would be substantially less than how much we still spend protecting our oil habit. And these costs would not be borne indefinitely. Once established, the ethanol fuel system would be competitive and self-sustaining and could lead to reduced costs—in oil, and perhaps also in military operations and American lives.

CHAPTER 7

RISING IN THE EAST

Coping with China's Ascent

THE UNITED STATES will confront two overriding national-security challenges for at least the next generation. First, Americans must effectively wage a long, twilight struggle against violent Islamic fundamentalists. Second, we must simultaneously cope with China's almost certain rise to great-power status. Perhaps no country in history, including the purposeful increase in global significance of the United States at the turn of the last century, has risen as rapidly as China. China's ascent has been, to date, a mostly positive development, given the alternative—a huge country mired in poverty. Nonetheless, the rapidity of China's rise, and the fact that it is occurring while China is still run by an autocratic government with outstanding territorial claims against American friends (Taiwan in particular), make the situation complex—and potentially hazardous for American interests. The manner in which the United States addresses these challenges will largely determine its continued ability to promote international security in the early twenty-first century.

American foreign policy makers have never faced two such vexing and dissimilar challenges at once. During World War II, the United States did fight on two geographically distinct fronts against two very different foes, but the military power employed to defeat the Axis was largely fungible and the tactics used on each front were largely similar. During the Cold War, undeniably the shaping experience of the current and last generation of foreign-policy and national-security practitioners, the United States faced a single, all-encompassing Soviet challenge that for decades defined the intellectual and organizational framework of U.S. foreign policy. The paramount sets of demands we face today are totally disparate—one driven by stateless terrorists operating globally; the other by a rising commercial, political, and military giant in East Asia.[1]

Confronting each task individually would be daunting and consuming. Facing them concurrently, as the United States inevitably will have to, may well prove overwhelming for a government apparatus and a national mindset better suited to singular efforts. Together, these two challenges mark a profound departure from previous eras in U.S. foreign policy. They represent a sharp turn for which the United States remains largely unprepared militarily, psychologically, and politically.[2] U.S. policymakers need to reincorporate grand strategy into their foreign policy and become more aware of the connections between policies, even when these policies address vastly different problems. At a minimum, Americans must reapportion their attention to acknowledge the dual challenges of China and the war on terrorism, and start regarding China with the same sort of urgency they attach to combating the Islamic jihad.

Clearly, China's rise offers great opportunities as well as challenges. But the rise of great powers throughout history has been dangerous, with the potential for rivalry, conflict, and even all-out war—and it is of manifest importance that these possibilities be avoided in regard to China. Many new realities of the international system make America's prospects for success fairly good in this regard, but only if we stay focused on the challenges ahead—and remain prepared to cope with the inevitable setbacks and dangers.

Until now, American strategies for dealing with these two challenges separately have been only partially successful. In the first phase of our campaign against the jihadi terrorists, we relied too heavily on military power and failed to employ an integrated strategy where military actions are but a single element of a multidimensional approach. Although the United States proved reasonably successful in Afghanistan, the lack of attention to the nonmilitary dimensions of strategy and other problems have resulted in an Iraq mission teetering on the edge of failure. With respect to the People's Republic of China (PRC), the United States has practiced a policy of "engagement" for more than a generation. This somewhat ill-defined approach relies heavily on commercial interaction to draw Beijing into the global community of nations. This, in a sense, is the rationale for the "stakeholder" approach to China championed by former Deputy Secretary of State Robert Zoellick during his tenure in government. It assumes that China's further economic development and integration into global economic processes will prevent it from adopting disruptive foreign policies. According to this prosperity-causes-peace framework, even undemocratic governments come to recognize that, in order to receive the superior benefits of economic interdependence, they must curb their foreign-policy ambitions. This perception is allegedly reinforced by the power of the market, which imposes its own sanctions (i.e., conflicts discourage foreign investment and increase insurance premiums and other costs). From this perspective, the more developed the Chinese economy, and the more enmeshed China becomes in the international economy, the less likely Chinese officials will be to take actions that could undermine their access to foreign trade, technology, and investment—the sources of their country's prosperity. A related argument holds that China's economic development hinders its ability to conduct a forceful external policy because prosperity promotes regional and societal autonomy and weakens the central government's authority.[3]

While China's growing prosperity has helped free hundreds of millions of its citizens from abject poverty, one could argue that the policy of "engagement" has succeeded too well. Or, perhaps more accurately, engagement plus America's increasing national fixation on challenges on the other side of the globe have created a dangerous combination. China is now beginning to get the better of the United States in open political and commercial contests. This trend promotes a host of values antithetical to those Americans cherish, including disrespect for civil rights, captive labor unions, unfriendly environmental policies, and autocratic governments. In addition, China's growing military power arouses justifiable unease, especially given its authoritarian political system and its tense relations with Taiwan.

Yet, in the end, some form of an engagement policy is our only viable choice. Most of the above problems would likely get worse, at least inside the PRC, if China were somehow deprived of global markets. Moreover, if the United States dared try to ostracize China at this point, it would almost surely fail because of resistance abroad—not to mention among many pro-trade groups at home. The key is not to bash China, but to have a sufficiently sophisticated understanding of the relationship that we can be encouraging and work together in some areas while standing firm and pushing for reforms in others. Doing this in an effective fashion should ensure that the United States will retain its strong alliance relationships in the Asia-Pacific region and beyond, rather than see China increasingly displace it as the most influential great power in the East.

HOW THE UNITED STATES IS (NOT) RESPONDING

Before the terrorist attacks of September 11, 2001, the Clinton and Bush administrations treated China's growing power as a priority issue with implications for a range of U.S. polices in East Asia and elsewhere. There were clear differences between the two countries over WMD proliferation, the limits of national sovereignty, and other fundamental matters. A series of events—including the 1995–96 Taiwan Strait Crisis, the May 1999 U.S. bombing of the Chinese embassy in Belgrade, and the April 2001 collision between a Chinese fighter and a U.S. EP–3 surveillance plane—marked their strained relationship. Clinton-administration officials sought to overcome these problems through a long-range strategy aimed at promoting China's domestic liberalization, global economic integration, and responsible international behavior.[4] Members of the George W. Bush administration worried more directly about the implications of China's growing economic and particularly military strength. Shortly before Bush's election, foreign policy adviser Condoleezza Rice characterized China as a "strategic competitor" that aspired to weaken the U.S. role in Asia.[5] These expressions of concern persisted in several early national-security documents and appeared to be generating countervailing policies from Beijing.

The September 11 attacks, the ensuing global war on terror, and the invasion of Iraq derailed this process of reassessment. Attention in Washington focused almost exclusively on exposing and destroying terrorist networks in Asia and elsewhere, and on eliminating their state sponsors. Administration representatives ceased characterizing China as a potential adversary or the United States as a balancing power in East Asia. They also professed unconcern about the possible implications for U.S. interests of China's ongoing economic growth, military modernization, and diplomatic initiatives (except in the case of North Korea, where Washington pressed Beijing to assume a *larger* role in resolving the nuclear-weapons crisis).[6] Several American officials have depicted the current bilateral relationship as the best in decades.

The United States and China have engaged in a wide-ranging program of dialogue and cooperation on the global war on terror and other security issues, including North Korea and WMD proliferation.[7] Exchanges between the two countries' militaries, largely suspended following the EP–3 episode, have been resumed at modest levels.[8] Economic relations remain good despite the heavy trade imbalance in China's favor. Although

Chinese officials resisted Operation Iraqi Freedom, their opposition manifested itself less visibly than that of many other governments, including some long-standing American allies.

The change in the Bush administration's approach toward China is perhaps most evident with respect to Taiwan, the one issue that might engender a direct PRC-U.S. military conflict.[9] During Bush's first few months in office, administration representatives concentrated on warning Beijing not to employ force against the island. In April 2001, President Bush publicly pledged to "do whatever it takes" to defend Taiwan. The administration made an unprecedented offer to sell Taipei four Kidd-class guided-missile destroyers, eight diesel submarines, twelve P–3 anti-submarine aircraft, and other weapons systems designed to enhance Taiwan's defenses against Chinese military threats.

In recent years, however, members of the administration have increasingly distanced themselves from Taiwanese efforts to assert greater independence from the mainland. U.S. officials, including President Bush himself in December 2003, have publicly rejected assertions that Taiwan already is sovereign and independent. Although U.S. representatives have complained about Taiwan's failure to spend more to counter China's increasing military capabilities, and its failure to consummate all of the arms sales negotiated in 2001, they have made these comments in the context of affirming support for maintaining the status quo and resuming the cross-strait dialogue.[10]

Blindsided by the events of 9/11 and fearing further attacks, U.S. policymakers justifiably launched a limited military counterattack against the agents of violent jihadism. The many unforeseen demands and avoidable complications that have since arisen in the U.S.-led global war on terror, however, have generated unintended consequences far beyond their immediate battlefields. As a result of its military operations in the Middle East, the United States is dangerously distracted from the rapidly changing strategic landscape of Asia at a time when China is making enormous strides in its military modernization, commercial conquests, diplomatic inroads, and application of soft power. Americans often speak of "managing" China's emergence as a dominant power, but this term understates China's increasing ability to manage American perceptions and actions while seeking to consolidate its newfound global gains.

Rather than seeking to weaken or confront the United States directly, Chinese leaders are pursuing a subtle, multifaceted, long-term grand strategy that aims to derive as many benefits as possible within the existing international system while accumulating the economic wherewithal, military strength, and other resources to reinforce China's continuing emergence as at least a regional great power. American officials have devoted insufficient attention to developing an effective response to this challenge. Too often, analysts of U.S.-Chinese relations focus on mechanics, such as the number of high-level Chinese-American exchanges, rather than substance, such as the content of these meetings. Managing the China challenge requires both a comprehensive understanding of China's economic, political, and military assets and policies, and an evaluation of how other countries are responding to them.

CHINA'S ECONOMIC ASCENT

China's economic successes over the past two decades have helped stimulate global commerce and improved the lives of millions of Chinese citizens. Unfortunately, they also have caused disturbing implications for the global balance of political and military power. As China's economy expands, so do the resources available to its leaders for pursuing diplomatic and military policies that will frequently conflict with American preferences.

China now has the fourth-largest economy in the world measured in dollars at current exchange rates. Its annual GDP growth throughout the past three decades—at more than 8 percent, the world's fastest—has served as a magnet for the influx of international capital. The country has surpassed the United States as the world's leading destination for foreign direct investment (FDI).[11] China also recently displaced Taiwan and Japan to become the world's second-largest producer of IT hardware, and now possesses the largest wired and wireless telecommunications networks in the world.[12] China's foreign-exchange reserves exceed $800 billion. Its total exports grew eightfold—to over $380 billion a year—between 1990 and 2003. If present trends continue, China's economy could become the second largest in the world by 2020.[13]

Chinese officials profess a commitment to integrating their country further into the world economy in order to both manage and exploit the process of globalization, but concerns about becoming dependent on foreigners have sustained efforts at self-reliance in many areas.[14] China's recent entry into the World Trade Organization already has enhanced its ability to influence global economic decisions and processes (e.g., its successful mobilization of international support in March 2002 to roll back

U.S. tariffs on imported steel). The PRC's open door toward most FDI has created a number of influential constituencies that lobby other governments against measures that could harm their access to the Chinese market. China's economic relations with a range of Asian, African, and Latin American countries have grown substantially in recent years, allowing the PRC to diversify its sources of energy and other imports and reinforce its credentials as a major world power.[15]

China's increasing cooperation with regional multilateral institutions (such as the Association of Southeast Asian Nations, or ASEAN, which signed a free-trade agreement with China in November 2004) and other Asian governments aims primarily to enhance China's assured access to vital resources (especially energy and other raw materials) and to promote its regional ascendancy.[16] A disturbing feature of China's growing economic weight in Asia, however, is its push for policies that would exclude or diminish the role of the United States in this important region—a practice Beijing has already employed with some success vis-à-vis Taiwan. China's successful drive for the convocation of the December 2005 East Asia Summit in Malaysia suggests a long-term ambition to build a new regional power structure that does not include Washington. The developing ASEAN–China Free Trade Area (ACFTA), which excludes the United States, will cover a region that is home to almost 2 billion people, with a forecasted aggregate GDP of $2 trillion, when it becomes fully operational by 2010 for the original six ASEAN members.[17] Some Chinese have called for an even more comprehensive East Asia Free Trade Area that would encompass China, ASEAN, Australia, India, Japan, New Zealand, and South Korea—an exclusionary combination that could deprive the United States of $25 billion in exports.[18] In the interim, Beijing has sought to expand the agenda of the ASEAN Plus Three (China, Japan, and South Korea) mechanism to address important regional economic and security issues without American participation.[19]

Although the Shanghai Cooperation Organization (SCO) originally had a security focus, it too has become an instrument with which China can promote its economic ties with other countries (in this case Russia and the newly independent states of Central Asia) within an institutional framework that excludes the United States. Its expanding network of full members (China, Russia, Kazakstan, Kyrgyzstan, Tajikistan, and Uzbekistan) and formal observers (India, Iran, Pakistan, and Mongolia) gives the SCO substantial potential. The present lack of international energy institutions linking supplier and consumer countries could provide an opening for the SCO to assume this role. Its roster of members and observers includes some of the world's largest oil and gas exporters and importers.

A more prosperous China is a good thing; a stronger China, though potentially problematic for the United States, is in large part a direct consequence of that greater prosperity; a China working to get along with its neighbors is clearly preferable to the alternative. But China's desire to exclude the United States from more regional forums is cause for concern—especially when juxtaposed, as has often been the case during the Bush administration, with insufficient American attention to the region (since China's efforts are more successful under such circumstances). Also deeply worrisome is China's willingness to emphasize economic interests to the detriment of human rights, as witnessed in its dealings with Iran and Sudan, and in its forced repatriation of North Korean refugees.

CHINA'S LEANER, MEANER MILITARY

With average annual increases of 15 percent during the past five years, China's military spending is one of the few sectors to outpace the country's economic growth.[20] Since the late 1990s, the Chinese government has accelerated efforts to modernize and upgrade the People's Liberation Army (PLA). The lack of transparency regarding Chinese defense expenditures obscures matters, but most foreign analysts estimate that, since the official figure excludes spending on military research and development, nuclear weapons, and major foreign-weapons imports, the PRC may spend the equivalent of between $50 billion to $100 billion annually on defense (up to three times the official Chinese budget figure of $35 billion).[21]

Whatever the true number, the success of the U.S.-led military operations in Iraq and the former Yugoslavia clearly has prompted the Chinese government to pursue improved capacities for power projection, precision strike, and the other attributes associated with the latest so-called revolution in military affairs (RMA).[22] For example, the PLA has emphasized developing rapid reaction forces capable of deploying beyond China's borders, and the PLA navy has been acquiring longer-range offensive and defensive missile systems, including a more effective submarine force (i.e. more operationally efficient and stealthy).[23] Chinese strategists have also sought to develop an "assassin's mace" collection of niche weapons that the PLA can use to exploit asymmetrical vulnerabilities in U.S. military defenses, such as America's growing military dependence on computers.[24]

Besides allowing the PRC to improve its traditionally weak indigenous defense industry, rapid economic growth has enabled China to become the world's largest arms importer. Russia has been an especially eager seller. Recently acquired Russian weapons systems include advanced military aircraft (e.g., Su–27s and Su–30s) and naval systems such as *Sovremenny*-class missile destroyers equipped with SS-N–22 Sunburn anti-ship missiles, and improved Kilo-class diesel attack submarines that would enhance a Chinese military campaign against Taiwan. China is also devoting more resources to manufacturing and deploying advanced indigenous weapons systems. The PLA's new, indigenously produced DF–31 and DF–31A intercontinental ballistic missiles, with initial operational dates in 2005 and 2007, respectively, are especially important because their mobility makes them hard to destroy. China's space program has resulted in its acquiring new surveillance, communication, and navigation satellites capable of coordinating military operations against Taiwan and other contingencies beyond Chinese territory.[25]

Despite its focus on winning the global campaign against terrorism, the Pentagon has not failed to notice China's military scale-up. In its 2005 annual report on China's military power, the Pentagon was careful to avoid incendiary rhetoric, but cautioned: "China faces a strategic crossroads. It can choose a pathway of peaceful integration and benign competition. China can also choose, or find itself upon, a pathway along which China would emerge to exert dominant influence in an expanding sphere. Or, China could emerge less confident and focused inward on challenges."[26] The latest Quadrennial Defense Review (QDR) Report, released in February 2006, likewise observes: "Of the major and emerging powers, China has the greatest potential to compete militarily with the United States and field disruptive military technologies that could over time offset traditional U.S. military advantages absent counter strategies." Although the authors acknowledge the need to encourage Beijing to cooperate with the United States "in addressing common security challenges, including terrorism, proliferation, narcotics, and piracy," they complain

China continues to invest heavily in its military, particularly in its strategic arsenal and capabilities designed to improve its ability to project power beyond its borders. Since 1996, China has increased its defense spending by more than 10 percent in real terms in every year except 2003. Secrecy, moreover, envelops most aspects of Chinese security affairs. The outside world has little knowledge of Chinese motivations and decisionmaking or of key capabilities supporting its military mobilization. The United States encourages China to take actions to make its intentions clear and clarify its military plans.[27]

The Chinese military buildup has moved U.S. Secretary of Defense Donald Rumsfeld to highlight publicly what he claims is a glaring contradiction: "Since no nation threatens China, one must wonder: Why the growing investment? Why these continuing large and expanding arms purchases? Why these continuing robust deployments?"[28] The unspoken answer is Taiwan. As the QDR observes: "Chinese military modernization has accelerated since the mid-to-late 1990s in response to central leadership demands to develop military options against Taiwan scenarios. The pace and scope of China's military buildup already puts regional military balances at risk."[29]

China now has hundreds of ballistic missiles aimed at Taiwan, as well as more than seven hundred warplanes capable of reaching the island without refueling. These capabilities are increasing annually.[30] Because China anticipates U.S. military intervention should a cross-strait conflict erupt, a major focus of the PLA's military preparations is a "decapitation strategy"—a quick strike to neutralize Taiwan's civilian and military command-and-control facilities. Such a strategy would require targeting key military capabilities while deterring or delaying an effective U.S. military response. In addition, China's improving submarine force increases the PRC's range of options for various types of blockade against Taiwan—and provides a deterrent against American intervention, since a sub that was lucky enough to be in the right spot could lurk until a U.S. warship came close and then possibly sink it. China's massive defense spending is shifting the balance of power against Taiwan, making a coercive solution increasingly attractive to Beijing.[31]

Although China's military buildup appears to be primarily motivated by a potential Taiwan contingency, many of its recent acquisitions could facilitate the projection of military power into more distant theaters of great importance to the United States, including Japan, India, Southeast Asia, and Australia. Some of the missile, air, and increasingly mobile ground forces directed today at Taiwan could be deployed to multiple points on China's periphery. The soon-to-be-fielded conventional land-attack cruise missiles, which could be deployed on China's new Type 093 nuclear-powered submarines, will give China a limited but useful global power-projection capability. In addition, Russia is now marketing Tu–22 Backfire and Tu–95 Bear bombers to the PLA, which could enable it to conduct air strikes against distant targets in Southeast Asia and else-where. Many PLA navy commanders still desire to acquire an aircraft carrier fleet, a traditional symbol both of global power-projection capabilities and great-power status.[32] The Chinese presence in Gwadar, Pakistan, lo-cated opposite the vital energy corridor of the Strait of Hormuz, also has a strategic dimension. For several years, China has been pursuing a "string of pearls" strategy to gain access to major ports from the Persian Gulf to Bangladesh, Cambodia, and the South China Sea.[33]

None of these developments is surprising; great powers expect to have strong militaries, and the United States certainly appreciates the logic of this position. But great powers often seek to disrupt the status quo with such newfound capabilities. Moreover, even those who criticize the United States and its global policies should recognize that modern-day America does not use its military to behave like the hegemons of old— grabbing up economic resources and setting terms of international com-merce that favor its own interests. To the contrary, it uses military power primarily to defend allies, keep open global trading routes enjoyed by all, and check the proliferation of dangerous weaponry. Thus, China's desire to compete with the United States raises questions, as Secretary Rums-feld noted, which may or may not have reassuring answers. The key for the United States is not to be shocked by China's behavior, but to en-courage the good possibilities of its growing power while being prepared to check any dangerous tendencies.

GENERAL TSU'S SOFT POWER

China's rising military might warrants attention and concern, but it should not obscure the larger power accumulation underway in Beijing. For the first time since the end of the Cold War, a nation is challenging U.S. "soft power"—the summation of economic leverage, cultural pull, and intellectual clout that has made the United States the preeminent force in the world. Professor Joseph Nye, former U.S. foreign-policy offi-cial and intellectual engineer of the "soft-power" concept, warns that "the rise of China's soft power—at America's expense—is an issue that needs to be urgently addressed."[34] A recent BBC poll of people in twenty-two countries highlighted the magnitude of this challenge. The survey found that nearly half the respondents saw Beijing's influence as positive; only 38 percent said the same for the United States.[35] Chinese representatives also have successfully modernized their diplomacy; for example, they have placed dozens of official policy papers on the Foreign Ministry's Web site and developed an effective approach toward media relations.[36] Beijing's hosting of the Summer Olympic Games in 2008 will reinforce China's status as a center of international culture and sports.

As part of a comprehensive "peaceful rise" public-relations strategy that they have been implementing since the mid-1990s, Chinese authorities have sought to assuage international anxieties about China's growing power and influence by downplaying territorial disputes, offering trade concessions, broadening cooperative dialogues, and promoting student and other cultural exchanges.[37] In Asia, China's quest to reassure its neighbors that its ascent does not threaten them, despite their ample historical reasons to fear otherwise, has proven surprisingly successful. This is all to the good—as long as regional leaders do not let down their guard, or allow themselves to be convinced by wishful thinking that China's rise is unequivocally and inevitably a benign development.

Many East Asian leaders profess to see China's rise as more of an economic opportunity than a diplomatic or military threat. Again, that is fine—as long as they do not entirely discount the latter possibility. But there are worrisome signs. These leaders maintain that their own countries' economic health depends in part on continued Chinese prosperity, and have eagerly embraced Beijing's proposals to reduce trade barriers and cooperate on transnational threats such as terrorism and infectious diseases. Japan's protracted economic stagnation has resulted in the PRC's becoming the leading growth engine for many countries. China's trade ties are growing with every Southeast Asian country. Few East Asian officials call for containing China. But they are also beginning to discount the importance of even hedging against a more aggressive future PRC. They also seem decreasingly inclined to assume that they would take America's side should, heaven forbid, the two great powers ever wind up in conflict.[38]

Perhaps most surprising is how much relations between India and China have improved in recent years. Those two countries have intensified their efforts to resolve their boundary disputes and conducted an unprecedented number of high-level military exchanges. For example, an April 2005 agreement specified steps India and China should take to demarcate their disputed boundary based on a "fair, reasonable, and mutually acceptable solution, through equal and friendly consultations."[39] Further, bilateral trade has increased to the point that China became India's second-largest trading partner in 2004, behind only the United States.

China also has improved its relations with Russia. In addition to holding an unprecedented number of high-level meetings, Chinese and Russian officials signed a bilateral friendship treaty in July 2001 and have proclaimed a strategic partnership, established a series of military confidence-building measures, and resolved the last disagreements over their long-disputed common border.[40] Russia has become the leading exporter of weapons to China, and bilateral energy ties, the main topic of Russian president Vladimir Putin's March 2006 visit to China, have also been expanding.[41]

Again, most of this sounds benign; in fact, most of it is actually to the good. But there are downsides that could get worse over time. For example, regarding Russia and China, the two authoritarian governments regularly defend each other, as well as other Eurasian governments, against Western criticism. The Iran, Sudan, and North Korea problems have already been noted. Most recently, Russian and Chinese officials endorsed the Uzbek government's controversial May 2005 military crackdown in Andijan, echoing Tashkent's allegations that the uprising represented a foreign-inspired terrorist plot aided by Western-backed nongovernmental organizations.

China and Russia cooperate more closely on Central Asia than any other region. Through the SCO, Russian officials acknowledge China's legitimate interests in Central Asia, while Beijing has an institutional mechanism to promote its objectives in close cooperation with Moscow. Since China shares many important goals with Russia in Central Asia (upholding the political status quo, curbing the growth of Islamic extremism, exploiting the region's energy resources, and balancing U.S. influence), China has been able to benefit from Russian initiatives in these areas and devote resources to other priorities. The two countries' economic activities in Central Asia thus far have been more complementary than competitive. Russian firms have focused on large-scale industrial and infrastructure projects, especially in the energy sector, whereas Chinese entrepreneurs have concentrated on selling cheap consumer goods, often through small-scale cross-border trade.

A growing number of authoritarian governments see China as an attractive ideological partner. Beijing's twin commitments to defending countries' national sovereignty and not interfering in other states' internal affairs appeal to dictators uneasy about the Bush administration's newfound dedication to spreading liberal democracy throughout the world. China's emerging status as a patron of the world's dictators club is particularly evident in Africa. Beijing's willingness to ignore human rights and related matters when disbursing aid earn it favor among several African dictators whose poor governance, opaque political systems, and refusal to implement the painful brand of economic or political reforms demanded by the United States make them unpopular in Washington. Because Africa also supplies an estimated quarter of Beijing's imported oil, it has been a breeding ground for convenient marriages between China and leaders of rogue states—not only Sudan's al-Bashir, but also Zimbabwe's Robert Mugabe and Angola's Jose Santos.[42] For example, China's extensive energy and military cooperation with Sudan has repeatedly led Chinese leaders to stymie efforts in the U.N. Security Council to coerce the Sudanese government into improving the human-rights situation in Darfur.[43]

Finally, China has made inroads into Latin America, long considered "America's backyard" because of the 1823 Monroe Doctrine. In April 2001, then-president Jiang Zemin spent almost two weeks in the region, visiting Argentina, Brazil, Cuba, Uruguay, and Venezuela. In November 2004, Chinese president Hu Jintao visited Argentina, Brazil, Chile, and Cuba, signing business deals worth billions of dollars. With half of China's FDI flowing to Latin America, Chinese officials predict that their FDI in the region could amount to $100 billion by the end of the decade.[44] China's investment already accounts for one-third of Latin America's total FDI.[45] Predictably, Chinese officials have cultivated relationships with the anti-American stalwarts Fidel Castro and Hugo Chavez to strengthen ties with Cuba and oil-rich Venezuela.[46] In March 2006, General Bantz J. Craddock, commander of USSOUTHCOM, warned the House Armed Services Committee that "increasing presence of the People's Republic of China (PRC) in the region is an emerging dynamic that must not be ignored."[47]

Although many of Washington's traditional allies in developing countries feel somewhat neglected by the Bush administration's current preoccupation with terrorism, Latin America's leftist leaders go further and blame the U.S.-supported international economic system for their countries' economic difficulties. Under the rubric of a "Global South" movement, these regimes have anointed China's Hu Jintao as their unofficial leader. President Hu has embraced this informal post. In 2004, he told an audience in Sao Paolo that China would spare no effort to help build a "democratic international order as well as multiple [approaches] to development models."[48] These were welcome words for leaders like Brazil's Luiz Ignacio Lula da Silva, who during an earlier trip to China said his government wanted a partnership with China that "integrates our economies and serves as a paradigm for South-South cooperation."[49]

Problems with the so-called Washington Consensus advocated by the World Bank and the International Monetary Fund—with its focus on curbing government spending, freeing domestic and foreign trade, and reducing government control of national economic assets—have led the developing world to pay closer attention to China's model. As described in a 2004 report by British foreign-policy expert Joshua Cooper Ramo, the "Beijing Consensus" preaches an innovative and export-led approach to growth.

It has three essential axioms. First, use high-technology "bleeding-edge innovation" rather than "trailing-edge technology" to kick-start development. Second, employ quality-of-life metrics (including equality and sustainability), rather than traditional per capita GDP measures, to assess progress toward development. Third, vigorously defend national sovereignty through economic, military, and other tools.[50] There is some merit to these ideas, and China certainly has put them to impressive use in its own development. Accordingly, even as Western officials and economists continue to challenge these policies because of their disruptive effects on international commerce and political development, the governments of Brazil, Russia, Vietnam, and other countries have dispatched state economists to study the Beijing Consensus.

Chinese officials seem to be using their value-neutral approach to other countries' political systems and practices to gain leverage in competition with American policymakers firmly committed to supporting democracy and human rights. As a result, China is forging a string of alliances across the globe with nations shunned by the United States—including Venezuela, Iran, Sudan, Burma, and Zimbabwe. China's strong-state approach to development has also earned it the respect of more reputable developing nations—from democracies such as India and Brazil to pseudo-authoritarian states such as Russia and Malaysia. Although competing more effectively with China should not lead U.S. policymakers to retreat from their promotion of democracy, they should bear in mind that China's laissez-faire attitude toward foreign political systems gives it certain inherent advantages in seeking supporters in the developing world.

CHINESE VULNERABILITIES

A comprehensive, unvarnished assessment of China's development strategy would expose the many problems associated with the country's successful achievement of high economic-growth rates. Some of the tensions of "market Leninism" include growing societal fault lines that threaten the long-term viability of the Beijing Consensus; an emergent middle-class increasingly impatient for property rights; rural discontent on the order of 87,000 peasant protests in 2005 alone; the deterioration of basic public services such as education and health care; increasing reliance on Internet-based information that the state can only partially control; 150 million transients wandering between village and city; a swiftly aging population that drains financial and other societal resources; and a 1.2 : 1 gender imbalance in favor of males resulting from government-enforced population policies (and selective abortions among Chinese parents, who typically prefer to have sons).[51] Chinese representatives also express concern about threats to China's internal security from foreign-supported terrorist groups, religious extremists, and ethnic separatists, especially in the impoverished western provinces of Tibet and Xinjiang.[52] At the March 2006 congress of the ruling Communist Party, Premier Wen Jiabao felt compelled to reaffirm the government's commitment to improving rural welfare and prosecuting corrupt local officials.

Less obvious but perhaps more severe industrial and political problems arise from the particular growth strategy that China employs to integrate itself into the world economy. First, the government has taken steps to circumscribe the emergence of an independent private sector, or associations among business leaders, that could press for unwanted political reforms. Second, Beijing policymakers have given state-owned enterprises (SOEs) a variety of privileges, including favorable access to certain capital, markets, and technologies. Third, other state policies have promoted FDI as part of an effort to introduce foreign technology and managerial practices into the Chinese economy. As a result of these policies, the Chinese private sector remains weak, SOEs are still inefficient, and foreign firms now control the bulk of China's advanced industrial and high-technology exports and enjoy prominent standing in many domestic markets. In addition, Chinese managers tend to pursue rent-seeking behavior, resort to excessive diversification while shunning inter-industry or inter-regional collaboration, and prioritize short-term gains over long-term investments.[53]

China's financial sector also suffers from serious weaknesses due to the faulty state policies that produce an enormous misallocation of national capital.[54] Sustaining the country's fragile banking system, which makes America's savings-and-loan problem of some years ago look like a minor accounting mistake, absorbs approximately one-third of China's annual GDP. Major banks have been recapitalized and are much stronger than they were a few years ago, but their ability to assess risk and opportunity accurately, and guide investment accordingly, remains quite limited.[55]

Most seriously from Beijing's perspective, all these problems may be undermining China's international economic competitiveness. Labor costs are rising at double-digit rates. The costs of imported oil and gas are soaring at a time when the Chinese economy is increasingly dependent on foreign energy sources. If continued, the forced revaluation of the renminbi could make Chinese goods less attractive on global markets. For example, Chinese textile and garment manufacturers have found it increasingly difficult to compete with their rivals in Bangladesh, Cambodia, and India. It remains uncertain whether China has managed to capitalize on its ephemeral window of cheap labor to generate sufficient internal momentum to fuel the country's further development after the middle class has grown to a scale that neutralizes China's comparative labor advantages. If it hasn't, this could mitigate the pace of China's rise in a way that alleviates some of the security worries expressed above. But it could also make China more worried about sources of raw materials, less inclined to improve environmental and labor practices, and otherwise less progressive in its policies.

Although analysts detect liberalizing and even democratizing trends within the country's authoritarian political system, most do not anticipate the regime's transformation or overthrow anytime soon.[56] The appeal of communism has clearly faded, but the Chinese leadership has been able to rely on nationalism and economic successes to bolster its position. Unfortunately, it remains in doubt whether China's democratization, should it occur, would make it a less challenging international rival of the United States.

China may democratize. China may attempt to seize Taiwan. China may democratize *and attempt to take Taiwan*. In the words of Ross Terrill, "traveling one road in economics and another in politics makes it difficult to arrive at a set destination."[57] Integrating even a democratic China with growing capabilities into the existing global order would require skillful management by U.S. and other policy makers. A protracted succession struggle, a violent dispute between Beijing and the provinces over their relative authority, or a collapse of the Chinese economy could draw the attention of China's leaders inward, but these developments all would present the international community with severe challenges. Even if one allows that a *democratic* China would be pacific, it does not follow that a *democratizing* China would pursue moderate foreign policies. Analysts of states moving from authoritarianism to democracy argue that their leaders have strong incentives to pursue aggressive foreign polices to acquire political support among aroused nationalist populations and unreconstructed authoritarian institutions such as the military.[58]

History is littered with failed strategies for dealing with rising states. The British and French attempts to contain a rising Imperial Germany at the turn of the last century had disastrous consequences. American and British approaches to the rise of Japanese power in Asia and the Pacific during the 1920s and 1930s also failed miserably. Indeed, the only modern example of a graceful transition of power was between Great Britain and the United States. The applicability of this pattern to the contemporary Sino-American relationship is dubious. The intimate relationship that spanned Washington and Whitehall throughout Britain's slow decline cannot in any way be equated with the complex, largely distrustful links that currently exist between Beijing and Washington. More promisingly, many economic and other indicators suggest that any U.S. decline is unlikely to occur as rapidly or comprehensively as Britain's did.

There are many features of the contemporary international system that give grounds for hope. Better modern-day communications between leaders, the clear benefits of economic globalization (for countries' GDPs, even if not for all workers), and the memories of the destructiveness of the world wars together with the stabilizing effects of nuclear deterrence all should improve the odds of peaceful coexistence and cooperation.

But nothing is foreordained. Even recent history shows that making predictions about the structure of great-power relations in Asia requires a certain humility and trepidation. Most often, practitioners and commentators alike erroneously assess the outcome of contested great-power transitions. Many analysts held the mistaken expectation that postwar

Japan was on course to displace the United States as the world's dominant economy. At present, many see an almost preordained Chinese ascent, notwithstanding the enormous domestic and international challenges that Beijing would need to overcome in the process. Yet, other analysts anticipate that India rather than China will eventually become Asia's new greatest power. Although such forecasts are premature, some evidence of the dimensions of the challenge that India could present to China is already apparent. For example, between 1999 and 2003, Indian companies delivered investment returns between 80 and 200 percent higher than those of their Chinese counterparts across six major industrial sectors (ranging from automobiles to telecommunications).[59]

Nor are matters entirely rosy, from Beijing's perspective, in the security realm. Chinese leaders fear, and perhaps anticipate, a serious confrontation with the United States at some point, with Taiwan, Tibet, or another issue serving as the catalyst. Chinese analysts typically describe American foreign policy as unilateral, militaristic, and unpredictable. Many have long perceived an American effort to encircle China.[60] The elevated U.S. military presence in Central Asia since September 2001, the growing U.S. defense ties with both India and Pakistan, and the modernization of American forces based in South Korea and Japan have reinforced these concerns. Chinese officials also look askance at Japanese leaders' increasing willingness to discard old taboos and assume a more prominent role in regional and even global security affairs in partnership with the United States.

In addition, Beijing remains uncertain about how best to manage the still-powerful independence movement in Taiwan. The issue presents an acute dilemma for China's leaders, whose individual and perhaps collective legitimacy could be undermined either by the "loss" of Taiwan or by the economic problems that would ensue from a military conflict over the island. Chinese authorities perceive a convergence of these problems in U.S. efforts to promote a cooperative network of regional ballistic-missile-defense (BMD) programs, which Beijing fears could lead to a de facto U.S.-Australia-Japan-ROK-Taiwan collective defense alliance. Another worry is the possibility of regime collapse or war in neighboring North Korea. Either development could produce a humanitarian disaster, with refugees surging across the Sino-Korean border, and long-term damage to East Asia's economies.

Chinese leaders' future foreign-policy intentions are even less predictable than the PRC's probable future capabilities. The factors that could affect whether China's future leaders challenge or uphold the international status quo are diverse and unfortunately largely indeterminate. They could include balance-of-power considerations, economic-resource needs, domestic political considerations, or perceived infringements on China's sovereignty or status.[61] During the last century, China radically altered its policy toward almost all the countries involved in East Asia.[62] Most spectacularly, Beijing shifted from allying with the USSR against the United States in the 1950s, to hostile neutrality toward both superpowers in the 1960s, to a defense alignment with Washington against Moscow in the 1970s and 1980s, to a policy of wary cooperation with Russia and restrained antagonism toward the United States in the 1990s, to professed support for American foreign-policy priorities since September 2001. These uncertainties surrounding the PRC's rise require a well-integrated, rather than an overly alarmist, approach to managing Chinese power.

SIX RULES FOR
FOGGY BOTTOM AND THE PENTAGON

The "engagement" policy that the United States has successfully practiced toward China for more than a generation is an ill-defined and inadequate approach for incorporating Beijing into the global community on Western terms in the era ahead. Although the United States has appropriately hedged its bets, not least by maintaining a robust military presence in the Asia-Pacific region, the "engaging" and "hedging" elements of the American strategy toward China are poorly integrated. Going forward, U.S. policy toward China will need to combine the two halves more effectively.

Most of China's neighbors pursue a largely successful self-reinforcing mixture of deep engagement and soft balancing regarding Beijing, shifting the emphasis in light of the particular question at issue.[63] Of course, an effective American policy toward China cannot and should not mechanically replicate the strategies pursued by Singapore, Thailand, and Vietnam to deal with the Chinese colossus on their border. Moreover, some of those countries may have thrown too much caution to the wind of late in their thinking about the PRC. Nevertheless, given the dimensions of the China challenge, it would behoove Washington to employ all available foreign-policy tools in a comprehensive and integrated manner. These include the cultivation of allies and friends, the targeted use of foreign assistance, the prudent strengthening and use of military power, the development of more robust intelligence capabilities, the waging of better public-education campaigns, and the credible demonstration of sustained political will.

Conducting an effective China policy will involve more than just interacting with Beijing. It must be embedded within an overall policy toward Asia that uses ties with key allies to act as a force multiplier for U.S. interests throughout the region. We offer six specific recommendations to execute our preferred approach.

Build Strong Partnerships

First, keep making new (old) friends. A regional plan is only as strong as the bilateral relations underpinning it. The United States must continue to build strong bilateral relations, particularly with Japan and India. If Japan feels threatened or abandoned, it will almost certainly remilitarize. Such a development would threaten the fragile security balance that has helped avert a major conflict in Asia during the past sixty years. Concerns about Beijing already are driving Tokyo to strengthen its self-defense capabilities—although, fortunately, thus far largely within the reassuring framework of the Japanese-American alliance. The Japanese provide approximately $5 billion annually in host-nation support for the roughly 50,000 U.S. forces based in Japan because they recognize their value in managing regional security challenges.[64] Yet, if China looked to eclipse American power in Asia, or if ties between Washington and Tokyo deteriorated, Japan would take even more vigorous measures to ensure its security, including perhaps reassessing its policy of nuclear abstention.[65]

The Bush administration has done much of the above rather well; U.S.-Japanese ties are strong at present. But the administration has been willing to see Sino-Japanese ties deteriorate without doing nearly enough to blunt or reverse this trend. This might seem to fit within our philosophy of hedging against untoward developments in China. But, in fact, a sophisticated Asia policy needs to avoid unnecessary provocations and any trend toward the formation of blocs of states. Tolerating or even welcoming a poor Sino-Japanese relationship as a way to strengthen the U.S.-Japanese alliance is an uninspired and unproductive approach for the United States.

In that spirit, Americans need to communicate more forthrightly to the Japanese their concerns about Prime Minister Junichiro Koizumi's annual visits to the Yasukuni war shrine and related actions that weaken Japan's soft power in Asia. At the same time, they should make a greater effort to urge the Chinese to improve Beijing-Tokyo ties by, among other things, reminding Chinese leaders about the dangers of risking military conflict with Japan, a close American ally. We should also remind China how far Japan has come in recognizing its own history, despite the occasional controversy over a textbook or the speech of a Japanese politician; these are now the exceptions rather than the rule. That said, Japanese are tired of being critiqued by an autocratic regime that seems bent on dwelling on the negative, so China needs to be careful about its behavior too.

American policymakers are also correctly devoting more attention to improving ties with India, the only country that can match China in terms of demographic weight—and one of the world's most important democracies and newest nuclear-weapons states. Efforts to strengthen bilateral cooperation in the fields of counterterrorism, defense, and economics would help reinforce India's position in Asia in the face of China's rise. In Southeast Asia, U.S. officials need to avoid taking steps that suggest a lack of interest in the region. Secretary of State Rice's decision to skip the July 2005 meeting of the ASEAN Regional Forum, for instance, sent precisely the wrong message to the other members about American concern regarding regional affairs.[66]

Keep Old Friends

Second, don't forget other old friends. Regional anxieties about the implications of China's growing strength lie just below the surface in most Asian countries. Some Asians worry that the PRC's growing capabilities eventually could result in China's achieving a kind of existential hegemony, with Beijing dominating Asian affairs even in the absence of a deliberate policy to do so. Concerns about the long-term growth of Chinese military power contribute to widespread support in Asia for keeping a robust U.S. military presence in the region, as well as a grudging tolerance for Japan's more activist security policies. Since these anxieties are normally not expressed openly for fear of antagonizing Beijing, policymakers in Washington might not fully appreciate the level of concern in Asia about the PRC's future direction. Such misperceptions are disturbing, since any American strategy for managing China will require the support of most of its neighbors to be effective.

The United States must make it a priority to reinvigorate its relationship with South Korea, especially in view of the damage done to the alliance during the last five years over the North Korea crisis in particular. Recent events such as the accidental deaths of two South Korean teenagers during a U.S. military training exercise and the U.S. refusal to grant South Korean authorities jurisdiction for crimes committed by American forces in their country have reinforced anti-American trends in that country. Deeper issues such as diverging assessments of the threat from North Korea and China's growing economic ties with the Republic of Korea have exacerbated this problem. The increasing potential of Chinese economic and military dominance of Southeast Asia may encourage South Koreans to place greater value on their security ties with the United States, but more effective U.S. policies are essential to facilitate this process. One key is not to force the issue of how the ROK would respond to any U.S.-Chinese conflict over Taiwan. Seoul has understandable reasons to be very reluctant to discuss such hypotheticals. Rather than force it to do so, the United States should strive to make the alliance work well on more immediate matters.

Commit More Resources

Third, American policymakers must become much more diplomatically active in the region to compare favorably with increasing Chinese diplomatic activism. In the economic realm, they need a strategy beyond the simple promulgation of bilateral trade accords. China has achieved substantial success recently in promoting a pan-Asian economic vision that excludes the United States. In previous decades, the United States pursued a more effective trans-Pacific vision of economic cooperation with Asia. During the second Reagan administration, for instance, the United States spearheaded the formation of the Asia-Pacific Economic Cooperation (APEC) project, which includes twenty-one nations from North and South America as well as from Asia.

Regrettably, in recent years, distractions such as NAFTA, China's entry into the WTO, and the East Asian financial crisis have resulted in less vigorous U.S. efforts to promote these trans-Pacific institutions. This has provided China with an opportunity to advance exclusionary models. Americans must reclaim a trans-Pacific economic vision as a means of reconnecting the United States to the newly forming "Asian" economic landscape. Given the rapidly growing trade deficit the United States has with ASEAN, such a vision should entail a more expansive economic-liberalization strategy.

The United States must remain ready to play hardball with China on matters such as the valuation of its currency and protection of intellectual property rights—all the while recognizing that in many ways, China is playing fairly by the rules set forth by global financial institutions and the market. America's twin trade and budget deficits are not principally China's fault, but are results of U.S. fiscal-policy profligacy as well as (somewhat contradictorily) the continued appeal of American financial markets for investors around the world. In other words, there are tensions and even contradictions in how to handle China in the economic-policy domain. We should not scapegoat the PRC or see its policies as primarily predatory; at the same time, we must be prepared to hold Beijing accountable for its policies while also improving our own. Again, China should be seen as neither complete partner nor absolute rival of the United States; it is a bit of both (though it is closer to the first in economic terms). The only way to handle such a complex policy topography is through constant attention, hard work, and frequent communication between U.S. political leaders and the American people. The American tendency to assume that Asia will take care of itself while the United States focuses primarily on Europe and the Middle East has never been smart policy and is now more untenable than ever. Such thinking must be rejected, and Asia must be strongly and prominently engaged, by the next U.S. president.

Keep the Military

Fourth, the United States must maintain its stabilizing military presence in Asia. Several changes resulting from the Pentagon's recent global posture review concern key U.S. allies in Asia. These sensitive shifts in the U.S. military presence in Asia should not be rushed or hyped. Instead, they should be explained as evolutionary movements rather than radical departures from established policies. The United States must maintain a forward deployed military presence in the region that is both reassuring to friends and a reminder to China that we remain the ultimate guarantor of regional peace and stability. Capital ships, stealthy submarines, expeditionary marine forces, and overwhelming airpower will likely offer the most effective military instruments for managing a range of Asian scenarios involving core U.S. interests. They also are essential for credibly backstopping American alliances and other security commitments in the region. More positively, we should make clear our eagerness to work with all Asian countries, including China, in pursuit of common security objectives such as countering terrorism, piracy, and WMD proliferation. Joint peacekeeping operations involving China, Japan, South Korea, and other countries could provide opportunities for expanded security dialogue among the participants.

Win Hearts and Minds

Fifth, recognize that a more promising and equally important battlefield for the "hearts and minds" struggle within Islam today lies in Southeast Asia, not the Middle East. The United States must launch a major diplomatic engagement strategy in the region, starting with Indonesia, the world's most populous Islamic nation. We should build on the opening provided by the successful U.S.-led post-tsunami relief effort in that country, an episode that throughout the region highlighted the economic and military strengths of the United States in comparison with China, whose stingy assistance did not warrant membership in the core group of leading aid-donating countries that took charge of the relief effort for a short period. In the aftermath of their shared experiences in this endeavor, the American and Indonesian governments agree that they have the potential to forge a long-term partnership. Achieving further progress will require expanding our recently renewed contacts with the Indonesian military, a key local ally against Islamic extremism. The global education initiative outlined in the last chapter, designed with countries such as Indonesia in mind, will provide more of a basis for partnership—and more of a contrast with China, should it remain withholding in its foreign assistance. In improving ties with Indonesia, the United States would simultaneously counter the twin problems of spreading Chinese influence and Islamist extremism in Southeast Asia.

Understand Domestic Politics

Sixth, the United States needs a more nuanced set of strategies for dealing with China's domestic situation, particularly the rising expectations of its growing middle class. Whereas China's newly enhanced diplomatic corps can detail the rifts in the American neoconservative movement with a knowledge rivaling that of media pundit Chris Matthews, U.S. officials have yet to appreciate fully the policy implications and opportunities arising from China's substantial domestic problems and resulting internal schisms. Such awareness does not require prohibiting U.S. high-technology companies from investing in the Chinese market, nor must it entail unwarranted concern about China's need to assure its access to foreign energy sources. But an effective strategy does mean exploiting hard-to-control information portals linking Chinese Internet users with the rest of the online world. It also means discouraging Chinese energy policies that could be both strategically and environmentally disastrous.

U.S. foreign policy must rebalance its energies between the Middle East and East Asia because a continuing preoccupation with the Middle East will have negative long-term ramifications for the American position in the world. The two challenges are not identical. The violent struggle with Islamic extremism is now an inescapable feature of American foreign policy and homeland-security efforts. In contrast, relations with China involve a complex mix of cooperation and competition, and are not necessarily destined to either evolve into strong friendship or degenerate into open hostility. China is neither Bill Clinton's "strategic partner" nor George W. Bush's "strategic competitor"—or perhaps it is both.

Our suggestions for managing this complicated relationship are by necessity nuanced and even abstract. So, in conclusion, we might offer one final concrete recommendation: The next U.S. president should make sure that one of the top three U.S. foreign-policy officials is first and foremost an Asia hand. Since the Nixon administration, secretaries of state have focused on Europe, Russia, and the Middle East, as have national security advisers. The Clinton administration's secretaries of defense, particularly Bill Perry and Bill Cohen, had considerable interest and expertise in Asia, but they have been exceptions rather than the rule. Richard Armitage came to his job as deputy secretary of state in the first George W. Bush administration with a great deal of background in East Asia, but he was only the second most powerful official in a department that was itself deemphasized in policymaking. China's rise is the dominant feature of the international system today, and the next president needs someone at his or her side who understands the implications of that rise in all their richness and complexity.

CHAPTER 8

A NEW NONPROLIFERATION STRATEGY

GEORGE W. BUSH and John Kerry agreed in 2004 that nuclear proliferation posed the principal threat to U.S. security of our times. They were right.[1]

The spread of nuclear weapons—or, more specifically, the spread of the materials, information, and expertise needed to make them—to new states is itself bad enough. But in a world of terrorist groups such as al Qaeda, nuclear weapons provide the potential means for Western cities to be largely leveled, with hundreds of thousands killed in a single blast. Whether or not most countries that obtain nuclear weapons would ever seriously consider using them, radical jihadists probably would—and their prospects for being able to purchase, steal, or otherwise obtain a nuclear device increase with each additional member of the nuclear club.[2]

Policymakers sometimes talk about proliferation as if one straightforward concept—deployment of missile defense, or more money for cooperative threat reduction, or a more multilateralist approach toward treaties—would solve much of the problem. Indeed, each of these policies has its place. But conservatives and neo-conservatives often talk as if arms control is generally a waste of time, and that only hard power (often of a unilateralist variety) matters. Those on the left, by contrast, often sound ready to rely exclusively on arms control, international law, and patient multilateral diplomacy when addressing the spread of dangerous weapons.

Neither position is right. Stopping proliferation is perhaps the classic case where it is essential to employ a blend of hard and soft power, of decisive American leadership with consensus-building diplomacy, of attempts to use treaties with a willingness to resort to military or economic coercion if they fail. This issue thus provides a golden opportunity for Hard Power Democrats as well as moderate Republicans and independents to pose a more viable way forward for the country than either the far left or far right often counsel. Handling specific cases correctly will always require calibration for the circumstances at hand—and will always be difficult. That said, the general goal of addressing the nuclear-proliferation problem effectively requires the United States to vigorously develop and employ several different types of foreign policy tools:

- strong military alliances to deter adversaries and reassure friends that they need not pursue nuclear weapons of their own
- continuation of cooperative-threat-reduction efforts beyond their current scope and beyond Russia
- de-emphasis of nuclear weapons in American security policy and reinvigoration of certain aspects of arms control
- individually tailored policies for the key problem states, most notably North Korea and Iran, with the ultimate goal being to achieve the sort of success that the Bush administration was able to accomplish in regard to Libya

The last of these is the most complex to implement. The next to last, about de-emphasizing nuclear weapons and reinvigorating some types of arms control, may be the most intellectually demanding but is ripe for a major breakthrough by a new administration not carrying the baggage or the anti–arms control prejudices of the Bush administration. Cooperative threat reduction requires more work but is moving in the right direction, albeit too slowly; again, a new administration can add some vigor (though, in fairness, the Bush administration has improved its approach after an initial reluctance). The first point is the easiest in one sense, since a solid foundation of American alliances has been laid in the decades since World War II. But sustaining this good state of affairs requires constant attention—and repairing some of the damage of recent years will take considerable effort.

In one sense, tackling specific proliferation challenges can create the most need for American hard power. That has certainly been seen in Iraq and could prove true elsewhere as well. However, it is also important to underscore, as we do in our treatments of the North Korea and Iran cases below, that hard power must be applied well, and in combination with what might be called soft power, to be constructive and useful. It must have international legitimacy (except in cases of extreme direct threat to the homeland, where America's self-defense right necessitates no consultation with others—though in such circumstances, support will usually be easily attainable). Creating this legitimacy is to a large extent a task for American soft power—that is, widespread international trust in U.S. leadership, which is obtained in turn largely by America's own support for a web of values, treaties, and international standards of good behavior that most other countries accept and that proliferators can therefore be punished for violating.

If and when military force is used, it must be used well and responsibly, including a long-term game plan for follow-through and ultimate success. As we argue below, it is quite difficult (though hardly impossible) to imagine plausible circumstances in Iran or North Korea where the use of military force would be America's wisest course of action in the coming years. But even if that is the case, hard power in a broader sense is relevant. Maintaining strong alliances, and conveying a willingness to employ force if absolutely necessary, are critical to American nonproliferation policy—just as they are for ensuring U.S. national security more generally.

U.S. ALLIANCES AND AMERICA'S
BROAD ROLE IN THE WORLD

Proliferation can only be stopped if countries that worry about their own security have some alternative way of protecting themselves against plausible threats. Only America has the global system of credible military alliances—and deployable military power—to help other countries protect themselves in key unsettled regions such as East Asia and the Middle East. Historically, its security umbrella made it far easier for friends and allies such as Germany, South Korea, Taiwan, and Japan not to pursue their own nuclear deterrents, and the same logic generally applies in today's world for many states.[3]

The importance of maintaining strong and credible American alliances as an anchor for the global security order is a major reason why future candidates for office will have to work to keep America engaged abroad. There may be a temptation to retreat into a more isolationist approach to the world, given the difficulties of the Iraq operation in particular, to say nothing of America's twin budget and trade deficits.[4] But for reasons of preventing nuclear proliferation, among many others, it is important that candidates resist this impulse.

In the convincing phrase Madeleine Albright coined in the 1990s, the United States truly is the "indispensable nation." Another useful metaphor from that era, Richard Haass's description of America as "reluctant sheriff," is also apropos. The United States may show greater skepticism about using its military muscle in the future than it did during much of the George W. Bush presidency, but it needs to play the role of international sheriff at times nonetheless (with the help of "posses" of like-minded states), because no other entity can do so.[5] Those moderates and progressives angry about Bush-administration unilateralism and arrogance must avoid overcompensating in such a way that they weaken America's critical role as a global leader.

America's centrality in the international order is another aspect of the reason why moderates and progressives must be careful when they suggest that multilateralism will be a core element of their foreign policy, as many do. While multilateralism is desirable, it should not be taken so far as to devolve simplistically into a "democratic" approach to world affairs in which each nation essentially gets equal say. As Harvard professor and former Pentagon official Joseph Nye argues, the United States should not act multilaterally when doing so would contradict core American values, delay responses to immediate threats to its security, or promote poor policies that might have been improved through a tougher (and more unilateral) bargaining process.[6] The United States will sometimes have to do things that are unpopular internationally; it will usually have to help forge consensus among nations rather than wait for it to develop; and it will generally have to act rather than hope that crises will go away on their own. On the subject at hand, this means that America needs to be ready to defend its allies without waiting for global approval or the formation of large coalitions to do so.

LOOSE NUKES AND COOPERATIVE THREAT REDUCTION

Helping Russia secure its huge arsenal of "loose" nuclear materials and weapons is the only way to ensure that criminal or terrorist groups do not get their hands on such lethal armaments. Only about half of the key Russian nuclear-related sites have received appropriate security improvements to date.[7] In addition, sensitive nuclear materials the world over need to be secured, even at civilian research facilities where no weapons programs have ever existed. At present, highly enriched uranium is found in many places where it is not needed for any scientific or commercial purpose, raising the risk of theft and subsequent catastrophe to unacceptable levels.

The United States has been spending roughly $1 billion a year for these purposes. Study groups, such as one led by former senator Howard Baker and the late Lloyd Cutler, have recommended major increases above this total, and other countries have pledged funds as well. There is a role for increased resources. But absorptive capacity has probably been a greater constraint on rapid progress than raw resources.

Democrats and other Bush-administration critics have tended to harp on the funding issue in recent years. While it is indeed important to keep resources up around the $1 billion a year mark, and ideally somewhat higher, the greater challenges probably lie within the area of forging a stronger partnership with Russia. This will be very difficult to do given current political problems in the relationship. If a stronger technical partnership on this matter can be made stronger, American resources—matching those provided by Russia—may usefully increase further. In particular, Russia needs to assess more comprehensively security at its nuclear sites, consolidate dangerous materials and weapons to a smaller number of sites, improve physical security measures as well as the quality of its security forces at that smaller number of sites, and back up all these ideas with rubles.

More countries with highly enriched uranium in research reactors need to be convinced to modify their reactors to run on lower-enriched uranium. The G8 can help in this effort at persuasion more than it has to date. If and when such measures are successful, more funds will be appropriate—including the $20 billion already pledged by other donors for global nuclear-security efforts.

A final issue within the general purview of cooperative threat reduction and nuclear safety and security concerns the new arsenals of the new nuclear powers. If India and Pakistan can be convinced to share some information about their facilities with the donor community, some help might be usefully provided them as well. At a minimum, weapons scientists and security specialists from these countries should be granted access to those who understand best practices in this field so that insights can be shared on matters such as safe nuclear-storage practices, permissive action links to prevent unauthorized usage, and background-check practices for nuclear-security personnel.

Others have written on the nuclear-security question in greater detail. But the basic points made above need to be a minimum body of knowledge for any political candidate serious about making progress in this critical area of threats to American and international security.[8] And on balance, while there are many more constraints than sheer lack of funds, modest increases in U.S. funding on the order of several hundred million dollars a year will be appropriate for such efforts even in the short term—with the possibility of much larger increases if constraints can be lifted on program effectiveness in Russia.

THE PROPER ROLE OF
TOUGH-MINDED ARMS CONTROL

Arms control has a place in preventing proliferation as well. However, on this point, moderates and progressives need to be careful how they make their arguments. Arms control does not make the world safer because dangerous countries emulate the behavior of the United States and other major powers, or because such extremist regimes care much about international treaties. Rather, Washington's ability to form a strong international consensus to coerce proliferating countries into better behavior depends on our ability to convince the world that that behavior is illegitimate and indefensible. Only with international support, for example, can U.N. Security Council sanctions be applied against dangerous regimes. Arms control establishes standards that then help us hold problem countries accountable when they violate those standards.[9]

With this general philosophy in mind, five specific arms-control concepts deserve discussion because of their relevance to the question of dealing with proliferation and proliferators. They are the ABM Treaty, the Comprehensive Test Ban Treaty (CTBT), the Proliferation Security Initiative (PSI), the Nuclear Non-Proliferation Treaty (NPT), and limits on the U.S. and Russian offensive nuclear-force postures. The George W. Bush administration withdrew from the ABM Treaty during its first term in office, refused to pursue the CTBT (after the Senate voted against ratification late in the Clinton years), created the PSI, tried with limited success to toughen the terms of the NPT, and made some progress on the last item with the Moscow Treaty of 2002.

The politics of the ABM Treaty are, of course, highly charged. The Bush administration reasonably argued when it came into office that a treaty designed to prevent countries from protecting themselves, whatever logic it had during the superpower competition of the Cold War (when practical defenses were infeasible), no longer made sense. In this, it actually built on its predecessor's legacy, since the Clinton administration developed a plan to deploy long-range interceptors in Alaska and California on roughly the schedule that the Bush administration actually made those systems operational. But, as previously noted, the Bush administration greatly increased the scope and the cost of the missile-defense effort (roughly doubling it from $5 billion a year to $10 billion a year, including the costs of short-range missile defenses), deployed it despite ongoing technical problems in the system itself, and withdrew from the U.S.-Russian ABM Treaty without making any serious effort to negotiate an amendment to it first.

On balance, the Bush administration's missile-defense deployment was reasonable, but somewhat rushed. It would have been preferable, for the sake of maintaining America's moral high ground on matters of arms control, to try to renegotiate the ABM Treaty before abandoning it. This legacy cannot be undone, but it should remind Americans that we now have a certain legitimacy deficit when it comes to holding other countries accountable to their arms-control obligations.[10]

That is where the CTBT debate comes in. The Bush administration has remained somewhat agnostic on the CTBT, choosing not to promote it but at the same time continuing to respect the self-imposed U.S. moratorium on nuclear testing that dates back to 1992. This approach has been far preferable to complete repudiation of the CTBT (along the lines of how the Bush administration has handled the Kyoto Protocol on climate change, the international criminal court, and the ABM Treaty). But it leaves the next U.S. president with a big choice to make about future policy, even as many conservatives favor development of new warheads. One type would be designed to penetrate the Earth to destroy deep underground targets without releasing lots of fallout; the other would be designed to remain highly reliable for decades to come, without frequent rebuilding. However, as a main inventor of the hydrogen bomb Richard Garwin and others have argued, the United States can maintain the reliability of existing warheads without testing simply by rebuilding each warhead to original specifications every few decades. It can also design and build a robust, reliable warhead without testing, since such warheads would by definition have large tolerances for error and little chance of fizzling out. Finally, the notion of Earth-penetrating bombs that release only minimal fallout has been shown to be implausible on technical grounds, as Michael Levi of the Council on Foreign Relations has convincingly argued.[11] On balance, the case for the CTBT is strong, in that any consequences for the American nuclear deterrent would be minimal while the potential benefits for nonproliferation policy could be substantial.[12] In short, the United States does not need to test to maintain a reliable nuclear arsenal. By contrast, potential proliferators would probably need to test in order to develop dependable weapons (or at least those advanced enough to be placed on a missile). And they can be pressured more effectively not to test if the world's major powers are themselves abstaining (it is worth noting that North Korea tested missiles, not nuclear weapons, in the summer of 2006—perhaps in part because it knew that testing the latter would cause a strong international response against it).

The Bush administration did create one totally new type of arms-control initiative during its time in office: the Proliferation Security Initiative. Involving neither a new treaty nor a governing board, it is nonetheless an effort to use multilateral mechanisms to limit the spread of dangerous weaponry and as such can be defined as arms control. The idea is to use existing national law from participating countries, which include a core of about 15 major players plus another 40 or more nations supportive of the idea, to target suspicious ships that come into their territorial waters. For example, a North Korean ship in Japanese or Australian seas could be stopped for a routine safety inspection, as existing legislation and existing norms on territorial waters permit. If that ship were then found to have illicit weapons components aboard, or contraband such as narcotics or counterfeit currency, its cargo could be seized. In fact, there have been a couple of successes along these very lines to date. Most notably, it was the sort of activity envisioned and encouraged by the PSI, together with traditional intelligence, that led to the rolling up of Libya's nuclear-related programs as well as much of Pakistan's A.Q. Khan proliferation network. Unfortunately, to take another case, the unwillingness of South Korea and China to participate in the PSI has limited its effectiveness against North Korea.

The NPT issue is perhaps the most directly relevant of all the arms-control concepts considered here. The NPT, signed in 1968, was essentially a deal between the world's nuclear haves and have-nots. The former promised to shrink and ultimately eliminate their nuclear arsenals (and also work toward a CTBT); the latter promised not to pursue their own nuclear weapons provided that they were granted help with nuclear energy programs. Alas, the latter provision has allowed countries with malevolent intent to gain access to nuclear technology under the guise of creating energy programs, but later to divert that technology toward weapons efforts. Recognizing that this loophole allowed North Korea to create nuclear capability far faster than it could have on its own, a number of countries, including the United States, have since tried to tighten the treaty.

One change has been to demand wider access for weapons inspections, to ensure that illicit facilities are not secretly created, through a procedure known as the Additional Protocol. The logic of this approach has been largely accepted by most countries. A second change has been to deny countries with problematic proliferation records the right to develop their own nuclear technology, be it for energy or weapons. Several types of ideas are on the table here. One is the preferred Bush-administration approach, advocating that no additional countries be allowed to develop enrichment or reprocessing technologies. This approach would be fine for America's interests if it were truly negotiable, but at present it does not seem to be, and the world's expected growing demand for nuclear power will further complicate such strict efforts to limit the spread of relevant technologies. More modest new restrictions would deny technology to countries with bad proliferation records (such as Iran). Another approach would require that any enrichment plants in countries not now possessing them be placed under multinational ownership and oversight (to increase transparency and make it harder for illicit weapons activities to be hidden).

Unfortunately, none of these ideas restricting access to the nuclear fuel cycle are presently codified in any new treaty or any formal revision to the NPT, meaning that many countries view them as more of a guideline than a strict rule. That fact gives states such as Russia and China an excuse to avoid pressuring countries like Iran in the current nuclear crisis involving that country.[13] The next administration needs to find a negotiable approach and promote it vigorously. Although the recommended Bush approach would be ideal, it is probably unrealistic. A somewhat less stringent variant, such as one combining the more modest ideas mentioned above with a guaranteed supply of subsidized nuclear fuel (and later with assistance in waste disposal),[14] will probably have to be selected instead.

Finally, the United States should continue to find practical ways to reduce the role of nuclear weapons in its security policy—even though the ultimate goal of nuclear abolition almost certainly remains unattainable anytime in the foreseeable future. Gradual further reductions in the size of U.S. and Russian arsenals are appropriate. There is no need for thousands of warheads and no credible scenario under which the use of such astronomical numbers of apocalyptic weapons could make sense. Even the need to remain decisively ahead of China (so that the PRC does not become tempted to catch up to American nuclear capabilities) can be confidently satisfied with 1,000 long-range warheads. A follow-on to the agreement President Bush and President Putin signed in 2002, known as the Moscow Treaty and limiting each side's long-range arsenal to about 2,000 weapons by 2012, should be negotiated. Roughly half as many warheads, together with sharp reductions in tactical nuclear arsenals, would make strategic (and budgetary) sense. Such cuts would do no harm whatsoever to America's deterrent while strengthening its legitimacy as an enforcer of international nonproliferation standards.[15]

INDIVIDUAL CASES

The nuclear-proliferation problem will haunt future Congresses and the next American president every bit as much as it has worried those of the past. The North Korean and Iranian nuclear programs remain unresolved and very difficult matters. Pakistan's possession of a nuclear arsenal is only slightly less troubling, given its potential for internal instability (and the large numbers of radical jihadists within its borders). In addition to the dangers associated with individual extremist countries' getting nuclear weapons, there is a possibility that accelerating global proliferation could reach a "nuclear tipping point" and lead to many more countries getting the bomb.[16]

The Bush administration's legacy on nuclear issues will be fairly complex. On Iraq, of course, the administration engaged in preventive war (often mislabeled as preemption, which refers to striking before an imminent enemy attack). On Libya, building on the George H. W. Bush and Clinton legacies, it impressively and successfully used a combination of incentives and coercion to convince Qaddafi to roll back his program.[17] On India, it effectively welcomed a generally responsible democracy into the nuclear club, though without gaining a major Indian contribution to the global nonproliferation effort in return.

On Iran, the verdict is still out. Unfortunately, on North Korea, the outcome has been quite poor. The George W. Bush administration was paralyzed for much of its first term in trying to choose between a hardline preference for facilitating regime change and a more flexible yet still tough conditional-engagement strategy. On balance, its focus on Iraq and its doctrine of preemption created a set of circumstances that made it much harder to prevent Pyongyang from roughly quadrupling its nuclear arsenal in the last half decade.

Each of these elements of nonproliferation and counterproliferation strategy requires some elaboration below. We focus in the end on the hot-spot countries that future members of Congress and the next president will have to face squarely and early in their new terms, beginning with South Asia but emphasizing Iran and North Korea. In neither case do we anticipate a likelihood of using military force, since the prospects for doing so at high effectiveness and reasonable cost are generally poor in both cases. But tough-minded policy is nonetheless needed, with a full consideration of punishing economic steps to be taken in the event that Pyongyang and Tehran stay embarked on nuclear paths. Still, toughness cannot be the only defining feature of American policy, since it precludes development of strong coalitions that will be needed to apply effective coercive instruments against North Korea and Iran. As we describe below, each country must be faced with a stark choice between international engagement and inducements should its behavior improve, and ostracization and sanctions otherwise. Offering the former credibly requires the effective use of American soft power—not as an alternative to hard power but in part to set up the predicate for employing more coercive policies with international support if and when engagement fails.

Syria

First, a brief word on Syria, which has occasionally been discussed as a possible target for American coercive action in recent years. This is understandable at one level. Syria is run by an old-fashioned (if relatively young) autocrat who supports anti-Israeli terrorism, who may have had a hand in the assassination of the Lebanese leader Hariri in 2005, and who has wavered in his willingness to clamp down on Iraqi Baathists since the U.S. military invasion of his neighbor to the east. But Syria's WMD programs focus primarily on chemical weapons, not nuclear or advanced biological arms. In addition, its support of terrorism, while serious, does not pose the same magnitude of threat to Western security as does al Qaeda, and its territorial ambitions appear to be far more modest than those of Iraq under Saddam or North Korea.

According to the CIA, "Russia and Syria have approved a draft cooperative program on cooperation on civil nuclear power. In principle, broader access to Russian expertise provides opportunities for Syria to expand its indigenous capabilities, should it decide to pursue nuclear weapons."[18] There is also some suspicion that Syria was a client of Pakistani scientist A. Q. Khan's nuclear trading network.[19] There is little direct evidence, however, of significant advances in Syria's nuclear program. According to then-under secretary of state John Bolton, the United States "continue[s] to watch for any sign of nuclear-weapons activity or foreign assistance that could facilitate a Syrian nuclear-weapons capability." Further, there is little definitive evidence of a sophisticated Syrian biological-weapons program. According to Bolton, "We believe Syria would need foreign assistance to launch a large-scale biological-weapons program right now." While Syria should be pressured to change numerous aspects of its foreign policy, and to eliminate verifiably its chemical weapons and any biological-weapons programs, its WMD capacity does not currently warrant consideration of the most extreme types of American and international responses.[20]

South Asia

India and Pakistan badly damaged the global nonproliferation order when they detonated nuclear weapons in 1998. But the nature of the problem is much different in regard to them than in regard to Syria, Iran, or North Korea. Pakistan is a U.S. security partner, cooperative in many aspects of the war on terrorism; India is a vibrant democracy and, increasingly, an international friend. As such, different types of policy steps are called for—in the spirit not of coercion but of judicious use of incentives to try to get these nations, at a minimum, to cap their nuclear programs.

Pakistan presents several major challenges to any American strategy aimed at controlling dangerous technologies in general, and nuclear weapons in particular. It has enough extremist elements within its political system that its arsenal's security requires considerable further attention and vigilance. Pakistan's apparent willingness to export sensitive nuclear technology to North Korea and, possibly, to Iran (or, at least, to turn a blind eye to such exports as the A.Q. Khan network carried them out unofficially) has been a major blow to cooperative export-control regimes. Its acquisition of nuclear weapons outside the Non-Proliferation Treaty has undeniably weakened the principle of international relations that additional countries should not acquire nuclear weapons. And some suspect that Pakistan would be willing to transfer whole nuclear weapons to other states; Saudi Arabia is sometimes mentioned in this respect.

Several mitigating circumstances have, however, pushed the United States toward a decidedly less confrontational policy vis-à-vis Pakistan than this indictment might suggest. In the immediate aftermath of the September 11, 2001, terrorist attacks, the United States urgently needed Pakistani overflight and basing rights and assistance in conducting its war against al Qaeda and the Taliban in neighboring Afghanistan. This led it to lift nuclear-related sanctions on Pakistan. While understandable at the time, this lax approach should not be the entire extent of future American policy toward Islamabad.

Where should we go from here? Rolling back Pakistan's nuclear capability is not a realistic goal of arms-control policy. Instead, the current focus should be to find a nonproliferation "halfway house" for Pakistan that encourages responsible stewardship of its nuclear weapons and related technologies. That halfway house should primarily aim to clamp down on nuclear-related exports by Pakistan, such as those of the infamous A. Q. Khan network. It should also seek to ensure the security of the country's arsenal through safety measures such as those described above in the discussion of cooperative threat reduction. Finally, policy should seek to cap the quantitative and qualitative development of the Pakistani arsenal (including prevention of future testing).

The United States and allies should use the promise of further economic aid and trade concessions, including the type proposed in chapter five, to improve Pakistan's export controls. At the same time, the United States might provide Pakistan technical assistance in implementing these controls. There is little unclassified knowledge as to the degree of official authorization for past proliferation-related activities, but it is prudent to assume that at least some may have been unauthorized. The United States should consider discussing methods for enhancing and implementing export controls, largely by sharing with Pakistani officials unclassified information about which technologies America restricts and how it monitors compliance at national borders. It should focus more on generalities than specifics, though, being careful not to transfer information that Pakistani citizens or others might use to evade U.S. export controls.

It would also be beneficial to bring Pakistan formally into the international nonproliferation regime, to give it a political stake in its success. The best way to begin this process would be for Pakistan (and India) to sign and ratify the CTBT. This underscores the importance of the United States' doing the same. Many American conservatives argue that when the United States signs arms treaties, it gains no real leverage over problem states, which will not be impressed by the good American example and will do what they wish anyway. However, this analysis is too simple. Among other things, it ignores the fact that, absent its own ratification of the CTBT, the United States has no plausible chance to convince India and Pakistan to sign the treaty, and much less ability to convince other friends and allies to pressure them to do so.

In parallel, the United States should try to convince Pakistan to terminate the production of all fissile material suitable for nuclear weapons, as all the major nuclear powers have. The Chinese example of a modest-sized deterrent could help in making the argument. So could continued American commitment to reducing its dependence on nuclear weapons, as argued above. When candidates try to explain their support for arms control, it will help them politically to argue that such American restraint can help the United States solve specific problems such as this one.

India's regime is more stable than Pakistan's and less inclined to support or condone any terrorist groups or rogue states. But there is still a major problem here, and the George W. Bush administration's willingness to wipe India's nuclear slate virtually clean in the interest of strengthening the bilateral relationship goes too far.

India is a democratic, peaceful state that has every bit as much inherent moral right to nuclear weapons as does, for example, its neighbor China. But in the interest of global stability—something India also requires for its economic development—New Delhi should be willing to look for ways to help shore up the nuclear-nonproliferation system. It may insist on keeping its weapons; in fact, it almost surely will. But there is a good deal that still can be done—not as a favor to America, but as a way to help undergird a more stable world. India must find a way to show restraint.[21]

India can do three different types of things to play a responsible role in preventing further global nuclear proliferation. In some cases, international cooperation or assistance may be of benefit to it. It can further improve export controls. Even while remaining outside the NPT, it can solidify the global nonproliferation regime by signing and ratifying the CTBT and ceasing fissile-material production. Finally, it can foster a stable strategic balance with Pakistan (and China) at the lowest possible force levels.

Unlike Pakistan, India has demonstrated a real political commitment to nuclear export controls. Thus, export-control engagement should focus on ensuring that India has the appropriate legal and institutional arrangements to effectively implement its export-control goals. In addition, the

United States should encourage India to formally declare its intent to comply with the Nuclear Suppliers Group guidelines restricting sensitive nuclear exports. This would improve international leverage in pressuring Pakistan to adopt similar standards.

Until steps such as these are taken, including Indian signing of the CTBT and an additional agreement to stop producing fissile material for any purpose, the United States should show more restraint in its nuclear cooperation with India than the Bush administration has done. (Various mechanisms for fostering the prospects of such ideas could be considered, such as a joint China-India-Pakistan regional pact to limit nuclear forces and stop the production of fissile material. It is not clear that such an idea would be negotiable, but there is no reason to oppose it if it proves workable.) Ideally, the United States might have tolerated shipments of uranium fuel to India, for example, but held off on other nuclear cooperation until New Delhi made progress on the arms-control and export-control fronts. As a fallback option, the United States should keep working to try to persuade India to find viable means of opposing more nuclear proliferation. The next American president will have the option, for example, of proposing that India and the United States together adopt the CTBT. [22]

Iran

The last two cases are different, and more severe. When accepted standards of arms control are violated, especially by countries with track records of aggression against their neighbors or their own peoples, stern measures may be needed, including economic sanctions and the use of military force. The threat of military force does not look very promising in regard to either North Korea or Iran at this point. In both situations, the more appealing policy approach is to maximize the economic leverage that can be mustered against these two dangerous regimes. In addition to the threat of coercion, incentives can play a role—especially if Tehran and Pyongyang are willing to begin to transform their government policies more broadly. Under such circumstances, the United States should make it clear that it would not promote regime change if the government in question verifiably and meaningfully committed to carrying out fundamental regime transformation (in policies and outlook, not necessarily in individuals or political parties).

Unlike the situation with North Korea, where its policy performance has been quite poor, the Bush administration has adopted a generally sound approach for dealing with Iran in recent years. But the situation remains very difficult. The problem posed by Iran is of the utmost seriousness: A state with strong links to terrorism is pursuing extremely dangerous technologies, and attempts to achieve greater arms-control transparency are being frequently stymied. The case for coercive measures is strong. Unlike North Korea, though, Iran has not already progressed to the point of having nuclear weapons. And unlike with Iraq, where non-military efforts at resolution failed for more than a decade, concerted diplomatic efforts with Iran began fairly recently. Finally, despite discouraging recent trends in Iran's politics, the country is not nearly so dictatorial as Iraq under Saddam or North Korea under Kim. Internal political reform may help the nonproliferation cause—and that reform process may be affected by how the outside world pressures Tehran.

There is no doubt that Iran has already transgressed many nonproliferation commitments. By lying to IAEA inspectors and conducting secret uranium-enrichment and plutonium-reprocessing experiments over two decades, Iran has explicitly violated its NPT obligations, which require transparency and monitoring for any such efforts (even when non-weapons-related). Compounding those specific violations, Iran has consistently supported international terrorism, including sponsoring Hezbollah and reportedly harboring al Qaeda leaders, and has a poor human-rights record, though not of the same scale as North Korea's or Iraq's under Saddam Hussein.

Iran is at present the world's number one state sponsor of terrorism by most metrics, given its active support for Hezbollah in particular.[23] Iran may be less likely than North Korea to sell fissile materials to terrorists to earn money, but it has been more likely to use terrorists as delivery vehicles to execute state policy. If it had a nuclear deterrent, it might be even less constrained about unleashing Hezbollah or other terrorist groups, no longer fearing American retribution as acutely. Iranian acquisition could directly spur regional competitors—Egypt, Saudi Arabia, Syria, and possibly others—to acquire their own nuclear weapons. And while failure in North Korea could be blamed in part on past policy errors, Iranian acquisition of an atomic bomb would suggest that the United States and the international community, even with their new focus on proliferation, and even with relatively early warning of a proliferation development, are effectively powerless to stop the spread of nuclear weapons. It would thus be an invitation to would-be proliferators.

TABLE 8.1   Iranian Nuclear Facilities by Region of Country

Coastal	Tehran-vicinity	Interior– North / East	Interior – South / West
Bushehr	Damavand	Arak	Ardakan
	Jabr Ibn Hagan	Bonab	Fasa
	Karaj	Chalus	Narigan
	Lashkar-Abad	Darkhovin	Saghland
	Ramandeh	Esfahan	Yazd
	Tehran	Gorgan	Zarigan
		Khondab	
		Mo-Allem Kalayeh	
		Natanz	
		Tabriz	

SOURCE: Iran Nuclear Reactors, Nuclear Threat Initiative, January 17, 2006. (http://www.nti.org/e_research/profiles_pdfs/Iran/iran_nuclear_sites.pdf, accessed February 7, 2006.)

NOTE: For the purposes of this table, the category of Tehran-vicinity includes any facilities within a 50 km-radius of Tehran. The line for dividing the interior was drawn from Abadan on the border with Iraq to Mashhad near the border with Turkmenistan, thus dividing Iran between Esfahan in the north/east and Yazd in the south/west. Darkhovin is a suspected uranium enrichment site. Mo-Allem Kalayeh is a suspected nuclear research center.

TABLE 8.2   Iranian Nuclear Facilities by Type

Mines	Research Sites	Enrichment Facilities	Heavy Water Production	Reactors
Narigan	Bonab	Arak	Khondab	Bushehr
Saghand	Chalus	Ardakan		
Yazd	Damavand	Darkhovin		
Zarigan	Esfahan	Esfahan		
	Gorgan	Fasa		
	Jabr Ibn Hagan	Jabr Ibn Hagan		
	Karaj	Lashkar-Abad		
	Mo-Allem Kalayeh	Natanz		
	Tabriz	Ramandeh		
	Tehran	Tehran		

SOURCE: Iran Nuclear Reactors, Nuclear Threat Initiative, January 17, 2006. (http://www.nti.org/e_research/profiles_pdfs/Iran/iran_nuclear_sites.pdf, accessed February 7, 2006.)

NOTE: For the purposes of this table, ore purification, conversion facilities and centrifuges are considered enrichment facilities; weapons development is considered research; milling plants are considered mines. Darkhovin is a suspected uranium enrichment site. Mo-Allem Kalayeh is a suspected nuclear research center. The Wisconsin Project on Nuclear Arms Control also lists Esfahan and Tehran as having reactors. Iran Nuclear Update, The Risk Report 2003, Volume 9, Number 5, The Wisconsin Project on Nuclear Arms Control, September-October 2003, (http://www.wisconsinproject.org/countries/iran/nuke2003.htm, accessed February 14, 2006.)

It is worth underscoring why an Iranian nuclear weapon would be such a bad thing. After all, some might say, with the world's five permanent U.N. Security Council members having the bomb, with South Asia having gone nuclear in the last decade, and with even North Korea's presumed arsenal apparently being tolerated (or at least not severely opposed) by the international community, why not simply tolerate a Mideast Muslim counter to Israel's presumed nuclear capability?

There are many responses to this flawed way of thinking, starting with the fact that Muslims already have the bomb (in Pakistan and India), which counters the notion that fairness somehow requires that we allow another country with a large Islamic population to obtain a nuclear capability. But the real arguments are threefold. First, over the past one to two decades, only the former Taliban government in Afghanistan rivaled Iran as a state sponsor of terrorism. Iran's support for Hezbollah and other groups has not only directly led to violence against Israel and American military forces in Saudi Arabia, but also to violence against Jewish populations in Latin America. Iran now appears to be having a hand in helping Iraqi insurgents improve the improvised explosive devices they have used with such deadly effect against coalition troops and indigenous security forces in Iraq. Given this record, there is at least some remote possibility that Iran would give nuclear capabilities to a terrorist group under extreme circumstances.[24]

Second, and more likely, Iran could become emboldened in other aggressive ways by possession of a bomb. In particular, it could step up support for violence against Israel or U.S. and other Western military forces in the Persian Gulf region. It could threaten its neighbors in the region, some of which govern territory or resources that Iran claims. Tehran could be emboldened by knowing that retaliation against its aggression could become more difficult if it had a nuclear deterrent.

Third, Iran's acquisition of a nuclear weapon would be one more serious blow against a nuclear-nonproliferation effort that has taken numerous hits of late. Thankfully, earlier forecasts of the nonproliferation regime's demise have not come to pass. President Kennedy and other observers in the 1960s thought the world might have a couple dozen nuclear powers by now. After the Cold War ended, it again seemed likely that many states would obtain the bomb. But most European powers and America's East Asian allies showed remarkable restraint throughout this period, as did most Arab states, and three former Soviet republics as well as South Africa actually denuclearized after the Cold War. However,

India, Pakistan, and North Korea have in recent years created a dangerous momentum that threatens to blow the lid off these past accomplishments and lead to a rampantly proliferating world. Iran's acquisition of the bomb, even as the world watched the entire process unfold right before its collective eyes, would increase the risks much more.

What is to be done? Clearly, a diplomatic solution remains far preferable to a military one. But Iran has already rejected compromise proposals, such as a dedicated facility on Russian territory that would provide it a guaranteed fuel supply. Perhaps another idea, even if less optimal, remains worth considering. For example, Iranian enrichment might be tolerated on a small scale, if delayed for a few years and then closely monitored.[25] This possibility, which has been suggested by the International Crisis Group, is far from ideal yet probably better than a complete failure of diplomacy.

If diplomacy does fail, five options remain. They are all-out war, limited military strikes, strong economic coercion, limited sanctions, and stronger support for Iran's political opposition.

All-out war is clearly a policy of extreme last resort. Iran has three times the population of Iraq, where our forces are already tied down, making occupation extremely foreboding as an option. Invasion would also risk radicalizing the generally pro-Western Iranian population. Limited sanctions and support for Iran's opposition would be weak responses given the severity of the postulated Iranian offense.

So the remaining options are targeted strikes, with airpower and perhaps covert operations, as well as strong economic sanctions. There is a case for the former, but it would probably radicalize Iran while setting its weapons program back no more than five to ten years. Further, in the face of targeted strikes, Iran could be expected to go underground, just as Iraq did in the 1980s after Israel attacked its Osirak reactor. Indeed, it is probably already doing so, using advanced tunneling equipment and hardening techniques learned from the North Koreans and others. Buying five to ten years might make sense if we could get a Mideast peace accord and stable Iraq in the meantime as a result—but the prospects for either seem mediocre already, and, if anything, Iran could be expected to increase its meddling in these problem areas after such a strike.

That leaves serious economic coercion as the essence of the preferred strategy. A full ban on the Iranian oil trade in all of its dimensions would deal a severe economic blow to Iran. Of course, it would deal a serious (if somewhat less severe) blow to the global economy too, given the fact that Iran accounts for 5 percent of global oil production in an already tight market. This fact makes the case for energy diversification on a much more aggressive scale than the world has pursued it to date. But the need for a different energy policy cannot be allowed to distract us from what may soon be needed here in a more immediate way—some real teeth in our efforts to prevent a dangerously nuclearizing world. Higher oil prices, despite their downsides, are a reasonable cost to pay given the stakes.[26] They could also galvanize support for energy diversification. That would not be enough to spare the United States considerable short-term economic pain. But it could place it in a substantially stronger strategic position over time.

North Korea

When it began to develop a uranium-enrichment program in the late 1990s, North Korea violated not only the 1994 Agreed Framework with the United States, under which it pledged not to develop or possess nuclear weapons, but also the Nuclear Non-Proliferation Treaty as well as the 1991 North-South denuclearization pact with Seoul. The Bush administration was right to challenge Pyongyang once it learned of this behavior in 2002. North Korea then claimed to withdraw from the NPT, but only after violating it—an action of questionable legitimacy. It also expelled International Atomic Energy Agency (IAEA) inspectors, putting itself further into contravention of its NPT obligations and removing necessary transparency.[27] Subsequently, in addition to keeping its secret uranium-enrichment program (which is probably not yet producing enough uranium for a weapon), North Korea reprocessed the plutonium in the spent fuel at the Yongbyon site, increasing the estimated size of its likely nuclear arsenal from one or two bombs to perhaps eight or even more.[28]

There are several reasons why such an arsenal poses a grave risk, each of which reflects more generic concerns described earlier. First, North Korea might sell some nuclear technology or even materials to terrorists or other states. Second, if North Korea someday collapses, its nuclear materials could fall into the hands of those who would sell them to the highest bidder. Third, U.S./ROK deterrence could be weakened if North Korea thought it had a nuclear trump card. Should war then result, the more bombs North Korea possessed, the greater its odds of successfully delivering a nuclear warhead against Seoul or another population center (even in the United States, probably by means other than missile attack). Finally, North Korean nuclear weapons could start a nuclear domino effect in Northeast Asia, possibly provoking Japan, South Korea, and Taiwan, which would in turn weaken global nonproliferation more broadly.

One might be tempted to argue that, with the cat out of the bag and North Korea possibly now in possession of about eight nuclear weapons (or at least enough reprocessed plutonium to build that many), we now have a fait accompli and the issue will recede in political significance. The Bush administration, by this logic, will be seen as having presided over the development of a North Korean arsenal—something Democrats can mention to point out that Republicans may not be as good at foreign policy as they like to argue. Indeed, this argument would be partly right, since Bush administration preemption doctrine gave North Korea an excuse to pursue more weaponry that many countries seem to have found at least partly plausible, and Bush administration inattentiveness to the North Korea problem in 2002 and 2003 allowed a serious problem to get even worse.

Still, taking the political blamemanship path is not a sufficient alternative strategy for Democrats or other administration critics. Doing so would be both too optimistic and too fatalistic. It would be fatalistic because it would give up too soon. North Korea's arsenal remains de facto rather than official, so there is still hope of walking it back. That hope is increased by the historical facts that the international community ultimately convinced South Africa, Ukraine, Belarus, and Kazakstan to denuclearize. Accepting North Korea as a nuclear power as if that is a tolerable development on the world stage is also too blithe in light of the associated dangers. In addition to the arguments noted above, North Korea may ultimately complete construction on two large reactors with the theoretical capacity to produce enough plutonium for dozens of bombs a year. If that construction progresses substantially, the same types of questions about preemptive strikes (actually, in this case, preventive strikes) will be raised as are being forced to the policy fore by Iran.

So a major new U.S. policy effort is needed. Congress probably cannot do this. But the next U.S. president should make a major push to undo North Korea's nuclear progress—especially that which has occurred during the George W. Bush presidency. Doing so will be very difficult, since the threat of military force is no longer useful to eliminate the relevant plutonium. That plutonium has now been reprocessed and moved, probably in 2003, so the tools available to American policymakers have declined in number. In addition, the world has largely accepted a de facto North Korean nuclear arsenal, since the DPRK has probably had more than half a dozen warheads for at least two years. That the world's diplomatic focus has not been on Pyongyang has conveyed a sense of either defeatism or complacency about the existence of the DPRK threat. A new American president will have to re-create a sense of crisis after the fact.

The core of a new policy should be to force North Korea to decide between either more or less economic and diplomatic engagement. In other words, the goal should be to make the status quo untenable for Pyongyang, forcing it to choose between a better relationship with the outside world as well as more trade, investment, and assistance on the one hand, or on the other, the prospects of pressure and coercion being applied against it. A situation in which North Korea keeps, or even expands, its nuclear arsenal while South Korea and China increase the largesse they direct toward that country is intolerable. It is also a very serious indictment of the performance of governments in Washington, Seoul, and Beijing that have allowed this to occur, as Pyongyang has effectively divided them from each other and split the coalition that was supposed to restrain it.

The United States and its regional partners South Korea, Japan, China, and Russia should offer Pyongyang a set of inducements as well as a clear threat indicating that the nuclear status quo, or worse, cannot and will not be accepted. In doing so, they should be careful not to set a precedent for rewarding illicit behavior by granting North Korea large benefits simply for undoing a nuclear program it should not have had in the first place. They should make more comprehensive demands—not only denuclearization, but also reductions in conventional forces, elimination of chemical arms, structural economic reform, the beginnings of human-rights improvements—as a condition for substantial increases in aid. If Pyongyang is prepared to make such a deal, Washington and other capitals should be clear that they are prepared to help finance a transition to a Vietnam-style economy in North Korea. Total aid packages in the range of $1 billion to $3 billion a year for several years—to help build infrastructure, revitalize agriculture, and improve the public health and even education systems—could be acceptable if North Korea were to move verifiably and decisively in this direction. (More modest reforms could be met with more modest, yet still generous, aid packages.) U.S. bans on trade and investment could also be lifted, provisionally at first and later in a permanent way; a temporary U.S. diplomatic presence could lead to full relations, a permanent embassy, and a peace treaty within several years.[29]

Failing that, China and South Korea in particular should curb their investment activities in North Korea as well as their trade relations. They are the two countries keeping the DPRK afloat. While humanitarian aid is desirable under any circumstances, types of assistance that prop up the regime only make sense if the regime is behaving in an acceptable—or at least a promising and improving—manner. That is, for the most part, not happening at present (on this point, Bush administration hardliners are right). But Washington has been unable to convince Seoul and Beijing to move to a policy of coercion so far. Its only chance of doing so in the future requires that it seriously attempt negotiations with North Korea first, with an eye towards inducing Pyongyang to attempt the path followed by Vietnam and China itself.

The Vietnam model is, admittedly, an ambitious vision. It would probably not appeal initially to Kim Jong-Il—who might worry that once reform processes were unleashed, he would suffer the fate of Ceausescu in Romania (shot by a firing squad) rather than that of the reformist leaders of modern-day Vietnam or China. But those latter two countries have shown the way. And they have done so while retaining a communist superstructure, which could make the idea potentially palatable to Kim Jong-Il and (regrettable as it may be in an ideal world) allow him to remain in power as he transformed his nation.

If pressure from the United States and other countries made the status quo untenable, Kim could be forced to choose between reform and slow strangulation of his state. Making such a choice seem inescapable will require remarkable diplomacy from the next U.S. president, given how unwilling South Korea and China would now be to apply coercion against the DPRK under virtually any circumstances. But by making it clear that Washington is willing to have a better relationship with Pyongyang under the right conditions, the next American president may be able to convince Seoul and Beijing to accept the other side of the coin too—threatening real punishment of North Korea if it does not denuclearize and otherwise reform. This is the kind of juxtaposition of hard power with soft power—and sincere effort at negotiation with more Machiavellian strategic planning should negotiation fail—that can distinguish hard power Democrats and moderate Republicans from the more ideological view of conservatives and neo-cons on North Korea. It does not mean assuming that Kim Jong Il can be dealt with successfully, if we only talk to his regime bilaterally, as some on the left sometimes seem to imply. Rather, it is inspired in large part by the recognition that a strategy of coercion cannot work under the present circumstances and that it will only be available to Washington after a more sincere effort at engagement has been vigorously attempted and shown to fail.

Of course, even if the basic deal had some appeal to Pyongyang, it might not be feasible to convince the DPRK to give up all of its nuclear capabilities immediately.[30] It might take several years to reach that final goal. But as long as any deal immediately and verifiably froze the DPRK's nuclear activities, and then quickly began to get plutonium out of North Korea, the United States could accept it.

Should negotiations fail, the option of coercive action would be the natural recourse. On the economic front, the goal should be to convince South Korea and China that their current level of economic engagement would be inappropriate if North Korea refused a reasonable deal. Moreover, with a new U.S. president in place, North Korea could no longer blame the Bush administration's preemption doctrine or axis-of-evil construct for its behavior. It would lose the excuse that it was in America's crosshairs, reducing whatever sympathy the world had occasionally felt for it during the Bush years.

Military options would not be totally off the table, especially if North Korea either threatened to sell nuclear materials abroad or continued construction on its large reactors. One possibility, though hardly a panacea, would be a "surgical" military strike against the large reactors. Even though it is too late to prevent North Korea from having the plutonium for perhaps eight bombs, it is not too late to prevent North Korea from becoming an industrial-scale producer of weapons. All-out war would run too high a chance of causing the very outcome that it was designed to prevent—detonation of at least one nuclear weapon in a major city, be it Seoul or Washington or Seattle. That said, the United States and the Republic of Korea would have to be braced for possible war after any limited use of airpower, since they would not be able to predict how North Korea might respond.[31]

The punitive option that would make the most sense after failed talks, however, would center on economics. Economic coercion may well become feasible if North Korea refused the model of Vietnam and insisted on retaining its nuclear weapons and its Stalinist ways. But the viability of a strategy of economic coercion, designed to so pressure Pyongyang that it would fear regime collapse and therefore have to reassess its earlier decision to have nuclear weapons, will depend not only on the outcome of the South Korean presidential elections in 2007 but on the willingness of the United States to first attempt the type of engagement strategy we propose above.

Getting proliferation policy right requires the kind of approach that Hard Power Democrats and other moderates naturally offer. Too often, those on the left place excessive reliance on arms control, as if international law and treaties will stop outlaws such as Kim Jong Il. Too often, those on the right dismiss any role for formal arms control. They forget that America's ability to devise coercive strategies to deal with problems like North Korea requires international consensus and cooperation— which in turn can only be created if proliferators are seen to be violating principles and rules that the rest of the world accepts and that are codified in some meaningful way.

Put differently, countering proliferation requires a mix of hard and soft power. If for no other reason, the soft power is needed even in dealing with the likes of tyrants such as Kim Jong Il to set up the conditions for strongly pressuring them after engagement strategies fail. In other words, even in dealing with the world's worst regimes, soft power is needed to set up the framework for the application of hard power. The Bush administration has belatedly come to this conclusion, it appears, in regard to Iran, but has never managed to do so in regard to North Korea. America's policy debate needs strong camps of proponents of such a blend, ideally within both main political parties, if it is to deal successfully with the most serious threat to its security in the years to come.

CONCLUSION

THIS BOOK BEGAN with an historical vignette that illustrates how wars can fundamentally reshape the domestic politics of the United States. Indeed, the Civil War is but one example of how national security and the fate of political parties are inextricably intertwined.[1] Political shocks animate the history of much of the last century, beginning with America's entry into the Great War. The bloody battlefields of World War I, the disillusionment associated with the Versailles Treaty, and the failure of the League of Nations helped to undermine Woodrow Wilson's liberal internationalism along with the fortunes of his Democratic Party. In the wake of these events, Warren Harding won a landslide victory in 1920 and set the stage for America's descent into isolationism, which would mark the country's approach to the world for the next generation.[2] Isolationists in the Republican Congress and among Eastern industrialists helped pass a series of Neutrality Acts in the 1930s and organized themselves formally as the America First Committee in an effort to keep the nation out of the messy politics of Europe and destructive foreign wars. The surprise Japanese attack on Pearl Harbor at once invalidated American isolationism, undermining the existing Republican Party in the process—effectively requiring its reinvention—and helped provide the context for an internationalist consensus that saw out the twentieth century.[3]

The John F. Kennedy presidential campaign and subsequent administration took an aggressive stance in international affairs (for instance, on the so-called missile gap and challenges posed by global communism), surprising Kennedy's Republican opponents by adopting a stance tougher than theirs. Yet it was Kennedy's initial intervention into Vietnam and

Johnson's dramatic escalation of U.S. military forces there that would set the scene for an historic rupture in American politics. The pain of Vietnam created a great divide within the Democratic Party, a rift that is still apparent today among many of the stalwarts in the party and in the running commentary about the Democrats and national security. The Vietnam War, probably more than any other foreign-policy issue, led to the remarkable reversals of fortune experienced by the Democratic and Republican parties on matters of national security ever since. The war's most ardent opponents, exemplified by the intellectuals of the New Left, decried America's "arrogance of power" and questioned the entire strategy of containment that had served as the lodestone of Democratic foreign policy since the Truman administration.[4] The subsequent conservative Republican misgivings over détente in the Nixon and Ford years, plus the neoconservative defections from the Democratic camp over matters such as Soviet adventurism in Afghanistan, Angola, and Ethiopia during the Carter administration, combined to create the underpinnings for the Reagan revolution, including the creation of the Committee on the Present Danger.[5]

These tectonic shifts in issue identification, party affiliation, and public perceptions suggest just how powerfully issues of war and peace reverberate inside domestic American politics in ways that are not always anticipated. We may well be in the midst of one of these historic shifts as a restless and divided body politic in the United States confronts an increasingly dangerous world with an unpopular war raging in Iraq and perhaps in Afghanistan as well.

The two major U.S. political parties tend to trade places or invert positions on critical issues over time. For instance, the Republican Party at the time of the Civil War led the bloody struggle against slavery while the Democratic Party of the day solidified its base in the South among the angry white gentry and workers. A century later, the Democratic Party championed the civil-rights movement for disenfranchised African Americans while Republicans countered with a subtle "Southern strategy" aimed at garnering the support of resentful Southern whites.[6] In the 1890s, it was the Republicans who were the staunch supporters of protectionist tariffs and balanced budgets; fast forward to the 1990s, and theirs had become the party more identified with free trade and massive budget deficits. Meanwhile, the Democrats, once seen as irresponsible spendthrifts, have seized the mantle of prudent government spending and fiscal responsibility as main campaign themes while raising and responding to public concerns over the dangers of unfettered trade trends.[7]

These profound intergenerational shifts in partisan philosophy and issue identification should serve as a cautionary note to those who would argue that the Republican advantages on war and national-security issues are permanent and immutable. While it is true that there are a range of powerful cultural and ideological factors that bind the U.S. military and its most fervent public supporters to the Republicans, several things are happening that at least suggest that the long-established and carefully nurtured Republican dominance on matters of national security is in jeopardy.

First, after ignoring or denying the problem for years, Democrats have begun to take notice of the fact that defense is the only major national issue on which the Republicans have held a decisive advantage in recent elections and have started to fight back. A number of private and public initiatives in recent years—including the Valley Forge Project, the Truman Democrats, the Wilderness Initiative, the Third Way project, and the national-security work of the Center for American Progress—have been launched to help rebuild national-security awareness, expertise, and bona fides within the Democratic Party. There are also a number of Iraq war veterans running for Congress in the upcoming elections, this time under the banner of the Democratic Party, bringing their military experiences, perspectives, and public appeal into the political arena on the side of the stubborn donkey. And Democrats are studying the playbooks of Republican electoral victories, seeking to replicate some of the organizational strategies so effectively utilized by the Vulcans, those senior defense and foreign-policy practitioners who closed ranks around Governor Bush in advance of the 2000 election, to project an image of seriousness and experience when it comes to national security.[8] (Some of these same trends are also occurring among moderate and internationalist Republicans who are gearing up themselves for 2008.)

Indeed, there are many signs that key figures and institutions within the Democratic Party are beginning to appreciate the political significance of this moment. Would-be candidates are speaking out more on defense issues, exchanging views with defense intellectuals and meeting regularly with members of the military, touring military bases and facilities, visiting the wounded in military hospitals, and talking with the families of the deployed. Loren B. Thompson, a noted military commentator at the Lexington Institute, has taken note and has this to say about a certain senator from New York: "Senator Hillary Clinton . . . has consistently supported the military throughout her tenure in the upper chamber. Not only did she back invading Iraq and wade into arcane military issues such as body armor, but defense companies in her state say she has been consistently, effectively supportive. Anyone who listens to her speak on military matters can see that she has become a real expert on issues like readiness and reserve forces."[9] And she is by no means alone on this score.

But it's not primarily Democratic initiative that is beginning to turn the tide on public attitudes on national security, not yet at least. It has primarily been Republican missteps that have created a potential opening for intrepid Democrats and moderate Republicans by creating a national need for a stronger debate and better set of choices on matters concerning the safety of the country. The Bush administration's bungling of Iraq and near-complete exclusion and subsequent alienation of moderate Republicans from its governing councils have also taken a toll on those who would generally be inclined to support the GOP on matters of the military and national service. Secretary Rumsfeld's flawed undertakings in Iraq, his sometimes dismissive and vindictive dealings with senior military officers, and his zeal for military reform have all combined to create a kind of perfect storm of dissatisfaction among members of the military and their most ardent supporters, including proponents of defense spending in Congress, much of the defense industry, and key segments of the officer corps. Some of his ideas have been welcome, especially on matters beyond Iraq (a subject on which it seems irrefutable that his historical legacy will be nothing short of tragic), and Democrats as well as Republican traditionalists can learn from his style of leadership, as long as they avoid the excesses. But the fact remains that the context he has created is one of such dissension and dissatisfaction that the country is ready for a transformed debate and for a new politics of national security.

As a consequence of all this and more, Democrats have an opportunity to gain substantial political ground and potentially even to trade places with Republicans in the competition for the loyalties of those who care the most about national security. At the same time, Republicans, increasingly aware of this danger, are gearing up for a fight over the future of their party and its approach to the world more intense than any they have engaged in since the early days of the Reagan movement.

This is a potentially epochal development in American politics, on par with the major shifts in American history described above, but one that will be fleeting or illusory unless Democrats tackle these issues with a deadly seriousness. Most of the recent returns that seem to signal a growing favor for the Democrats in polling on military issues reflect a deeper disenchantment with Republicans as opposed to a compelling attraction to the competing Democratic vision (when there happens to be one). This means, for Democrats, that time's a-wasting. Democrats will have to be more than the anti-Bush politicians to gain an advantage more enduring than a temporary boost from the next election. They will need the kind of idea-driven agenda, and confident preoccupation with matters of national security, that has generally been conceded to the GOP in recent decades. And moderate Republicans will themselves have to take a page out of the neocon playbook, campaigning on vision rather than simple competence and reason (however welcome large doses of the latter might be at the moment).

To date, Democrats and even moderate Republicans have proven unequal to the task of meeting Bush's philosophical certitude and one-party rule with an ideological or practical alternative. Partisan differences have been greatly exaggerated, however, by the president's aggressive foreign policy. As a result of that divide, the unpopularity of the Iraq war, and the president's dismal poll numbers, Democrats are beginning to define a vision. There are signs that the Democratic Party's brain trust and political elite are coalescing around four possible approaches to foreign-policy and national-security challenges, and there are similar groupings among Republicans thinking anew about foreign policy as well.

The first Democratic perspective argues that the real flaw in the Bush administration is not in the conception of its national-security strategy but rather in its implementation. Adherents of this position believe that the president essentially got it right on both Afghanistan and Iraq (perhaps less so on the latter, but now that we are deeply engaged, there is no choice but to finish the mission), and that his efforts to fortify the military and create new capacities for heightened homeland security should be embraced. Clearly, Democrats would do a much better job at alliance management, but the essential course that Bush chose after 9/11 should not be radically altered.

This perspective, while certainly a minority position inhabited by a smallish band of centrists, is clearly discernible among the elite foreign-policy ranks of the party, who might usefully be described as "hard-power Democrats." Advocates of this approach will recoil from any suggestion that their governing philosophy is in any way derivative of

the Bush administration's approach, so poisonous will be the politics—
both within and between the parties—in the run-up to the 2006 and
especially the 2008 elections. This group appreciates the need for
America to employ hard power (and occasionally to crack heads) to advance its interests but believes that Democrats can do it much more effectively, without alienating much of the world in the process.

A second group of Democrats believes that most of the true challenges
to global security cannot be effectively dealt with through military means,
and that the insecurity many Americans feel is a direct result of the powerful forces of globalization. To many of these "globalists," Iraq is a dangerous and potentially debilitating sideshow that saps the country's resources from other consequential challenges. Among this cohort there is
genuine desire to broaden the definition of national security to include a
host of other conditions: the dramatic changes in the global economy and
the need to prepare Americans for fierce global competition; the rise of
radical jihadism on a global scale, which requires a war of ideas not
weapons; the spread of dangerous infectious diseases such as avian flu
and HIV/AIDS; and the need to face up to the harsh realities of global
climate change produced by a global economic engine run on petroleum
that funnels enormous financial resources to the most illiberal political
regimes on the planet.

The globalists are, in many ways, the angriest and most perplexed by
the Bush ascendancy. While Bush is apt to pronounce on vexing issues in
simple, declarative, black-and-white terms, members of this faction
within the Democratic camp are likely to respond to queries about the
complexities of a particular problem with an admission that it *is* a complex problem, as opposed to providing a simple (and probably wrong) answer with great certainty. Globalists appreciate that while the United
States has been the single most important catalyst for globalization, the
American people are not well prepared for dealing with some of the
downsides and back alleys of globalization, from job losses to international
terrorism.[10] There is probably also an unspoken anxiety among this "challenges of globalization" cohort that their positions are difficult to explain
to the American people and ultimately easy to demagogue or simply dismiss in political discourse.

The third group, the "modest-power Democrats," believe that it is
time for the United States to step back from global politics, given both
pressing domestic issues such as the needs to restore American competitiveness and rebuild areas destroyed by Hurricane Katrina, and the cor-

rosive effect of many recent American initiatives, particularly the war in Iraq. Public-opinion polls depicting tattered American prestige suggest that a little American retrenchment may be a good thing for all concerned. The modest-power Democrats are not only unhappy with Bush, they are deeply suspicious of the entrenched Washington Democratic establishment—and the so-called Clinton Democrats, whom they see as "Republican-lite" and whom they blame for not standing up to the Bush administration.[11] These Democrats have come to appreciate some of the limits to American power, and their modern variant of McGovern's "come home, America" is not so much isolationist as concerned with pulling back from the hyper-interventionism and overextension of the Bush era. This group also realizes that past campaigns promoting a kind of global retrenchment—e.g., by the Republicans around World War II and the Democrats at the end of Vietnam—have generally fared poorly politically, so they will argue primarily for pulling back from activities already regarded as unpopular.

The fourth group of Democrats with a world view are those from labor or environmental communities who are profoundly anxious about the path and pace of global capitalism. While small in number and essentially absent from the Washington national security scene, these "old school leftists" are active on university campuses and in the blogosphere as well as traditional venues such as union halls. While approaching problems with very different perspectives, their worries revolve around job losses in critical industries in the U.S. and exploitation abroad. These groups tend to be deeply suspicious of trade and international agreements designed to promote greater global commercial intercourse.

These global rejectionists are not generally content to express their views through the traditional vehicles of policy influence—op-eds, positions papers, and petitions—instead often reverting to more activist tools of direct action, including angry demonstrations and other publicity-seeking activities. While this fourth group is comprised of often strange bedfellows with little in common, their collective anger around specific issues such as trade and the environment have the potential to profoundly influence Democratic positions and attitudes.

Yet Democrats are not alone in having to contend with competing ideologies and approaches when it comes to foreign policy. After five years in power (including four years of controlling both the executive and legislative branches), the Republican Party is often perceived as unified, especially concerning national-security questions. Yet, as with any party with a president in office, the responsibility of governance and the desire to hold office often cloaks the internal battles and debates. In recent months, these fissures have become ever more apparent. And many expect that these differences will only become more important as the 2008 campaign race heats up. Within the Republican Party, four main national-security cliques can be delineated.

The "Oldsmobile conservatives" are traditional Wall Street Republicans who believe in internationalism and the power of institutions and alliances but are traditional realists, hesitant of making values (even democratic ones) a core part of American foreign policy at the expense of other interests. They tend to be skeptical of military intervention for reasons short of defensive purposes and are reluctant to shape the internal politics of other states. The catchword for these conservatives is *stability*. Perhaps best exemplified by George H. W. Bush, this cohort spent the first years of the George W. Bush presidency on the defensive—many of its members were in government, but they tended to lose the most crucial debates.

Neoconservatives, or "nationalist transformationalists" as they are occasionally called, believe deeply in American exceptionalism and the power of democracy and American values. They advocate that America should use its hard (military) power to promote both, but remain skeptical about international institutions such as the United Nations. These neoconservatives are not afraid of creating short-term instability in the name of altering the status quo to make it more congenial to American interests. Their perspective has been ascendant during the George W. Bush presidency, as several key neoconservative players were the "Vulcans" who advised Bush as a candidate for president in 2000 and then went on to dominate national-security decisionmaking during the president's first term. This cadre has also developed an influential network of advocates outside of government.[12]

The "America firsters" in the Republican Party are very suspicious of American engagements abroad as well as international institutions, and they focus on issues such as immigration and foreign ownership of U.S. assets. They also tend to focus on state-based threats such as China. Their ideological approach has a long history in the policy debates about America's role in the world—some have called them "Jacksonians," and they identify with former leaders such as Robert A. Taft and Jesse Helms—although they have been in retreat for many years, and remain relatively marginalized within today's national-security community.[13] But public anxieties about the loss of jobs to foreign workers overseas (or immigrants in the United States) and the challenges of globalization have given this clique new life.

The "faith-based interventionists" believe that America has a moral purpose and that while it must fight terrorism, it also must act to deal with humanitarian crises in places such as Africa and North Korea. They also view many world events through a religious prism, which significantly influences their views on the Middle East in general and the Israeli-Palestinian conflict in particular.[14] This group's rise has coincided with the emergence of religious conservatives and evangelicals as a powerful constituency within the Republican Party, and has gained increased attention with President George W. Bush's frequent references to religion as a motivating force for his policies.[15] Another distinguishing characteristic of this cohort is that it is represented by numerous activist organizations that provide humanitarian assistance on the ground.[16]

So Republicans, too, have their own divisions and debates when it comes to foreign policy. And the unprecedented global challenges confronting the United States create at least the possibility of a major political realignment or a return to bipartisan approaches around specific problems. The significance of such a tectonic evolution in American politics cannot be underestimated.

For Democrats, the struggles among their four schools will be critical to determining their party's future—whether it can win office again, and if it does, how it will govern America during a critical moment in our history. Ever since the disappointing outcome of the 2004 election, Democrats have been haunted with a deep anxiety: Is the party that prided itself on understanding the lives of common Americans now out of touch? With a strong foreign-policy and national-security platform coupled with a compelling approach to critical domestic issues such as the economy, the environment, and health care, the Democrats can compete again. And so can moderate and other internationalist Republicans who are currently vying for influence inside their own party. But to do so will require a sophisticated political strategy that essentially combines the "hard power" and "globalist" approaches to the world while resisting strenuously any suggestion of a retreat from global affairs. At the heart of this approach must be a renewed appreciation for the centrality of national security in modern politics.

Democrats and moderate Republicans should aspire to achieve a blend of hard power with a hard-headed and informed view of globalism, leading with the former politically and to some extent even substantively, but incorporating elements of a globalist approach to governance. They would have a broader view of the world and of American national security interests than classic conservatives or neo-cons. These hard power Democrats and moderates would differ from conservatives and neo-cons on more grounds than simply competence in the execution of policy—an area where the latter have, principally because of the Iraq experience, raised doubts about their ability to remain focused on the mundane matters of implementing big ideas. For example, such Democrats and moderate Republicans would emphasize alliances much more in the use of force—but at the same time without sounding as if they were giving the U.N. or other countries a veto over American pursuit of its own national security interests.

Hard power Democrats and moderates wouldn't necessarily have avoided the Iraq invasion but they would have taken the extra time to build up a larger and more effective coalition; they would be prepared threaten force against an overly aggressive China or a dangerous North Korea as the Clinton administration did in the mid–1990s, but only in the context of a broader diplomatic effort that went the extra mile to avoid the possibility of conflict; they would be willing to launch an operation like NATO's 1999 Kosovo war even without U.N. permission, as the Clinton administration did; they would be willing to use more force against a group like al Qaeda in the late 1990s even when the public wasn't so clearly ready to risk casualties in such an operation (as the Clinton administration did not); they would also be prepared to intervene militarily to stop a genocide like that in Rwanda in 1994 even if doing so didn't fit within a classic, limited definition of U.S. national security interests.

There are, however, two enormous challenges associated with this potential realignment in national politics when it comes to the hard-core issues of war and peace: the Republican Party and the Democratic Party themselves. First, the GOP will not relinquish political territory on the national-security ramparts without a hard fight. Republicans still see national security as playing to their natural advantages on broad cultural, geographic, and political grounds, despite an increasingly unpopular war. And just as in the last campaign when President Bush and his operatives came after Senator Kerry on what he thought was his strong suit—national-security experience—you can reliably expect Republican candidates to fight tenaciously to hang on to the uniformed as well as the general national-security voter who has been a critical part of their base of support across the country and particularly in so-called Red America.

Indeed, the major Republican candidates as well as the national party machinery will almost certainly reprise the strategy described at the outset of this book—the Lincoln-led effort to depict Democrats as unworthy on national-security grounds—to characterize at least some Democrats as weak and even dishonorable when it comes to Iraq and other critical national-security questions. Democrats who appear "timid and right" on these issues will only play into the inevitable Republican strategy for winning the national-security vote on the basis of symbolism rather than substance. Indeed Karl Rove has said as much. As one battle hardened Republican political operative noted, "On national security, we are like the Green Bay Packers of the 1960s. They were known for telling opposing teams *exactly* which running play was coming, and the other guys still couldn't stop them. That's especially disheartening—to know exactly which play is coming and still not be able to mount an effective counter. That's what the Republicans will continue to do to Democrats in political contests until you show us that you can stop us."[17] Although reviving America's international economic competitiveness, reaffirming the U.S. commitment to global partnerships and multilateral diplomacy, and improving living standards in the developing world are each and all manifestly important objectives, Democrats and like-minded moderates and internationalists will need to go beyond stating these soft-power objectives and offer hard solutions—including some that could involve the unashamed application of military power—to the most immediate threats facing the United States.

The second hurdle lies within the Democratic Party. While the Democratic Party is virtually united in its critique of Republican mismanagement on Iraq and elsewhere, there is significant disagreement on how to advance an alternative governing agenda for management of national-security issues— beginning with what to do next in Iraq, if and when power comes their way. There are also those within the Democratic Party who argue that a platform that highlights areas where the party holds clear advantages—for instance, health care, competitiveness, and labor—can afford to downplay security issues. And there are even some who say that the entire Bush approach for using military power to advance national interests has been fundamentally rejected by the American people and that now is the time for a kinder and gentler approach to security challenges. We have argued in this book that politicians and strategists on both sides of the aisle do this at their, and the nation's, peril.

In doing so, we have tried to offer a detailed and specific set of proposals designed to improve the national-security standing of the United States in the world. This is advice also intended to improve the quality and tenor of the national-security debate in this country, and while it is probably most relevant politically for Democrats, it is offered equally to moderate and internationalist Republicans, independents . . . anyone, really, with an interest in resurrecting a more effective America on the global stage. Some of our ideas build on other Democratic proposals and even Bush-administration initiatives. There is no shame in that; indeed, the country needs to create the type of foreign-policy consensus it often championed in the twentieth century. That said, it needs a vigor in its new foreign-policy vision, a commitment to purpose, and a devotion of energy and resources that the Bush administration has generally lacked outside the immediate realms of Afghanistan and Iraq.

In the military and national-security arena, we offer several specific instances where, if diplomacy fails and dangers gather, Democrats must be prepared to consider and pursue military options to safeguard vital American interests. We also argue that there needs to be a more careful calibrating and understanding of civil-military affairs in the modern context of national security, drawing some inspiration from Secretary Rumsfeld while avoiding his excesses. The nation also needs somewhat larger ground forces and more special-force capabilities in the time ahead for ongoing operations in places such as Afghanistan and Iraq along with other global responsibilities. (The Bush administration has rightly advocated the latter while generally opposing the former.) These and other demands mean that it will not be practical to cut defense spending in coming years, despite the increase of more than $100 billion in the core annual budget during the Bush administration, and candidates of all stripes should say as much. To deal with Iraq-like contingencies and post-conflict reconstruction demands of the future, a major effort to develop better stabilization forces is also essential.

We argue for a comprehensive strategy to better position the United States in a long struggle against fundamentalist radicals. It should include a broad education effort here at home to increase Arabic-language competence, not only to improve cross-cultural awareness and sensitivity but also to create the basis for a much stronger generation of intelligence specialists, language-competent military officers, and hardheaded American diplomats. The United States also should work with other major countries to promote a vigorous educational-reform agenda for developing countries—couched in the language of multilateralism and development but motivated in large part by the need to help Islamic states strengthen their societies and engage their populations with the realities, the challenges, and the opportunities of the modern world. Without such a strategy, we will continue to lose the long-term war on terror despite whatever fleeting progress we may make in the short term—an idea that Secretary Rumsfeld himself advanced in 2003 and 2004, but which the Bush administration has failed to deliver upon.

The United States also needs a major new national commitment to boosting the ethanol-fuel system to relieve some pressures on foreign energy supplies from unstable parts of the Middle East. Energy policy has become popular in the United States, but there is a chance that our national focus in dealing with it will fade if and when gas prices decline. There is also a strong likelihood that the market itself will not catalyze the major shift in policy that we now need—and that technology now promises. Among other measures, the country needs a national energy economics board to help calibrate tax policy and other incentives to spur supply as well as demand of alternative fuels.

Taken together, these policies and others can help repair America's tattered image in the world and rebuild its "soft power" in the process. In refocusing on hard power, it would be a mistake to forget its essential complement. By getting the former right, Democrats and internationalist Republicans create opportunities to promote the latter too.

In the international arena, we make the case for a more vigorous and robust approach to tackling proliferation in North Korea and elsewhere around the globe. Here, the goal has to be to sharpen the stark choice offered would-be proliferators—more engagement with the world on the one hand, or punishment and coercion by a united international front on the other. The Bush administration has failed in this effort because its international standing is so low that it cannot credibly threaten the stick and often lacks imagination and sincerity in how it employs carrots.

There is also a manifest need to acknowledge more seriously and anticipate the arrival of China on the international scene as a great power. This will require moving beyond the competing, and equally wrongheaded,

recent paradigms of China as strategic partner or strategic rival. It is neither, or perhaps both, and a sound policy framework for dealing with its
impressive yet challenging rise will require recognizing as much.

On homeland security, some progress has been made, and we need to
recognize these achievements. Any politician who implies that because
we still have vulnerabilities here at home previous efforts to protect the
country have failed does not recognize the inherent difficulty of this enterprise. A new leader must build upon the Bush foundation to include
more resources and incentives for a number of critical programs. Protecting private-sector infrastructure tops the list, but we also need other
types of efforts, including a renewed focus on preventive strategies and
programs to create capacity for monitoring and intercepting would-be
terrorists at the local level (as New York City but few other municipali-
ties have done to date). New National Guard structures and capacities
for homeland security will also be necessary to meet the anticipated
challenges of the post–9/11 age, including the creation of regional organizations to facilitate coordination between states and National Guard
units on the one hand and first-responder communities and other local
actors on the other.

Again, these ideas should by no means be seen as meant exclusively for
Democrats; no, indeed. The intention here is to augment the prepared-
ness and capabilities of the nation, so if some of these proposed policies
influence the broader political debate and even attract positive Republican attention, so much the better. Again, a stronger Democratic Party on
the issues of national security will improve the quality of the national debate on how best to keep the nation safe and, as a consequence, improve
the quality and seriousness of American politics in the process.

The American people have largely lost faith and confidence in the current course of the nation, including on national-security issues, but they
have yet to embrace an alternative. They await a concrete set of policy
plans showing how Democrats in particular will manage both the traditional and nontraditional challenges confronting the country. Democrats
will need to offer a credible, comprehensive, and forward-looking national-security strategy that complements a robust program of domestic
initiatives to gain active and enduring public support. Just as important,
Democrats must do all this while displaying and demonstrating an intrinsic self-confidence on matters involving both soft and hard power. Democrats, and many internationally minded Republicans, are amply capable of dealing with the new transnational and multilateral issues—energy

matters, health and environmental concerns—that are indeed becoming as morally imperative and strategically significant as traditional national-security issues. But without a firm grounding in the details and demands of hard security matters, Democrats may not have the opportunity to demonstrate their dexterity on this broader agenda of critical tasks.

The rallying cry for the last successful Democratic presidential campaign was the memorable "It's the economy, stupid" made famous by the Clinton war room. But now it is the very real issues of war—rather than the appropriation of martial metaphors for campaign organizations—that animate the most important matters before the nation. As such, the rallying cry for this generation of Democrats and moderate, internationalist Republicans needs to be, "It's national security first" that focuses the attentions of would be candidates and political strategists alike. Without such a hardheaded approach to the world and to the conduct of national campaigns, Republican internationalists are likely to wind up the bridesmaids to the real policymakers in their own party again. Democrats are apt to remain on the political sidelines, left to contemplate what went so terribly wrong.

Notes

INTRODUCTION

1. See Melinda Lawson, *Patriot Fires: Forging a New American Nationalism in the Civil War North* (University of Kansas Press, 2002).
2. For an excellent description of this episode and other examples of Rove's intrepid political style, see Nicholas Lemann, "The Controller: Karl Rove is working to get George Bush reelected, but he has bigger plans," *The New Yorker*, May 12, 2003.
3. For a discussion of Karl Rove's political game plan for the future of the Republican Party, see E. J. Dionne Jr., "Rove's Early Warning," *Washington Post*, January 24, 2006.
4. For an excellent article on how political scientists explain this intense era of partisanship, see Carl Cannon, "How Political Scientists Explain the New Partisanship," *National Journal*, January 21, 2006.
5. For a wonderful treatment of the contradictions and challenges in the modern formulation and execution of American foreign policy, see Derek Chollet, "A Consensus Shattered," *The National Interest* (Spring), pp. 73–75.
6. Ibid.
7. Ibid.
8. For similar views about how Democrats need to reshape their approach to national security, see Peter Beinart, *The Good Fight: Why Liberals and Only Liberals Can Win the War on Terror* (2000) and Will Marshall, editor, *With All Our Might: A Progressive Strategy for Defeating Jihadism and Defending Liverty* (New York: Rowman and Littlefield Publishers, Inc., 2006).

CHAPTER 1

1. Peter Beinart, "A Fighting Faith," *The New Republic*, December 13, 2004. One analysis cited by Galston and Kamarck found more than 70 percent of voters placing the broad area of defense and foreign policy at the top of their

priorities list. See William A. Galston and Elaine C. Kamarck, "The Politics of Polarization," The Third Way Middle Class Project, October 2005, p. 18.

2. CNN, "Election Results," November 3, 2004, available at www.cnn.com/election/2004 [accessed 1/13/2005]. [Please note: This link no longer works.]

3. Kerry 2004 platform, ontheissues.org [accessed 2/4/2006].

4. Loren Griffith, "Where the Democrats Went Wrong," Truman National Security Project, May 2005, p. 3, available at www.trumanproject.org.

5. Ibid.

6. David McCullough, *Truman* (Simon & Schuster, 1992), pp. 891–911.

7. For an excellent account of the Democrats' history on national-security policy, see Peter Beinart, *The Good Fight: Why Liberals—and only Liberals—Can Win the War on Terror and Make America Great Again* (Harper Collins, 2006).

8. Acceptance Speech of Senator George McGovern, Democratic National Convention, Miami Beach, Florida, July 14, 1972.

9. Les Gelb, "The Essential Domino: American Politics and Vietnam," *Foreign Affairs*, April 1972.

10. Inaugural address of Jimmy Carter, January 20, 1977.

11. William Galston and Elaine Kamarck, "The Politics of Polarization," Third Way, September 2005, p. 15.

12. 2000 CNN Exit Poll, January 6, 2001; 13,130 respondents.

13. Gallup poll, August 24–26, 2001; national telephone poll; 814 respondents; +/- 3 percent margin of error.

14. *Los Angeles Times* poll, January 31–February 3, 2002; national telephone poll; 1,545 respondents; +/- 3 percent margin of error.

15. NBC News/*Wall Street Journal*, January 10–12, 2004; national telephone poll; 1,002 respondents; +/- 3.1 percent margin of error.

16. Michael Moore, *Dude, Where's My Country?* (Warner Books, 2003), p. 95.

17. "About Code Pink," http://www.codepink4peace.org/article.php?list=type&type=3. [accessed 6/18/2006].

18. Andrew J. Bacevich, *The New American Militarism: How Americans Are Seduced by War* (Oxford University Press, 2005), p. 37.

19. The American National Election Studies, *The ANES Guide to Public Opinion and Electoral Behavior* (University of Michigan, Center for Political Studies), available at www.electionstudies.org. [accessed 2/2/2006].

20. Andrew Bacevich describes the way Norman Podhoretz shaped the neoconservative discourse by inserting the rhetoric of "isolationism" into a critique of McGovern's, and therefore the Democrats', platform, *The New American Militarism* p. 75.

21. Bacevich, *The New American Militarism,* p. 39.

22. Susan L. Marquis, *Unconventional Warfare: Rebuilding U.S. Special Operations Forces* (Brookings, 1997), pp. 1–5.

23. Bacevich, *The New American Militarism*, p. 118.
24. Gallup poll, Election Polls—Vote by Groups, 1984–1988, available at http://poll.gallup.com/ [accessed 2/5/2006].
25. Bacevich, *The New American Militarism*, p. 118.
26. Gallup poll, Election Polls—Vote by Groups, 1984–1988, available at http://poll.gallup.com/ [accessed 2/5/2006].
27. Bacevich, *The New American Militarism*, p. 118.
28. Michael Rust, "In General, an Important Decision," *Insight on the News*, vol. 9, no. 32, August 9, 1993.
29. Ibid.
30. Richard L. Berke, "Unaccustomed Role for Clinton at Sea," *New York Times*, March 13, 1993.
31. On pay, see Office of the Under Secretary of Defense for Personnel and Readiness, Defense Manpower Requirements Report, Fiscal Year 2001 (May 2000), table 6–2, available at dticaw.dtic.mil/prhome/docs/fy2001.pdf [accessed January 2006]; Korb.
32. Eric Schmitt, "Settling In: The Armed Services; Joint Chiefs Fighting Clinton Plan to Allow Homosexuals in Military," *New York Times*, January 23, 1993.
33. Transcript of Bill Clinton's speech, "Remarks announcing the new policy on gays and lesbians in the military," Weekly Compilation of Presidential Documents, July 26, 1993, v. 29, no. 29, p. 1369(3) [accessed 2/3/2006].
34. Schmitt, "Settling In: The Armed Services; Joint Chiefs Fighting Clinton Plan to Allow Homosexuals in Military," *New York Times*, January 23, 1993.
35. Bill Clinton, *My Life* (Alfred Knopf, 2004), p. 485.
36. Steven Lee Myers, "Testing of a President," *New York Times*, November 14, 1998.
37. Rowan Scarborough, "Major gets minor rebuke for slamming Clinton; General rules 'adulterous liar' article," *Washington Times*, November 14, 1998.
38. Daniel J. Rabil, "Please, impeach my commander in chief," *Washington Times*, November 9, 1998.
39. *Congressional Quarterly Weekly*, January 5, 1999.
40. Elizabeth Becker, "A Call to Stick to the Budget Riles Some in the Military," *New York Times*, December 12, 1999.
41. Michael O'Hanlon, *How to Be a Cheap Hawk* (Brookings, 1998), p. 23.
42. See, for example, Ivo H. Daalder and Michael E. O'Hanlon, *Winning Ugly: NATO's War to Save Kosovo* (Brookings, 2000), pp. 1–21.
43. See Ken Owen, Director of Media Relations, DePauw University, "Draft Needed, But Unlikely, Moskos Tells DePauw Forum," September 30, 2004, available at www.collegenews.org/x3679.xml, accessed on July 17, 2006.

44. Elizabeth Becker, "A Call to Stick to the Budget Riles Some in the Military," *New York Times*, December 12, 1999.

45. Remarks by Governor George W. Bush delivered at The Citadel, South Carolina, September 23, 1999.

46. Ibid.

47. Quoted in Benjamin Wallace-Wells, "Corps Voters," *The Nation*, November 2003.

48. David Rieff, "Who Botched the Occupation?"*New York Times Magazine*, November 2, 2003, pp. 44, 58.

49. AP-IPsos poll, March 10, 2006.

50. Joseph Carroll, "Americans Continue to Say Iraq Is the Nation's Top Problem," Gallup Organization, Princeton, N.J., July 13, 2006, available at http://poll.gallup.com/content/default.aspx?ci=23761&pg=1.

51. Peter D. Feaver, "Whose Military Vote?" *Washington Post*, October 12, 2004, p. A23.

52. Dave Moniz, "Troops in Survey Back Bush 4-to-1 Over Kerry," *USA Today*, October 3, 2004.

53. Betros, L. *West Point: Two Centuries and Beyond* (McWhiney Foundation Press, 2004), p. 6.

54. Gordon Trowbridge, "Poll: U.S. Troops' Support for Bush, War in Iraq Declined During 2005," *Defense News*, January 2, 2006, p. 14; and Gordon Trowbridge, "Troops Sound Off: Military Times Poll Finds High Morale, But Less Support for Bush, War Effort," available at www.militarycity.com/polls/2005_main.php, accessed July 16, 2006.

55. For further details, see Tara Sonenshine, "Reporting on the War; chaos takes a toll on newsgathering," *The Baltimore Sun*, April 7, 2006, p. 15A.

56. John Mueller, *Policy and Opinion in the Gulf War* (University of Chicago Press, 1994), p.70. Cited in William M. Darley, "War Policy, Public Support, and the Media," *Parameters*, Summer 2005, pp. 121–134.

57. Eric V. Larson, "Casualties and Consensus: The Historical Role of Casualties in Domestic Support for U.S. Military Operations," MRC–726-RC, RAND, April 25, 1996. Quoted in Darley, "War Policy."

58. Trowbridge, "Poll: U.S. Troops' Support for Bush."

59. Betros, L. *West Point: Two Centuries and Beyond* (McWhiney Foundation Press, 2004), p. 7.

60. This depends on one's definition of "Midwest." Gore did capture the traditionally Democratic electoral votes of Minnesota, Iowa, Wisconsin, and Illinois.

61. The *ANES Guide to Public Opinion and Electoral Behavior* shows that in 2004, 29 percent of the voters polled "leaned independent," 28 percent were "weak partisans," and 33 percent considered themselves "strong partisans." The number of independent voters, having steadily risen since 1952, repre-

sents an opportunity for both parties, especially given the close margins of the last two elections.

62. Gallup poll at http://gallupbrain.com [accessed 2/5/2006]. [This URL does not presently work.]

63. See David C. King and Zachary Karabell, *The Generation of Trust: How the U.S. Military Has Regained the Public's Confidence Since Vietnam* (American Enterprise Institute, 2003), pp. 4, 17, 44.

64. David McCullough, *Truman*, p. 534.

65. James Traub, "The Things They Carry," *New York Times Magazine*, January 4, 2004.

66. Stephen Hess, *The Little Book of Campaign Etiquette* (Brookings, 1998), pp. 99–100.

67. Rachel Kleinfeld and Matt Spence, "Creating Truman Democrats," *Truman Project Paper Series*, January 2005, p. 2.

68. Ibid.

69. See, for example, Congressman Steny Hoyer et al., "Ensuring America's Strength and Security: A Democratic National-Security Strategy for the Twenty-First Century," September 2005.

70. William A. Galston and Elaine C. Kamarck, "The Politics of Polarization," The Third Way Middle Class Project, October 2005, p. 19.

71. Kleinfeld and Spence, "Creating Truman Democrats," January, 2005, p. 6.

72. Ibid., p. 2.

73. Ibid., p. 10.

74. Jeffrey Record, "Why the Strong Lose," *Parameters*, Winter 2005–2006, pp. 24–25.

CHAPTER 2

1. A private conversation with a senior advisor to Governor Bush who was appointed to a senior position in the foreign policy bureaucracy.

2. National Commission on Terrorist Attacks Upon the United States, *The 9/11 Commission Report* (Government Printing Office, 2004).

3. For an exploration of the complexities of trying to fashion a democracy in Iraq, see Ambassador L. Paul Bremer III, *My Year in Iraq* (Simon and Schuster, 2006). Although we are quite critical of the U.S. effort in Iraq ourselves, and think that a much better and more effective policy could have been devised, any fair reading of this book shows just how difficult and contentious any nation-building effort there was bound to be.

4. Bob Woodward, *Plan of Attack* (Simon and Schuster, 2004), pp. 8, 37.

5. Anthony H. Cordesman, *The Iraq War: Strategy, Tactics, and Military Lessons* (CSIS, 2003), pp. 149–165.

6. Bob Woodward, *Bush at War* (Simon and Schuster, 2002), pp. 201–251.

7. For similar arguments on some of these points, see Michael O'Hanlon, "Iraq Without a Plan," *Policy Review*, No. 128, December 2004/January 2005, pp. 33–46.

8. Michael R. Gordon and General Bernard E. Trainor, *Cobra II: The Inside Story of the Invasion and Occupation of Iraq* (Pantheon Books, 2006).

9. Bremer, *My Year in Iraq*, pp. 14, 106–107.

10. Associated Press, "Powell Says He Urged More Troops for Iraq War," *Philadelphia Inquirer*, April 30, 2006.

11. See George Packer, *The Assassins' Gate: America in Iraq* (Farrar, Straus, and Giroux, 2005), pp. 100–250; Gordon and Trainor, *Cobra II*.

12. Gordon and Trainor, *Cobra II*, p. 142.

13. For a sense of where Pentagon thinking may well have been on this subject, see David Frum and Richard Perle, *An End to Evil: How to Win the War on Terror* (Random House, 2003), p. 37.

14. Packer, *Assassins' Gate*, pp. 126–132; Gordon and Trainor, *Cobra II*, p. 464.

15. Michael Elliott, "So, What Went Wrong?" *Time*, October 6, 2003, pp. 34–37.

16. See Conrad C. Crane and W. Andrew Terrill, *Reconstructing Iraq: Insights, Challenges, and Missions for Military Forces in a Post-Conflict Scenario* (Army War College, 2003); Edward P. Djerejian, Frank G. Wisner, Rachel Bronson, and Andrew S. Weiss, *Guiding Principles for U.S. Post-Conflict Policy in Iraq* (Council on Foreign Relations, 2003), pp. 5–6; and Ray Salvatore Jennings, "After Saddam Hussein: Winning a Peace If It Comes to War," *U.S. Institute of Peace Special Report 102* (U.S. Institute of Peace, February 2003).

17. See Tom Clancy with General Tony Zinni and Tony Koltz, *Battle Ready* (G. P. Putnam's Sons, 2004), pp. 18–22.

18. See Tommy Franks, *American Soldier* (HarperCollins, 2004), p. 419.

19. See Anthony H. Cordesman, *The Iraq War: Strategy, Tactics, and Military Lessons* (CSIS, 2003), pp. 493–508.

20. This point is made in Gordon and Trainor, pp. 356–359.

21. George Packer, "War After the War: What Washington Doesn't See in Iraq," *The New Yorker*, November 24, 2003, pp. 4 and 8.

22. CNN, "Bremer: More Troops Were Needed After Saddam's Ouster," October 5, 2004, available at www.cnn.com.

23. Jim Krane, "U.S. Officials: Iraq Insurgency Bigger," *Philadelphia Inquirer*, July 9, 2004; Thomas E. Ricks, *Fiasco: The American Military Adventure in Iraq* (New York: Penguin Books, 2006).

24. For trends in Iraq in this period, see the Brookings Institution's Iraq Index at www.brookings.edu/iraqindex.

25. Brookings Institution Iraq Index.

26. Program on International Policy Attitudes, "What the Iraqi Public Wants," College Park, Maryland, January 31, 2006, available at www.worldpublicopinion.org, accessed March 17, 2006.

27. International Republican Institute, "Survey of Iraqi Public Opinion, March 23–31, 2006," April 27, 2006, available at www.iri.org, accessed July 17, 2006.

28. Edward Wong and Dexter Filkins, "Sectarian Strife: In An About-Face, Sunnis Want U.S. to Remain in Iraq," *New York Times*, July 17, 2006, p. A1.

29. For one alternative, see Kenneth M. Pollack et al., *A Switch in Time: A New Strategy for America in Iraq* (Brookings, 2006).

30. The generally reasonable Democratic national-security strategy does this; see Senate and House Democrats, "Real Security: Protecting America and Restoring Our Leadership in the World," March 2006, p. 3.

31. Rosa Brooks, "The 2,000 Dead Aren't The Only Victims," *Los Angeles Times*, October 29, 2005.

32. Erik Eckholm, "A New Kind of Care in a New Era of Casualties," *New York Times*, January 31, 2006.

33. Juan Gonzales, "Vets' Ills Mounting Fast," *New York Daily News*, February 7, 2006; Greg Jaffe, "For Nate Self, Battlefield Hero, Trauma Takes a Toll," *Wall Street Journal*, October 6, 2005.

34. Richard Allen Greene, BBC News, "U.S. Veterans' Invisible Wounds," August 16, 2005, at http://news.bbc.co.uk/2/hi/americas/4122602.stm [accessed 6/20/2006].

35. Eason Jordan, "Dying to Tell the Story?" *International Herald Tribune*, February 7, 2006.

36. Robert Mahoney, ed., *Attacks on the Press in 2005* (Committee to Protect Journalists, 2006), p. 190.

37. "Iraq Coalition Casualties: Contractors—A Partial List," http://www.icasualties.org/oif/Civ.aspx [accessed 2/19/2006].

38. "Civilians Reported Killed by Military Intervention in Iraq," at http://www.iraqbodycount.net [accessed 2/19/2006]. [As of 6/20/06, Iraq Body Count gives 42,889 as the maximum number of reported Iraqi deaths.]

39. Serah Sewall, "What's The Story Behind 30,000 Iraqi Deaths?" *Washington Post*, December 18, 2005.

40. Steve Kosiak, *The Cost of U.S. Military Operations in Iraq and Afghanistan through Fiscal Year 2006 and Beyond* (Center for Strategic and Budgetary Assessments, 2006), at http://www.csbaonline.org/4Publications/Archive/U.20060104.WarSpending/U.20060104.WarSpending.pdf [accessed 6/20/2006].; and Congressional Budget Office, "Estimated Costs of U.S. Operations in Iraq Under Two Specified Scenarios," Washington, D.C., July 13, 2006, p. 1, available at www.cbo.gov, accessed on July 14, 2006.

41. Congressional Budget Office, *The Budget and Economic Outlook: Fiscal Years 2007 Through 2016* (Congressional Budget Office, 2006), p. xiii; and Congressional Budget Office, "Current Budget Projections," March 3, 2006.

42. Peter Bergen and Alec Reynolds, "Blowback Revisited: Today's Insurgents in Iraq are Tomorrow's Terrorists," *Foreign Affairs*, November/December 2005; Daniel Benjamin and Steven Simon, *The Age of Sacred Terror: Radical Islam's War Against America* (Random House, 2003) and *The Next Attack: The Failure of the War on Terror and a Strategy for Getting It Right* (Times Books, 2005).

43. National Intelligence Council, *Mapping the Global Future* (Government Printing Office, December 2004), p. 94, at http://www.foia.cia.gov/2020/2020.pdf [accessed 6/20/2006].

44. Sean Rayment, "Secret MoD Poll: Iraqis Support Attacks on British Troops," *London Sunday Telegraph*, October 23, 2005.

45. Joshua Kurlantzick, "The Decline of American Soft Power," *Current History*, December 2005, pp. 419–424.

46. Pew Global Attitudes Project, "America's Image Slips, But Allies Share U.S. Concerns Over Iran, Hamas," June 13, 2006, available at http://pewglobal.org/reports, accessed 7/17/2006.

47. Sonni Efron, "Prison Abuse as Hurting U.S. Credibility," *Los Angeles Times*, January 14, 2005.

48. BBC News, "US Senate Backs Detainee Rights," October 6, 2005, at http://news.bbc.co.uk/1/hi/world/americas/4314304.stm [accessed 6/20/06].

49. Associated Press, "Turkish Movie Depicts Americans as Savages," February 2, 2006, at http://www.cnn.com/2006/WORLD/europe/02/02/turkish.movie.ap/.

50. See the Pew Research Center for the People and the Press and the Council on Foreign Relations, "America's Place in the World 2005," Washington, D.C., November 17, 2005, available at www.cfr.org, accessed July 17, 2006.

51. Pew Research Center for the People and the Press in association with the Council on Foreign Relations, *America's Place in the World 2005* (Pew Research Center, November 2005), at http://people-press.org/reports/pdf/263.pdf [accessed 6/20/2006].

52. "The Isolationist Temptation," *The Economist*, February 11, 2006, pp. 27–28.

53. Edward Wong and Dexter Filkins, "Sectarian Strife: In An About-Face, Sunnis Want U.S. to Remain in Iraq," *New York Times*, July 17, 2006, p. A1.

54. Edward P. Joseph and Michael O'Hanlon, "Iraqi Constitution Must Deliver Oil to Sunnis or It Won't Deliver," *Christian Science Monitor*, August 11, 2005.

55. Kenneth Pollack, "A Switch in Time," Brookings Institution, February 2006.

56. Gordon and Trainor, *Cobra II*, p. 160.

57. Joseph A. Christoff, *Rebuilding Iraq: Stabilization, Reconstruction, and Financing Challenges*, GAO–06–428T, Government Accountability Office, February 8, 2006, at http://www.gao.gov/new.items/d06428t.pdf [accessed 6/20/2006].

58. Nina Kamp, Michael O'Hanlon, and Amy Unikewicz, "The State of Iraq: An Update," *New York Times*, December 14, 2005.

59. David C. Hendrickson and Robert W. Tucker, "Revisions in Need of Revising: What Went Wrong in the Iraq War," Strategic Studies Institute, U.S. Army War College, December 2005, p. 1.
60. Kenneth Katzman, "Iraq: U.S. Regime Change Efforts and Post-Saddam Governance," Congressional Research Service, November 21, 2005, p. 24.
61. Anthony H. Cordesman, "Iraq's Evolving Insurgency: The Nature of Attacks and Patterns and Cycles in the Conflict," Center for Strategic and International Studies, February 3, 2006, p. iii.
62. Rowan Scarborough, "White House Eyes Billions for Iraq Maintenance," *Washington Times*, January 31, 2006.
63. See Michael O'Hanlon, "Don't Stop Rebuilding Iraq," *Washington Post*, January 24, 2006, p. A17.
64. The authors thank Carlos Pascual for several of these ideas; personal communication, May 23, 2006.
65. John Mueller, "The Banality of 'Ethnic War,'" *International Security,* vol. 25, no. 1, Summer 2000, p. 42; Chaim Kaufmann, "Possible and Impossible Solutions to Ethnic Civil Wars," *International Security,* vol. 20, no. 4, Spring 1996, pp. 136–175; Barry R. Posen, "Military Responses to Refugee Disasters," in Michael E. Brown, Owen R. Cote Jr., Sean M. Lynn-Jones, and Steven E. Miller, eds., *Nationalism and Ethnic Conflict,* revised edition (MIT Press, 2001), pp. 193–232; and Stephen John Stedman, "Introduction," in Stephen John Stedman, Donald Rothchild, and Elizabeth M. Cousens, eds., *Ending Civil Wars: The Implementation of Peace Agreements* (Lynne Rienner Publishers, 2002), pp. 1–40.

CHAPTER 3

1. The Clinton administration probably deferred too quickly to General Hugh Shelton in 1998, electing to use cruise missiles rather than commandos or other more muscular, albeit risky, measures to attack al Qaeda camps in Afghanistan. To be sure, there were good military arguments against risking American forces in a raid that might come up empty in a country far from U.S. reinforcements. That said, the United States wound up taking similar risks in 2001 after the 9/11 attacks. It would have been difficult to overrule the best advice of the nation's top general on this matter Nevertheless, it would have been appropriate, at a minimum, to engender more debate and a fuller consideration of options before proceeding with any one of them. Since Special Operations CINC General Peter Schoomaker (now Army chief of staff) was reportedly sympathetic to the idea of a more aggressive approach, such a debate might have opened up new possibilities for the United States. See National Commission on Terrorist Attacks Upon the United States, *The 9/11 Commission Report* (Government Printing Office, 2004), chapter 4.

2. See David Halberstam, *War in a Time of Peace: Bush, Clinton, and the Generals* (Scribner, 2001).
3. See Dana Priest, *The Mission* (W. W. Norton and Co., 2003), pp. 249–250; Ivo H. Daalder and Michael E. O'Hanlon, *Winning Ugly: NATO's War to Save Kosovo* (Brookings, 2000); and Peter D. Feaver, *Armed Servants: Agency, Oversight, and Civil-Military Relations* (Harvard University Press, 2003), p. 279.
4. Bob Woodward, *Plan of Attack* (Simon and Schuster, 2004), pp. 8, 37.
5. Bob Woodward, *Bush at War* (Simon and Schuster, 2002), pp. 201–251.
6. Eliot A. Cohen, *Supreme Command: Soldiers, Statesmen, and Leadership in Wartime* (Free Press, 2002).
7. See Michael O'Hanlon, "Iraq without a Plan," *Policy Review*, No. 128, December 2004/January 2005, pp. 33–35.
8. See Jared Diamond, *Guns, Germs, and Steel* (W. W. Norton and Co., 1997).
9. Barry Posen, "Command of the Commons: The Military Foundation of U.S. Hegemony," *International Security*, vol. 28, no. 1, Summer 2003, pp. 5–46; for a related argument, see Michael O'Hanlon, *Technological Change and the Future of Warfare* (Brookings, 2000), pp. 106–167.
10. On the importance of America's transparent system, see G. John Ikenberry, "Institutions, Strategic Restraint, and the Persistence of American Postwar Order," *International Security*, vol. 23, no. 3, Winter 1998/99, pp. 43–78.
11. Matt Moore, "Worldwide Military Spending Up Sharply," *Philadelphia Inquirer*, June 10, 2004.
12. Donald Rumsfeld, *Quadrennial Defense Review Report* (Department of Defense, February 2006).
13. For summaries of some of these changes, see Michael O'Hanlon, *Defense Policy Choices for the Bush Administration*, 2nd ed. (Brookings, 2002), pp. 1–62; Michael O'Hanlon, *Defense Strategy for the Post-Saddam Era* (Brookings, 2005), pp. 1–38. For an alternative way in which the Army might be restructured to face current challenges, see Hans Binnendijk and Stuart E. Johnson, eds., *Transforming for Stabilization and Reconstruction Operations* (National Defense University, 2004).
14. President George W. Bush, Budget of the U.S. Government, Fiscal Year 2007: Historical Tables (Government Printing Office, 2006), pp. 134–136; Department of Defense, FY 2007 Department of Defense Budget, February 6, 2006, available at www.defenselink.mil. Of the approximately $440 billion requested for the Department of Defense in 2007, the breakdown by service was $130 billion for the Air Force, $112 billion for the Army, $111 billion for the Navy, $17 billion for the Marine Corps, and $70 billion for defense-wide activities. Categorized differently, $152 billion was to be for operations and maintenance; $111 billion for military personnel; $84 billion for procurement; $73 billion for research, development, testing, and evaluation; and $19 billion for miscellaneous purposes such as military construction.

15. See "Should the Draft Be Reinstated?" *Time*, December 29, 2003, p. 101.
16. Helen Dewar, "Hagel Seeking Broad Debate on Draft Issue," *Washington Post*, April 22, 2004, p. 25.
17. See Donald H. Rumsfeld, "Rumors About a Draft Are False," *Salt Lake City Desert News*, October 28, 2004; Hulse, C. "Military Draft? Official Denials Leave Skeptics," *New York Times*, July 3, 2004, p. 1.
18. Ole R. Holsti, "A Widening Gap Between the U.S. Military and Civilian Society? Some Evidence, 1976–1996," *International Security*, vol. 23, no. 3, Winter 1998/99, p. 13.
19. David C. King and Zachary Karabell, *The Generation of Trust: How the U.S. Military Has Regained the Public's Confidence Since Vietnam* (American Enterprise Institute, 2003), p. 44.
20. Center for Strategic and International Studies, *American Military Culture in the Twenty-First Century* (Center for Strategic and International Studies, 2000), pp. 32–33.
21. Adebayo Adedeji, *Educational Attainment and Compensation of Enlisted Personnel* (Congressional Budget Office, 2004), p. 14.
22. King and Karabell, *The Generation of Trust*.
23. On the latter figure, see Dave Moniz and Tom Squitieri, "Front-Line Troops Disproportionately White, Not Black," *USA Today*, January 21, 2003, p. 1. Some additional statistics: Enlisted personnel are 85 percent male and 15 percent female. Fifty percent of all enlistees are married. The enlisted force consists of 95 percent high-school graduates and 5 percent GED-equivalent degree holders. The officer corps is 8.3 percent African American and about 4 percent Hispanic, meaning that minority officer representation is far from proportional to the racial profile of the enlisted force, but much greater than minority representation in equivalent leadership positions in many other professions in the United States. The officer corps is also highly educated, with 91 percent holding at least a bachelor's degree and 11 percent holding at least one advanced degree. See Department of Defense, Population Representation in the Military Services (2001), available at http://www.dod.mil/prhome/poprep2003/download/ExecSum2003.pdf. Michael E. O'Hanlon, Defense Strategy for the Post-Saddam Era (Brookings, 2005), pp. 54–57.
24. For a good overview of how one U.S. military service improved dramatically after Vietnam, see Robert H. Scales Jr., *Certain Victory: The U.S. Army in the Gulf War* (Brassey's, 1994), pp. 1–38.
25. Jeff St. Onge and Jon Steinman, "Army Lowers Recruit Standards," *Philadelphia Inquirer*, April 7, 2006.
26. For a description of the total-force policy of the post-Vietnam era, see Michael D. Doubler, *I Am the Guard: A History of the Army National Guard, 1636–2000* (Government Printing Office, 2001), pp. 269–300; Janine Davidson, "A Citizen Check on War," *Washington Post*, November 16, 2003, p. B7.

27. For a review of the debate of that time, see Steven Kull and I.M. Destler, *Misreading the Public: The Myth of a New Isolationism* (Brookings, 1999), pp. 81–112.

28. For an illuminating study of why military service should be viewed as a profession, albeit one with problems, see Don M. Snider and Gayle L. Watkins, project directors, and Lloyd J. Matthews, ed., *The Future of the Army Profession* (McGraw-Hill, 2002).

29. Kathy Roth-Douquet and Frank Schaeffer, *AWOL: The Unexcused Absence of America's Upper Classes from the Military—and How It Hurts Our Country* (Smithsonian Books, 2006), chapter 9.

30. Harvard University, "Remarks of Harvard University President Lawrence H. Summers ROTC Commissioning Ceremony," June 9, 2004, available at http://www.president.harvard.edu/speeches/2004/rotc.html [accessed 2/2/2005].

31. See Nina Kamp and Michael O'Hanlon, "Iraq Index," at www.brookings.edu/iraqindex [accessed 3/31/06].

32. International Institute for Strategic Studies, *The Military Balance 2005/2006* (Routledge, 2005), pp. 48–106.

33. See Michael E. O'Hanlon, *Expanding Global Military Capacity for Humanitarian Intervention* (Brookings, 2003), pp. 56–57.

34. Julian Lindley-French and Franco Algieri, *A European Defence Strategy* (Bertelsmann Foundation, May 2004), p. 10.

35. See "G8 Action Plan: Expanding Global Capability for Peace Support Operations," Sea Island, Georgia, June 2004, available at www.g8usa.gov/d_061004c.htm; Anthony Lake, Christine Todd Whitman, Princeton N. Lyman, J. Stephen Morrison, and an Independent Task Force, *More than Humanitarianism: A Strategic U.S. Approach Toward Africa* (Council on Foreign Relations, 2006), pp. 80–88.

36. Samuel L. Berger, Brent Scowcroft, and an Independent Task Force, *In the Wake of War: Improving U.S. Post-Conflict Capabilities* (Council on Foreign Relations, 2005), p. 37; Newt Gingrich, George Mitchell, and the Task Force on United Nations Reform, *American Interests and U.N. Reform*, 2005), p. 33; and Michael O'Hanlon, *Expanding Global Military Capacity for Humanitarian Intervention* (Brookings, 2003), pp. 98–105.

37. See Adam Talaber, *The Long-Term Implications of Current Defense Plans and Alternatives: Summary Update for Fiscal Year 2006* (Congressional Budget Office, 2005), pp. 2, 20; Executive Office of the President, Budget of the U.S. Government, Fiscal Year 2007: Historical Tables (Government Printing Office, 2006), pp. 88–89.

38. For a somewhat different view on specific weapons platforms, see Lawrence J. Korb, Caroline P. Wadhams, and Andrew J. Grotto, *Restoring American Military Power: A Progressive Quadrennial Defense Review* (Center for American Progress, January 2006), pp. 57–68.

39. See, most notably, Admiral William A. Owens with Ed Offley, *Lifting the Fog of War* (Farrar, Straus, and Giroux, 2000).

40. National Defense Panel, "Transforming Defense," Washington, 1997, pp. 7–8.

41. See Michael O'Hanlon, *Technological Change and the Future of Warfare* (Brookings, 2000), pp. 32–105.

42. James M. Lindsay and Michael E. O'Hanlon, *Defending America: The Case for Limited National Missile Defense* (Brookings, 2001), p. 6.

43. See Bradley Graham, "Interceptor System Set, But Doubts Remain," *Washington Post*, September 29, 2004, p. 1.

44. James Glanz, "Pointed Questions on Missile-Defense System," *New York Times*, March 12, 2004.

45. See Geoffrey Forden, "Budgetary and Technical Implications of the Administration's Plan for National Missile Defense," Congressional Budget Office, 2000, p. 10; Lindsay and O'Hanlon, *Defending America*, p. 115.

46. Steven M. Kosiak, *Matching Resources with Requirements: Options for Modernizing the U.S. Air Force* (Center for Strategic and Budgetary Assessments, 2004), p. 41.

47. For more information on these and other weapons programs, see the database maintained by John Pike of GlobalSecurity.org at www.globalsecurity.org/military/systems.

48. Anthony H. Cordesman, *The Iraq War: Strategy, Tactics, and Military Lessons* (CSIS, 2003), p. 254.

49. David A. Fulghum and Robert Wall, "Prices at the Pump," *Aviation Week and Space Technology*, March 22, 2004, p. 27.

50. Bill Sweetman, "In the Tracks of the Predator: Combat UAV Programs Are Gathering Speed," *Jane's International Defense Review* (August 2004), pp. 48–55.

51. Hampton Stephens, "USAF: Indian Exercises Showed Need for F/A–22, Changes in Training," *Inside the Air Force*, June 4, 2004, p. 1.

52. Robert Wall, "Changing Story," *Aviation Week and Space Technology*, May 10, 2004, p. 35.

53. Alderman and Company, First Quarter Newsletter (2004), available at www.aldermanco.com.

54. Michael Sirak, "U.S. Air Force to Buy STOVL Variant of Fighter," *Jane's Defence Weekly*, February 18, 2004, p. 6.

55. Congressional Budget Office, Budget Options, March 2003, pp. 25–26.

56. Robert Wall, "Weighty Decisions," *Aviation Week and Space Technology*, March 22, 2004, p. 26; David A. Fulghum and Robert Wall, "Escalation," *Aviation Week and Space Technology*, March 22, 2004, pp. 24–25.

57. For a fuller discussion, see Michael Levi and Michael O'Hanlon, *The Future of Arms Control* (Brookings, 2005).

58. See, for example, Department of the Army, Army Modernization Plan 2003, pp. 47–52, D–24 through D–25.

59. Joshua Kucera, "Iraq Conflict Raises Doubts on FCS Survivability," *Jane's Defence Weekly*, May 19, 2004, p. 8.

60. For concurring views, see F. Stephen Larrabee, John Gordon IV, and Peter A. Wilson, "The Right Stuff," *National Interest*, no. 77, Fall 2004, p. 58; and Joseph N. Mait and Richard L. Kugler, "Alternative Approaches to Army Transformation," *Defense Horizons*, no. 41, 2004, p. 1.

61. See Peter A. Wilson, John Gordon IV, and David E. Johnson, "An Alternative Future Force: Building a Better Army," *Parameters*, Winter 2003–2004, pp. 19–39. As one example of the type of issue that needs to be studied, the question of the Stryker's weight remains unanswered. It may be too heavy for easy air transport in C–130 aircraft. See Thomas E. Ricks, "GAO Calls Stryker Too Heavy for Transport," *Washington Post*, August 14, 2004, p. 4.

62. Department of Defense, "Program Acquisition Costs by Weapon System," February 2004, p. 49; Congressional Budget Office, "Budget Options," March 2003, p. 14.

63. Elaine M. Grossman, "Christie: V–22's 'Vortex Ring State' May Yet Pose Operational Problems," *Inside the Pentagon*, December 18, 2003, p. 3.

64. Lt. Col. Kevin Gross, "Dispelling the Myth of the V–22," *Proceedings*, September 2004, pp. 38–41.

65. Comments of Assistant Secretary of Defense David S. C. Chu at a special hearing before a subcommittee of the Committee on Appropriations of the United States Senate, July 19, 1990, Senate Hearing 101–934, 101st Congress, 2nd session (Government Printing Office, 1990), p. 51; L. Dean Simmons, "Assessment of Alternatives for the V–22 Assault Aircraft Program," Institute for Defense Analyses, June 1990, Senate Hearing 101–934, p. 17.

66. See Michael O'Hanlon, *Defense Policy Choices for the Bush Administration*, 2d. ed. (Brookings, 2002), pp. 117–119.

67. Melissa Tryon, "Reconciling Democrats and the Military," in Will Marshall, ed., *With All Our Might: A Progressive Strategy for Defeating Jihadism and Defending Liberty* (Rowman & Littlefield Publishers, Inc., 2006), p. 146; David R. Segal et al., "Attitudes of Entry-Level Enlisted Personnel," in Peter D. Feaver, Richard H. Kohn, and Lindsay P. Cohn, eds., *Soldiers and Civilians: The Civil-Military Gap and American Security* (MIT Press, 2001), p. 177. For related background, see Ole R. Holsti, "A Widening Gap Between the U.S. Military and Civilian Society? Some Evidence, 1976–1996," *International Security*, vol. 23, no. 3, Winter 1998/99, pp. 5–42; Thomas E. Ricks, "The Widening Gap Between the Military and Society," *Atlantic Monthly*, July 1997, pp. 67–78; and Kathy Roth-Douquet and Frank Schaeffer, *AWOL: The Unexcused Absence of America's Upper Classes from Military Service—and How It Hurts Our Country* (HarperCollins, 2006), pp. 219–237.

68. See Sumit Ganguly, *Conflict Unending: India-Pakistan Tensions Since 1947* (Columbia University Press, 2001).

69. See Stephen Philip Cohen, *The Idea of Pakistan* (Brookings, 2004), pp. 97–130.

70. See International Crisis Group, "Unfulfilled Promises: Pakistan's Failure to Tackle Extremism," (January 16, 2004, available at http://www.crisisgroup.org/home/index.cfm?id=2472&l=1.

71. Christopher Langton, ed., "The Military Balance 2003–2004," International Institute for Strategic Studies, pp. 140–142.

72. See Roth-Douquet and Schaeffer, *AWOL*.

73. The more extreme idea of allowing foreigners to serve as a route to U.S. citizenship, as advocated by Max Boot and others, also warrants consideration.

74. Richard K. Betts, "The Delusion of Impartial Intervention," *Foreign Affairs*, vol. 73, no. 6, November/December 1994, pp. 20–33; Stephen John Stedman, "Alchemy for a New World Order," *Foreign Affairs*, vol. 74, no. 3, May/June 1995, pp. 17–18.

75. Select Bipartisan Committee to Investigate the Preparation for and Response to Hurricane Katrina, "A Failure of Initiative," U.S. Congress, February 2006, pp. 218–230; Government Accountability Office, "Hurricane Katrina: Better Plans and Exercises Needed to Guide the Military's Response to Catastrophic Natural Disasters," GAO–06–643, May 2006.

76. Frances Fragos Townsend, Assistant to the President for Homeland Security and Counterterrorism, "The Federal Response to Hurricane Katrina: Lessons Learned," The White House, February 2006, p. 55.

77. Lane Pierrot, "Structuring U.S. Forces After the Cold War: Costs and Effects of Increased Reliance on the Reserves," Congressional Budget Office, September 1992.

78. Lynn E. Davis, David E. Mosher, Richard R. Brennan, Michael D. Greenberg, K. Scott McMahon, and Charles W. Yost, *Army Forces for Homeland Security* (RAND Corporation, 2004), pp. 22–31.

79. General Tony Zinni and Tony Koltz, *The Battle for Peace: A Frontline Vision of America's Power and Purpose* (Palgrave Macmillan, 2006), p. 7.

80. National Intelligence Council, *Mapping the Global Future* (Government Printing Office, 2004), pp. 93–97.

81. Susan E. Rice, "The Threat of Global Poverty," *National Interest*, no. 83, Spring 2006, pp. 76–82.

82. Office of the Coordinator for Reconstruction and Stabilization (S/CRS), Fact Sheet, Department of State, Washington, D.C., March 8, 2005, available at www.state.gov/s/crs [accessed 6/25/2006].

83. Clark A. Murdock and Michele A. Flournoy, *Beyond Goldwater-Nichols: U.S. Government and Defense Reform for a New Strategic Era, Phase 2 Report* (Center for Strategic and International Studies, July 2005), p. 64.

84. E-mail from Jessica Garcia, Office of Foreign Disaster Assistance, USAID, to Nina Kamp, Brookings Institution, February 27, 2006.

85. Murdock and Flournoy, *Beyond Goldwater-Nichols,* pp. 6–7.

86. Tom Brokaw, "Diplomats for Tough Duty," *Washington Post*, August 14, 2005, p. B7.

87. Office of the Special Inspector General for Iraq Reconstruction, "Iraq Reconstruction: Lessons in Human Capital Management," Report No. 1, January 2006.

88. Office of the Coordinator for Reconstruction and Stabilization, "Post-Conflict Reconstruction Essential Tasks," Department of State, Washington, D.C., April 2005.

89. Neyla Arnas, Charles L. Barry, and Robert B. Oakley, "Harnessing the Interagency for Complex Operations," Defense and Technology Paper 16, National Defense University, 2005, pp. 18–19.

90. Other candidate countries, however unlikely they may be to fracture or fall apart, with populations of 40 million or more include Nigeria, Sudan, Pakistan, Bangladesh, Indonesia, and the Philippines, to say nothing of Mexico (or Colombia).

91. Seth G. Jones, Jeremy M. Wilson, Andrew Rathmell, and K. Jack Riley, *Establishing Law and Order After Conflict* (RAND Corporation, 2005), p. 132.

92. Murdock and Flournoy, *Beyond Goldwater-Nichols,* pp. 59–61.

93. Samuel R. Berger, Brent Scowcroft, and Independent Task Force, *In the Wake of War: Improving U.S. Post-Conflict Capabilities* (Council on Foreign Relations, 2005), pp. 19–23.

94. Associated Press, "National Guard in Short Supply, Some States Fear," *Honolulu Advertiser*, May 17, 2004.

CHAPTER 4

1. President George W. Bush, "Address to a Joint Session of Congress and the American People," September 20, 2001, available at www.whitehouse.gov/news/releases/2001/09/print/20010920–8.html [accessed 6/26/2006]; President George W. Bush, "State of the Union Address," January 29, 2002, available at www.whitehouse.gove/news/releases/2002/01/print/20020129–11.html [accessed 6/26/2006]; and President George W. Bush, "National Security Strategy of the United States of America," September 17, 2002, available at www.whitehouse.gov/nsc/nssall.html [accessed 6/26/2006].

2. For more on some of these issues, see Richard A. Falkenrath, "The 9/11 Commission Report: A Review Essay," *International Security,* vol. 29, no. 3, Winter 2004/05, p. 184.

3. Mark Mazzetti, "Spymaster Tells Secret of Size of Spy Force," *New York Times*, April 21, 2006.

4. John A. Kringen, "How We've Improved Intelligence," *Washington Post*, April 3, 2006, p. 19.

5. Charles Doyle, "The USA PATRIOT Act: A Sketch," *CRS Report for Congress* (Congressional Research Service, April 18, 2002).

6. Richard A. Posner, "A New Surveillance Act," *Wall Street Journal*, February 15, 2006, p. 16; Philip Bobbitt, "Why We Listen," *New York Times*, January 30, 2006, p. A27.

7. Jim VandeHei, "Rift Between Parties Over NSA Wiretapping Grows," *Washington Post,* January 26, 2006, p. 4.

8. Vicky O'Hara, "Terrorist Funding," National Public Radio, Morning Edition, November 20, 2003; Speech of George W. Bush at the FBI Academy, Quantico, VA, September 10, 2003; and Philip Shenon, "U.S. Reaches Deal to Limit Transfers of Portable Missiles," *New York Times*, October 21, 2003, p. A1.

9. Tom Ridge, "Since That Day," *Washington Post*, September 11, 2003, p. 23.

10. Martin Enserink, "Facing a Security Deadline, Labs Get a 'Provisional' Pass," *Science*, November 7, 2003, p. 962.

11. There may be some gaps in these types of protective measures to date, but the overall level of security is generally good. See Statement of Jim Wells, General Accounting Office, "Nuclear Regulatory Commission: Preliminary Observations on Efforts to Improve Security at Nuclear Power Plants," GAO–04–1064T, September 14, 2004.

12. John Moteff, "Computer Security: A Summary of Selected Federal Laws, Executive Orders, and Presidential Directives," Congressional Research Service Report for Congress RL32357, April 16, 2004, p. 2.

13. David Johnston and Andrew C. Revkin, "Officials Say Their Focus Is on Car and Truck Bombs," *New York Times*, August 2, 2004, p. A13.

14. President George W. Bush, Speech on Terrorism at the National Endowment for Democracy, October 6, 2005, available at "http://www.whitehouse.gov" [accessed October 6, 2005].

15. Eric Lichtblau, "Finance Centers Are Said to Be the Targets," *New York Times*, August 2, 2004, p. 1.

16. Shaun Waterman, "Al Qaeda Warns of Threat to Water Supply," *Washington Times*, May 29, 2003, p. 6; and Eric Lichtblau, "U.S. Cites al Qaeda in Plan to Destroy Brooklyn Bridge," *New York Times*, June 20, 2003, p. 1; Eric Lichtblau, "Government Report on U.S. Aviation Warns of Security Holes," *New York Times*, March 14, 2005, p. A1; Matthew Brzezinski, *Fortress America* (Bantam Books, 2004), pp. 16–17.

17. See Gilmore Commission (Advisory Panel to Assess Domestic Response Capabilities for Terrorism Involving Weapons of Mass Destruction), Fifth Annual Report, *Forging America's New Normalcy: Securing Our Homeland, Preserving Our Liberty* (RAND Corporation, 2003), p. 1; Alan B. Krueger and David D. Laitin, "'Misunderestimating' Terrorism," *Foreign Affairs*, vol. 83, no. 5, September/October 2004, p. 9; and Susan B. Glasser, "U.S. Fig-

ures Show Sharp Global Rise in Terrorism," *Washington Post*, April 27, 2005, p. 1.

18. Warren P. Strobel, "U.S.: Terrorist Attacks Increased Last Year," *Philadelphia Inquirer*, April 21, 2006.

19. Richard Benedetto, "Americans Expect Attacks, Poll Finds," *USA Today*, July 12, 2005, p. 1.

20. Will Marshall and Jeremy Rosner, "Introduction: A Progressive Answer to Jihadist Terror," in Will Marshall, ed., *With All Our Might: A Progressive Strategy for Defeating Jihadism and Defending Liberty* (Rowman & Littlefield Publishers, Inc., 2006), p. 2.

21. See Marc Sageman, *Understanding Terror Networks* (University of Pennsylvania Press, 2004).

22. The Advisory Panel to Assess Domestic Response Capabilities for Terrorism Involving Weapons of Mass Destruction (Gilmore Commission), "Implementing the National Strategy," December 2002, p. 11; Douglas Farah and Peter Finn, "Terrorism, Inc.," *Washington Post*, November 21, 2003, p. 33. On the assertion that modern terrorist groups watch and learn from each other, see Bruce Hoffman, "Terrorism Trends and Prospects," in Ian O. Lesser, Bruce Hoffman, John Arquilla, David Ronfeldt, and Michele Zanini, *Countering the New Terrorism* (RAND, 1999), pp. 8–28; on the nature of al Qaeda and affiliated as well as sympathetic organizations, see Paul R. Pillar, *Terrorism and U.S. Foreign Policy* (Brookings, 2001), pp. 54–55.

23. Cited in Daniel L. Byman, "Homeland Security: We're Safer Than You Think," *Slate*, August 2, 2004.

24. Leyla Linton, "Al Qaeda, Taliban Can Still Launch Attacks, Report Says," *Philadelphia Inquirer*, February 16, 2005.

25. Washington in Brief," *Washington Post*, July 17, 2004, p. A5.

26. Byman, "Homeland Security," *Slate*; ABC News, "No 'True' Al Qaeda Sleeper Agents Have Been Found in U.S.," abcnews.com, March 9, 2005.

27. Bill Gertz, "Goss Fears WMD Attack in U.S. 'A Matter of Time,'" *Washington Times*, February 17, 2005, p. 3.

28. Dana Priest and Josh White, "War Helps Recruit Terrorists, Hill Told," *Washington Post*, February 17, 2005, p. 1.

29. National Intelligence Council, *Mapping the Global Future* (Government Printing Office, 2004), p. 94.

30. Richard K. Betts, "The Soft Underbelly of American Primacy: Tactical Advantages of Terror," *Political Science Quarterly*, vol. 117, no. 1, Spring 2002, p. 30.

31. On jamming, see "U.S. Homeland Defense Strategists," *Aviation Week and Space Technology*, September 6, 2004, p. 20.

32. Peter D. Zimmerman with Cheryl Loeb, "Dirty Bombs: The Threat Revisited," *Defense Horizons*, no. 38, January 2004.

33. Lawrence M. Wein and Edward H. Kaplan, "Unready for Anthrax," *Washington Post*, July 28, 2003, p. A21.

34. Clark Kent Ervin, *Open Target: Where America Is Vulnerable to Attack* (New York: Palgrave Macmillan, 2006), pp. 79–115.

35. Statement of Richard Falkenrath before the Senate Committee on Homeland Security and Governmental Affairs, January 26, 2005, pp. 14–15. Available at www.brookings.edu.

36. Ibid., pp. 12–14.

37. For a similar critique of Congress's role, see 9/11 Commission, *The 9/11 Commission Report* (W.W. Norton and Co., 2004), pp. 420–422.

38. Statement of Richard Falkenrath before the Senate Committee, p. 4.

39. For more detail on these suggestions, see Michael d'Arcy, Michael O'Hanlon, Peter Orszag, Jeremy Shapiro, and James Steinberg, *Protecting the Homeland 2006/2007* (Brookings, 2006).

40. This could also be of great importance in addressing such scenarios as a possible mutation of the H5N1 bird-flu virus to a form highly dangerous to humans. See, for instance, Kendall Hoyt, "Bird Flu Won't Wait," *New York Times*, March 3, 2006.

41. Michael d'Arcy, Michael O'Hanlon, Peter Orszag, Jeremy Shapiro, and James Steinberg, *Protecting the Homeland 2006/2007* (Brookings, 2006), pp. 122–124.

42. James Steinberg, "Intelligence Reform," in Michael d'Arcy, Michael O'Hanlon, Peter Orszag, Jeremy Shapiro, and James Steinberg, *Protecting the Homeland 2006/2007* (Brookings, 2006), pp. 27–30; Jeremy Shapiro, "International Cooperation on Homeland Security," in d'Arcy, O'Hanlon, Orszag, Shapiro, and Steinberg, *Protecting the Homeland 2006/2007*, pp. 58–69.

43. Michael d'Arcy, "Technology Development and Transportation Security," in d'Arcy, O'Hanlon, Orszag, Shapiro, and Steinberg, *Protecting the Homeland 2006/2007*, pp. 135–39.

44. Stephen E. Flynn and James M. Loy, "A Port in the Storm Over Dubai," *New York Times*, February 28, 2006, p. A19.

CHAPTER 5

1. National Intelligence Council, *Mapping the Global Future* (Government Printing Office, 2004), p. 93.

2. See "Rumsfeld's War on Terror Memo," *USA Today*, May 20, 2005, available at www.usatoday.com/news/washington/executive/rumsfeld-memo.htm [accessed 6/26/2006].

3. Zeyno Baran, "Fighting the War of Ideas," *Foreign Affairs*, vol. 84, no. 6, November/December 2005, pp. 68–79.

4. President George W. Bush, The National Security Strategy of the United States of America, March 2006, p. 9, available at http://www.whitehouse.gov/nsc/nss/2006/ [accessed 6/26/2006].

5. Susan E. Rice, "The Threat of Global Poverty," *National Interest,* no. 83, Spring 2006, pp. 76–82.

6. World Bank, *World Development Report 2006: Equity and Development* (Oxford University Press, 2005), pp. 292–297.

7. Office of the Coordinator for Counterterrorism, U.S. Department of State, "Country Reports on Terrorism 2004," April 2005, pp. 72–73; World Bank, *World Development Report 2006,* pp. 292–297.

8. International Crisis Group, "Weakening Indonesia's Mujahidini Networks: Lessons from Laluku and Poso, Asia Report No. 103, October 2005, available at www.crisisgroup.org.

9. Stephen P. Cohen, *The Idea of Pakistan* (Brookings, 2004), pp. 15–200; Daniel Byman, *Deadly Connections: States that Sponsor Terrorism* (Cambridge University Press, 2005), pp. 167–185; and Office of the Coordinator for Counterterrorism, U.S. Department of State, "Country Reports on Terrorism 2004", pp. 73–75, 103.

10. Byman, *Deadly Connections,* pp. 79–115.

11. See International Crisis Group, "Reforming Egypt: In Search of a Strategy," Middle East/North Africa Report No. 46, October 2005, available at www.crisisgroup.org; U.S. Department of State, "Country Reports on Human Rights Practices 2005", p. 6, available at www.state.gov/g/drl/rls/hrrpt/2005/61550.htm [accessed 6/26/2006].

12. Office of the Coordinator for Counterterrorism, U.S. Department of State, "Country Reports on Terrorism," pp. 67–68.

13. Martin Indyk, Presentation at Brookings Panel Discussion, "President Bush's National Security Strategy: Is the U.S. Meeting Its Global Challenges?" Brookings Institution, Washington, D.C., March 21, 2006, pp. 21–22, available at www.brookings.edu.

14. Pew Global Attitudes Project, "American Character Gets Mixed Reviews: U.S. Image Up Slightly, But Still Negative," Pew Research Center, Washington, D.C., June 23, 2005, p. 1, available at www.pewglobal.org; Testimony of Andrew Kohut before the Subcommittee on Oversight and Investigations of the U.S. House of Representatives Committee on International Relations, November 10, 2005, available at pewglobal.org/commentary/display.php?AnalysisID=1001 [accessed 6/26/2006]; and Andrew Kohut, Carroll Doherty, and Richard Wike, "America's Image Slips, But Allies Share U.S. Concerns Over Iran, Hamas," Pew Research Center, Washington, D.C., June 13, 2006, p. 1, available at www.pewglobal.org.

15. Olivier Roy, *Globalized Islam: The Search for a New Ummah* (Columbia University Press, 2004).

16. On Lebanon, see Fouad Ajami, "The Autumn of the Autocrats," *Foreign Affairs,* vol. 84, no. 3, May/June 2005, pp. 20–35.

17. Tamara Cofman Wittes, "Progress of the 'Freedom Strategy' in the Middle East," *Arab Reform Bulletin*, February 2006.

18. Michael Herzog, "Can Hamas Be Tamed?" *Foreign Affairs*, vol. 85, no. 2 (March/April 2006), p. 91.

19. Reza Aslan, "The Struggle for Islam's Soul," in Will Marshall, ed., *With All Our Might: A Progressive Strategy for Defeating Jihadism and Defending Liberty* (Rowman & Littlefield Publishers, Inc., 2006), p. 27.

20. Thomas Carothers and Marina Ottaway, eds., "Getting to the Core," in *Uncharted Journey: Promoting Democracy in the Middle East* (Carnegie Endowment, 2005), pp. 256–267.

21. Robin Wright, *Sacred Rage: The Wrath of Militant Islam* (Simon and Schuster, 1985), p. 288.

22. Mona Yacoubian, "Promoting Middle East Democracy II: Arab Initiatives," U.S. Institute of Peace Special Report 136, U.S. Institute of Peace, Washington, D.C., May 2005, pp. 1–9.

23. Tamara Cofman Wittes, "The Promise of Arab Liberalism," *Policy Review*, July 2004.

24. Edward Gresser, "Reviving Muslim Economies," in Marshall, ed., *With All Our Might*, pp. 69–83.

25. President George W. Bush, The National Security Strategy of the United States of America, March 2006, pp. 26–28.

26. For a similar argument in regard to Pakistan specifically, see Stephen J. Solarz, "Pakistan's Choice: Partner or Problem?" in Marshall, ed., *With All Our Might,* pp. 119–120.

27. World Bank, *World Development Report 2006*, p. 285; United Nations, "The Millenium Development Goals Report, 2005,", p. 10, available at www.un.org. and http://milleniumindicators.un.org.

28. U.S. Department of State, "International Affairs Function 150: Fiscal Year 2007 Budget Request," February 2006, pp. 13, 21, 64–70.

29. World Bank, *The World Bank Annual Report 2005: Year in Review* (World Bank, 2005), pp. 41, 53.

30. 9/11 Public Discourse Project, "Final Report on the 9/11 Commission Recommendations," December 2005, pp. 4–5, available at www.9–11pdp.org [accessed 6/27/2006].

31. Madeleine K. Albright, Vin Weber, Steven A. Cook, and Independent Task Force, *In Support of Arab Democracy: Why and How* (Council on Foreign Relations, 2005), p. 41.

32. Lael Brainard, Vinca La Fleur, and Brookings Blum Roundtable, *Expanding Enterprise, Lifting the Poor: The Private Sector in the Fight Against Global*

Poverty (Brookings, 2005), pp. 1–18; Albright, Weber, Cook, and Independent Task Force, *In Support of Arab Democracy*, pp. 36–41.

33. See Tamara Cofman Wittes and Sarah E. Yerkes, "The Middle East Partnership Initiative: Progress, Problems, and Prospects," *Saban Center Middle East Memo #5*, November 29, 2004, available at www.brookings.edu.

34. Michael A. Levi and Michael B. d'Arcy, "Untapped Potential: U.S. Science and Technology Cooperation with the Islamic World," U.S. Policy Towards the Islamic World Analysis Paper #8, Brookings Institution, April 2005.

35. Robert Satloff, *The Battle of Ideas in the War on Terror* (Washington Institute for Near East Policy, 2004), pp. 78–80.

36. Lael Brainard, "Fulfilling the Promise of the Millennium Challenge Corporation," in Chuck Sudetic, ed., *Restoring American Leadership* (The Century Foundation, 2005), pp. 82–88.

37. Lael Brainard, Carol Graham, Nigel Purvis, Steven Radelet, and Gayle E. Smith, *The Other War* (Brookings, 2003), pp. 1–16; Joseph E. Stiglitz, *Globalization and Its Discontents* (W. W. Norton and Co., 2003), pp. 242–243.

38. Peter Bergen, "A Guide to the Hunt," *Washington Post*, February 26, 2006, p. B1.

39. Richard W. Stevenson, "Eight Leaders Hail Steps on Africa and Warming," *New York Times*, July 9, 2005, p. A1.

40. United Nations Development Programme and Arab Fund for Economic and Social Development, *Arab Human Development Report 2002* (United Nations Development Programme, Regional Bureau for Arab States, 2002), pp. 1–13, 51–63.

41. Alexander Evans, "Understanding Madrasahs," *Foreign Affairs,* vol. 85, no. 1, January/February 2006, pp. 9–16; Jessica Stern, *Terror in the Name of God: Why Religious Militants Kill* (HarperCollins, 2003), p. 293; and Marc Sageman, *Understanding Terror Networks* (University of Pennsylvania Press, 2004), p. 74.

42. Bradley Graham, "Foreign-Language Learning Promoted," *Washington Post,* January 6, 2006, p. 4.

43. Jay Mathews, "Strides in 'Critical Languages' Remain Small," *Washington Post*, March 14, 2006, p. A4.

44. Satloff, *The Battle of Ideas in the War on Terror* (Washington Institute for Near East Policy, 2004), p. 11.

45. Report of the Advisory Group on Public Diplomacy for the Arab and Muslim World, "Changing Minds, Winning Peace," U.S. Advisory Commission on Public Diplomacy, October 2003, p. 27.

46. For a succinct explanation of the importance of the issue, see Stephen W. Van Evera, "Why U.S. National Security Requires Mideast Peace," MIT Center for International Studies Report, April 2005.

47. For more on Telhami's views, see Shibley Telhami, *The Stakes: The Consequences of Power and the Choice for Peace* (Boulder, Colorado: Westview Press, 2002), pp. 95–130.

48. Martin Indyk and Tamara Wittes, "Dual Dilemmas: U.S. Policy Options for the Israeli-Palestinian Predicament," Saban Center Middle East Memo #9, Brookings Institution, May 19, 2006, available at www.brookings.edu.

49. On settlements, see Gershom Gorenberg, "Israel's Tragedy Foretold," *New York Times*, March 10, 2006; on Israel's need for strong-armed tactics, see Avi Dicter, "How to Win the War Against Terrorism," Remarks at Saban Center Symposium, Brookings Institution, September 22, 2005.

50. Speech by President William Jefferson Clinton at the U.S.-Islamic World Forum, Doha, Qatar, January 12, 2004, available at www.brookings.edu/fp/research/projects/islam/clinton20040112.pdf [accessed 6/27/2006].

51. Report of the Advisory Group on Public Diplomacy for the Arab and Muslim World, *Changing Minds, Winning Peace*, p. 49.

52. Larry Diamond and Michael McFaul, "Seeding Liberal Democracy," in Marshall, ed., *With All Our Might*, p. 62.

53. 9/11 Public Discourse Project, "Final Report on the 9/11 Commission Recommendations," p. 5.

54. Report of the Advisory Group on Public Diplomacy for the Arab and Muslim World, *Changing Minds, Winning Peace*, pp. 9–10, 34–36.

55. Secretary of Defense Donald Rumsfeld, Quadrennial Defense Review Report, February 2006, p. 9.

56. George W. Bush, National Strategy for Combating Terrorism, The White House, February 2003, p. 29; 9/11 Commission, *The 9/11 Commission Report* (W.W. Norton and Co., 2004), pp. 363–364.

57. Shibley Telhami, *The Stakes: America and the Middle East* (Westview Press, 2002), pp. 37–66.

58. Isobel Coleman, "Women, Islam, and the New Iraq," *Foreign Affairs*, vol. 85, no. 1, January/February 2006, pp. 24–38; Bernard Lewis, "Freedom and Justice in the Modern Middle East," *Foreign Affairs*, vol. 84, no. 3, May/June 2005, pp. 36–51.

59. Zbigniew Brzezinski, *The Choice: Global Domination or Global Leadership* (Basic Books, 2004), pp. 47–59.

60. Claudia Deane and Darryl Fears, "Negative Perception of Islam Increasing," *Washington Post*, March 9, 2006, p. A1.

CHAPTER 6

1. Naomi Oreskes, "Beyond the Ivory Tower: The Scientific Consensus on Climate Change," *Science*, vol. 306, no. 5702, December 3, 2004, p. 1686, available at www.sciencemag.org/cgi/content/full/306/5702/1686 [accessed

6/27/2006]; Jeffrey Kluger, "Polar Ice Caps Are Melting Faster Than Ever," *Time,* March 26, 2006, available at www.time.com/time/archive/print-out/0,23657,1176980,00.html [accessed 6/27/2006]; and Eileen Claussen, "Foreword," in Camille Parmesan and Hector Galbraith, *Observed Impacts of Global Climate Change in the U.S.* (Pew Center on Global Climate Change, 2004), pp. ii–v.

2. 9/11 Public Discourse Project, "Final Report on 9/11 Commission Recommendations," December 5, 2005, p. 4, available at www.9–11pdp.org.

3. Amory B. Lovins, E. Kyle Datta, Odd-Even Bustnes, Jonathan G. Koomey, and Nathan J. Glasgow, *Winning the Oil Endgame: Innovation for Profits, Jobs, and Security* (Rocky Mountain Institute, 2005), p. 9.

4. Senator Hillary Rodham Clinton, "Remarks of Senator Hillary Rodham Clinton at the National Press Club on Energy Policy," Washington, D.C., May 23, 2006, p. 14, available at Clinton.senate.gov/news/statements/details.cfm?id=255982&& [accessed 6/27/2006].

5. National Intelligence Council, *Mapping the Global Future* (Government Printing Office, 2004), p. 59.

6. President's Energy Policy Development Group, *National Energy Policy* (Government Printing Office, 2001), pp. x, 8–1, and 8–13.

7. See Ivo Daalder and Philip Gordon, "We Should Strike Iran, But Not with Bombs," *Washington Post*, January 22, 2006, p. B3.

8. Edward L. Morse, Amy Myers Jaffe, et al. on an independent task force cosponsored by the James A. Baker Institute at Rice University and the Council on Foreign Relations, *Strategic Energy Policy: Challenges for the 21st Century* (Council on Foreign Relations, 2001), p. 16; Gal Luft, "An Energy Pearl Harbor?" *Washington Post*, March 5, 2006, p. B2.

9. See Energy Information Administration, *International Energy Outlook 2005* (Department of Energy, 2005), tables A2 and A4, available at www.eia.doe.gov/oiaf/ieo/index.html; John Zarocostas, "Skyrocketing Oil Costs Feared in Nuke Standoff," *Washington Times*, January 24, 2006, p. 11.Oil provides about 40 percent of the world's energy, counting that used for transportation as well as heating, industrial production, and other uses. Coal and natural gas each provide nearly a quarter of the total world energy requirement, with the rest coming from nuclear energy or renewables.

10. Energy Information Administration factsheets, Department of Energy, 2002, available at http://www.eia.doe.gov/emeu/cabs/topworldtables1_2.html [accessed 6/27/2006].

11. Gal Luft, "An Energy Pearl Harbor?" p. B2.

12. About 10,000 foreign troops could be required for maintaining order for the million or so people living in that region. A modern American Army or Marine division could, by patrolling an open area and making use of modern sensors and aircraft, surely cover one hundred to two hundred miles of front.

Putting these missions together might imply a total of some three American-sized divisions plus support for a sustained operation to secure the coastal regions of Saudi Arabia. The resulting total force strength might be 100,000 to 150,000 personnel.

13. For a similar view, see Gary Hart, *The Shield and the Cloak: The Security of the Commons* (Oxford University Press, 2006), p. 141.

14. William Kaufmann put his 1992 estimate at $66.6 billion, for a U.S. force structure of similar size and posture to the current one. That would translate into roughly $95 billion in 2006 dollars. See William W. Kaufmann, *Assessing the Base Force: How Much Is Too Much?* (Brookings, 1992), p. 3.

15. Moreover, estimates that the U.S. Armed Forces spends up to $100 billion a year on Persian Gulf military security are unconvincing. Even if we could eliminate our need for Persian Gulf oil altogether, we probably would not cut military expenditures by nearly that amount. While the cost is surely significant, probably extending into the tens of billions of dollars annually, the U.S. military has very few forces dedicated exclusively to that part of the world. Were American military commitments to the region to disappear because of an end to the oil trade (itself a dubious assumption), U.S. conventional forces would almost surely not be reduced radically. Possible scenarios from East Asia to South Asia to other regions would probably lead the United States to retain most of its existing force structure. For a fuller discussion, see Michael O'Hanlon, *Defense Strategy for the Post-Saddam Era* (Brookings, 2005), pp. 95–120.

16. For an important early article in this debate, see R. James Woolsey, "The New Petroleum," *Foreign Affairs,* vol. 78, issue 1, January/February 1999, pp. 88–102.

17. John M. Amidon, "A 'Manhattan Project' for Energy," *Joint Forces Quarterly,* Issue 39, Fall 2005, p. 74.

18. President George W. Bush, "State of the Union Address," January 31, 2006, available at www.whitehouse.gov/stateoftheunion/2006/print/index.html [accessed 6/27/2006].

19. Steven Ginsberg, "Hybrid Perks May Become Problems," *Washington Post,* February 14, 2006, p. B8.

20. Justin Blum, "Fuel for Growth: Despite Controversy, Ethanol Is in High Demand, Lifting Farm Fortunes," *Washington Post,* February 18, 2006, p. D1.

21. Lawrence J. Korb and Robert O. Boorstin, *Integrated Power: A National Security Strategy for the 21st Century* (Center for American Progress, 2005), p. 62

22. An additional fact: Some 70 percent of all petroleum currently consumed in the United States goes to transportation. On the overall role of petroleum in the economy, see President's Energy Policy Development Group, *National*

Energy Policy (Government Printing Office, 2001), p. 8–3; Amory B. Lovins, E. Kyle Datta, Odd-Even Bustnes, Jonathan G. Koomey, and Nathan J. Glasgow, *Winning the Oil Endgame: Innovation for Profits, Jobs, and Security* (Rocky Mountain Institute, 2005), p. 1.

23. President's National Energy Policy Development Group, *National Energy Policy,* pp. 5–14 and 5–15.

24. National Commission on Energy Policy, *Ending the Energy Stalemate: A Bipartisan Strategy to Meet America's Energy Challenges* (National Commission on Energy Policy, 2004), p. xii.

25. On these matters, see Office of Fossil Energy, Department of Energy, "FutureGen: Integrated Hydrogen, Electric Power Production and Carbon Sequestration Research Initiative," Department of Energy, March 2004, pp. 1–9; Timothy E. Wirth, C. Boyden Gray, and John D. Podesta, "The Future of Energy Policy," *Foreign Affairs,* vol. 82, issue 4, July/August 2003, pp. 132–155; John Deutch and Ernest J. Moniz, "A Plan for Nuclear Waste," *Washington Post,* January 30, 2006, p. A17; and Steve Fetter, "Climate Change and the Transformation of World Energy Supply," Stanford University, May 1999, pp. 26, 40, and 58–62, available at http://iis-db.stanford.edu/pubs/10228/fetter.pdf [accessed 6/29/2006].

26. Lovins, Datta, Bustnes, Koomey, and Glasgow, *Winning the Oil Endgame*, p. 123.

27. There are limits on most such possibilities, though. For example, solar energy makes sense in certain places for local applications (and while it would be no mean feat, all the world's current energy consumption could in theory be satisfied by solar panels of 10 percent efficiency on just 0.1 percent of the world's land surface). But it still costs five to ten times as much per kilowatt hour as coal or gas for industrial-scale electricity generation, not even counting transmission or storage costs. See Robert F. Service, "Is It Time to Shoot for the Sun?" *Science,* vol. 309, July 22, 2005, pp. 548–551, available at www.sciencemag.org; Michael Parfit, "Powering the Future," *National Geographic,* vol. 208, no. 2, August 2005, p. 18.

28. Nuclear power already provides nearly 20 percent of the world's electricity at a total of more than four hundred sites. See Richard L. Garwin and Georges Charpak, *Megawatts and Megatons: A Turning Point in the Nuclear Age?* (Alfred A. Knopf, 2001), pp. 1–4, 107–205.

29. See, for example, Timothy Egan, "Seeking Clean Fuel for a Nation, and a Rebirth for Small-Town Montana," *New York Times,* November 21, 2005, p. A16.

30. Nicholas D. Kristof, "100-M.P.G. Cars: It's a Start," *New York Times*, February 5, 2006, p. WK13.

31. George P. Shultz and R. James Woolsey, "Oil and Security," Committee on the Present Danger Policy Paper, August 2005, available at www.fightingterror.org.

32. See Steve Fetter, "Climate Change and the Transformation of World Energy Supply," p. 40.

33. National Commission on Energy Policy, *Ending the Energy Stalemate*), p. 108.

34. Lovins, Datta, Bustnes, Koomey, and Glasgow, *Winning the Oil Endgame*, p. 125.

35. The states are quite active on a number of these issues already, but their level of effort varies greatly. See Energy Future Coalition, *Challenge and Opportunity: Charting a New Energy Future* (Energy Future Coalition, 2003), p. 94, available at www.energyfuturecoalition.org.

36. Lovins, Datta, Bustnes, Koomey, and Glasgow, *Winning the Oil Endgame*, pp. 44–78 (especially p. 66).

37. David Luhnow and Geraldo Samor, "Bumper Crop: As Brazil Fills Up on Ethanol, It Weans off Energy Imports," *Wall Street Journal*, January 9, 2006, p. A1.

38. For a challenge to the Lovins et.al. view, see John Deutch, "Biomass Movement," *Wall Street Journal*, May 10, 2006.

39. Samantha Slater, "Ethanol: Boom or Bubble?" Briefing Slides, National Corn Growers Association, April 3, 2006.

40. Roel Hammerschlag, "Ethanol's Energy Return on Investment: A Survey of the Literature, 1990–Present," *Environmental Science and Technology*, February 8, 2006; George P. Schultz and R. James Woolsey, "Oil and Security," Committee on the Present Danger paper, August 2005, available at www.fightingterror.org.

41. Lovins, Datta, Bustnes, Koomey, and Glasgow, *Winning the Oil Endgame*, pp. 186–190.

42. Sholnn Freeman, "Ford's Chief Makes Case for Federal Help," *Washington Post*, November 23, 2005, p. D1; Michael O'Hanlon and David Sandalow, "Regaining Energy Leverage Over Iran," *Washington Times*, February 1, 2006.

43. Senate Democratic Communications Center, "Democrats Announce Sweeping New Energy Legislation," U.S. Senate, May 17, 2006.

44. Justin Blum, "Fuel for Growth: Despite Controversy, Ethanol Is in High Demand, Lifting Farm Fortunes," *Washington Post*, February 18, 2006, p. D2.

45. Speech by Senator Richard Lugar on Energy Policy, Brookings Institution, March 13, 2006, p. 11, available at www.brookings.edu.

46. Center for American Progress, "America is Addicted to Oil," February 2006, available at www.americanprogress.org.

47. National Commission on Energy Policy, *Ending the Energy Stalemate: A Bipartisan Strategy to Meet America's Energy Challenges* (National Commission on Energy Policy, 2004), p. 75, available at www.energycommission.org.

48. Senator Hillary Rodham Clinton, "Remarks of Senator Hillary Rodham Clinton at the National Press Club on Energy Policy," May 23, 2006, p. 10, avail-

able at Clinton.senate.gov/news/statements/details.cfm?id=255982&&. [accessed 6/29/2006].

49. Larry Rohter, "With Big Boost from Sugar Cane, Brazil Is Satisfying Its Fuel Needs," *New York Times*, April 10, 2006.

50. Lovins, Datta, Bustnes, Koomey, and Glasgow, *Winning the Oil Endgame*, pp. 103–111.

51. Senator Hillary Rodham Clinton, "Remarks of Senator Hillary Rodham Clinton at the National Press Club on Energy Policy," pp. 6–7.

CHAPTER 7

1. For an excellent treatment of measurements associated with China's rise, see Bergsten, C. F., Gill, B., Lardy, S. R., Mitchell, D., *China The Balance Sheet: What the World Needs to Know About the Emerging Superpower* (New York: Public Affairs, 2006).

2. This is a point powerfully made by James F. Hoye, Jr., "A Global Power Shift in the Making: Is the United States Ready?" *Foreign Affairs* (July–August 2004), pp 2–3.

3. See, for example, Adam Segal, "Practical Engagement: Drawing a Fine Line for U.S.-China Trade," *The Washington Quarterly*, 27/3, Summer 2004, pp. 157–173; James Shinn, ed., *Weaving the Net: Conditional Engagement with China* (Council on Foreign Relations, 1996).

4. Discussions of the Clinton administration's policies toward China can be found in James Mann, *About Face: A History of America's Curious Relationship with China, from Nixon to Clinton* (Alfred A. Knopf, 1999); Patrick Tyler, *A Great Wall: Six Presidents and China* (Century Foundation, 1999); and Robert L. Suettinger, *Beyond Tiananmen: The Politics of U.S.-China Relations, 1989–2000* (Brookings, 2003).

5. Condoleezza Rice, "Promoting the National Interest," *Foreign Affairs*, vol. 79, no. 1, January/February 2000.

6. Morton Abramowitz and Stephen Bosworth, "Adjusting to the New Asia," *Foreign Affairs*, vol. 82, no. 4, July/August 2003, pp. 120, 125–127.

7. Reviews of these developments appear in Thomas J. Christensen and Michael A. Glosny, "China: Sources of Stability in U.S.-China Security Relations," in *Strategic Asia 2003–04: Fragility and Crisis*, edited by Richard J. Ellings and Aaron L. Friedberg (National Bureau of Asian Research, 2003), pp. 53–79; David M. Lampton, "The Stealth Normalization of U.S.-China Relations," *The National Interest*, no. 73, Fall 2003, pp. 37–48.

8. Kurt M. Campbell and Richard Weitz, "The Limits of U.S.-China Military Cooperation: Lessons from 1995–1999," *The Washington Quarterly*, vol. 29, no. 1, Winter 2005, pp. 169–186.

9. Diverging opinions about what conditions might lead China to employ force against Taiwan appear in Kurt M. Campbell and Derek J. Mitchell, "Crisis in the Taiwan Strait? *Foreign Affairs*, vol. 80, no. 4, July/August 2001, pp. 14–25; Thomas J. Christensen, "The Contemporary Security Dilemma: Deterring a Taiwan Conflict," *The Washington Quarterly*, vol. 25, no. 4, Autumn 2002, pp. 7–21; and Robert S. Ross, "Navigating the Taiwan Strait: Deterrence, Escalation Dominance, and U.S.-China Relations," *International Security*, vol. 27, no. 2, Fall 2002, pp. 48–85.

10. For a review of the administration's changing policies toward Taiwan, see Andrew Peterson, "Dangerous Games across the Taiwan Strait," *The Washington Quarterly*, vol. 27, no. 2, Spring 2004, pp. 23–41; Michael D. Swaine, "Trouble in Taiwan," *Foreign Affairs*, vol. 83, no. 2, March/April 2004, pp. 39–49.

11. See *China the Balance Sheet: What the World Needs to Know About the Emerging Superpower* for an in depth discussion of the various economic indicators of China's astonishing economic performance.

12. U.S. Department of Commerce, "ExportIT China: Telecommunications and Information Technology Market Opportunities for Small and Medium-Sized Enterprises," April 2003, pp. vii–ix.

13. James F. Hoge, Jr., "A Global Power Shift in the Making: Is the United States Ready?," *Foreign Affairs* vol. 83, no. 4, July/August 2004, p. 3.

14. This tension is discussed in Evan A. Feigenbaum, *China's Techno-Warriors: National Security and Strategic Competition from the Nuclear to the Information Age* (Stanford University Press, 2003).

15. Zha Daojiong, "China's Energy Security: Domestic and International Issues," *Survival*, vol. 48, no. 1, Spring 2006, pp. 179–190.

16. See, for example, Yong Deng and Thomas G. Moore, "China Views Globalization: Toward a New Great-Power Politics?" *The Washington Quarterly*, vol. 27, no. 3, Summer 2004, pp. 117–136; Catherin Dalpino and Juo-yu Lin, "China and Southeast Asia," in *Brookings Northeast Asia Survey 2002–2003*, edited by Richard Bush and Catherin Dalpino (Brookings, 2003), pp. 83–84.

17. Free trade between China and Burma, Cambodia, Laos, and Vietnam is envisaged by 2015.

18. Greg Mastel, "How China Threatens America . . . And What Can Be Done," *The International Economy: The Magazine of International Economic Policy*, Spring 2005, p. 43, at http://www.findarticles.com/p/articles/mi_m2633/is_2_19/ai_n15787112 [accessed 6/29/2006].

19. Robert Sutter, "China's Regional Strategy and Why It May Not Be Good for America," in David Shambaugh, ed., *Power Shift: China and Asia's New Dynamics*, (University of California Press, 2005), pp. 297–298.

20. An extensive description of China's growing military capabilities appear in the annual U.S. Department of Defense reports to Congress on Chinese military power.

21. The most recent CIA estimate is that China's military expenditure in 2005 amounted to $81.4 billion; see U.S. Central Intelligence Agency, *The World Factbook* (2006), available at http://www.cia.gov/cia/publications/factbook/rankorder/2067rank.html [accessed 6/29/2006]. For forecasts of future Chinese military spending, see Keith Crane et al., *Modernizing China's Military: Opportunities and Constraints* (RAND, 2005). The methodological difficulties in analyzing China's defense spending are assessed in Richard A. Bitzinger, "Just the Facts, Ma'am: The Challenge of Analysing and Assessing Chinese Military Expenditures," *China Quarterly*, no. 173, March 2003, pp. 164–175.

22. Chinese ambitions to use a RMA to amplify their military power are documented in Michael Pillsbury, *China Debates the Future Security Environment* (National Defense University Press, 2000), pp. 278–304.

23. Lyle Goldstein and William Murray, "Undersea Dragons: China's Maturing Submarine Force," *International Security*, vol. 28, no. 4, Spring 2004, pp. 161–196.

24. The Editors, "The Assassin's Mace," *The New Atlantis*, no. 6, Summer 2004, pp. 107–110.

25. For a comprehensive assessment of China's military buildup, see David Shambaugh, "China's Military Modernization: Making Steady and Surprising Progress," in *Strategic Asia 2005–06: Military Modernization in an Era of Uncertainty* (National Bureau of Asian Research, 2005), pp. 67–103.

26. U.S. Department of Defense, The Military Power of the People's Republic of China 2005: Annual Report to Congress, July 2005, p. 7.

27. U.S. Department of Defense, Quadrennial Defense Review Report, February 2006, p. 29.

28. Remarks delivered by Secretary of Defense Donald H. Rumsfeld, Shangri-La Hotel, Singapore, June 4, 2005, at http://www.defenselink.mil/speeches/2005/sp20050604-secdef1561.html [accessed 6/29/2006].

29. Department of Defense, Quadrennial Defense Review Report, p. 29.

30. Department of Defense, The Military Power of the People's Republic of China, p. 4.

31. Diverging evaluations of Taiwan's ability to deter or defeat a PLA military attack appear in Michael A. Glosny, "Strangulation from the Sea? A PRC Submarine Blockade of Taiwan," *International Security*, vol. 28, no. 4, Spring 2004, pp. 125–160; Michael O'Hanlon, "Why China Cannot Conquer Taiwan," *International Security*, vol. 25, no. 2, Fall 2000, pp. 51–86; and David Shambaugh, "A Matter of Time: Taiwan's Eroding Military Advantage," *The Washington Quarterly*, vol. 23, no. 2, Spring 2000, pp. 119–133.

32. Thus far, their political leaders have resisted acquiring a carrier for fear of provoking a premature naval arms race with the United States; see Robert S. Ross, "Assessing the China Threat," *The National Interest,* Fall 2005.

33. Bill Gertz, "China Builds Up Strategic Sea Lanes," *Washington Times*, January 18, 2005; Declan Walsh, "The New China: U.S. Uneasy as Beijing Develops a Strategic String of Pearls," *The Guardian*, November 10, 2005.

34. For excellent recent pieces on the rise of Chinese soft power, see Joseph Nye, "The Rise of China's Soft Power," *Wall Street Journal Asia*, December 29, 2005, Bates Gill and Y. Huang, "Sources and Limits of China's Soft Power; *Survival*, Summer, vol. 48, no. 2, 17–36, and Josh Kurlantzick, "China's Charm: Implications of Chinese Soft Power," *Carnegie Endowment Policy Brief,* June, no. 47.

35. BBC World Service, "22-Nation Poll Shows China Viewed Positively by Most Countries Including Its Asian Neighbors," March 2005, available at http://www.pipa.org/OnlineReports/China/China_Mar05/China_Mar05_rpt.p df [accessed 6/29/2006].

36. Evan S. Medeiros and M. Taylor Fravel, "The Changing Face of Chinese Diplomacy," *Asian Wall Street Journal*, November 25, 2003.

37. A good example of the public-relations themes can be found in Zheng Bijian, "China's 'Peaceful Rise' to Great-Power Status," *Foreign Affairs*, vol. 84, no. 5, September/October 2005.

38. Rommel C. Banlaoi, "Southeast Asian Perspectives on the Rise of China: Regional Security after 9/11," *Parameters: US Army War College Quarterly*, vol. 33, Summer 2003, pp. 98–107.

39. Nirmala George, "Border Deal Reached with China," *Washington Times*, April 12, 2005. See also Jo Johnson, "China and India Pledge to Boost Trade and End Border Dispute," *Financial Times*, April 12, 2005.

40. Richard Weitz, "Why Russia and China Have Not Formed an Anti-American Alliance," *Naval War College Review*, vol. 56, no. 4, Autumn 2003, pp. 39–61.

41. Lyle Goldstein and Vitaly Kozyrev, "China, Japan, and the Scramble for Siberia," *Survival*, vol. 48, no. 1, Spring 2006, pp. 163–178.

42. Peter Brookes and Ji Hye Shin, "China's Influence in Africa: Implications for the United States," *Heritage Backgrounder*, no. 1916, February 22, 2006, available at http://www.heritage.org/Research/AsiaandthePacific/bg1916.cfm [accessed 6/29/2006].

43. Stéphanie Giry, "Out of Beijing" *The New Republic,* November 15, 2004.

44. Mark Magnier, "U.S. Is Watching China's Latin American Moves," *Los Angeles Times*, April 15, 2006.

45. Willy Lam, "China's Encroachment on America's Backyard," *China Brief*, vol. 4, no. 23, November 24, 2004), available at http://www.jamestown.org/images/pdf/cb_004_023.pdf [accessed 6/29/2006].

46. Stephen Johnson, "Balancing China's Growing Influence in Latin America," *Heritage Foundation Backgrounder*, no. 1888, October 24, 2005, available at http://www.heritage.org/Research/LatinAmerica/loader.cfm?url=/commonspot/security/getfile.cfm&PageID=84474 [accessed 6/29/2006].

47. Posture Statement of General Bantz J. Craddock, United States Army Commander, United States Southern Command, Before The 109th Congress, House Armed Services Committee, March 9, 2005, available at http://www.house.gov/hasc/testimony/109thcongress/FY06%20Budget%20Misc/Southcom3–9–05.pdf [accessed 6/29/2006].

48. Cited in Lam, "China's Encroachment on America's Backyard."

49. Cited in Joshua Kurlantzick, "Cultural Revolution: How China is Changing Global Diplomacy," *The New Republic*, June 27, 2005, available at http://www.cerium.ca/article1267.html [accessed 6/29/2006]. See also Humphrey Hawksley, "Chinese Influence in Brazil Worries U.S.," BBC News, April 3, 2006, available at http://news.bbc.co.uk/2/hi/americas/4872522.stm [accessed 6/29/2006].

50. Joshua Cooper Ramo, "The Beijing Consensus," Foreign Policy Centre, 2004, pp. 11–12, available at http://fpc.org.uk/fsblob/244.pdf [accessed 6/29/2006].

51. Chinese socioeconomic strengths and weaknesses are summarized in C. Fred Bergsten et al., *China: The Balance Sheet: What the World Needs to Know Now About the Emerging Superpower* (PublicAffairs, 2006), pp. 18–72.

52. The threat of ethnic separatism in China is discussed in Graham E. Fuller and S. Frederick Starr, *The Xinjiang Problem* (Central Asia-Caucasus Institute, Paul H. Nitze School of Advanced International Studies, 2004); Joshua Kurlantzick, "The Unsettled West: China's Long War on Xinjiang," *Foreign Affairs*, vol. 83, no. 4, July/August 2004, pp. 136–143.

53. George Gilboy, "The Myth Behind China's Miracle," *Foreign Affairs*, July/August 2004.

54. Martin Wolf, "Why is China Growing so Slowly?" *Foreign Policy*, January/February 2005, available at http://www.carnegieendowment.org/publications/index.cfm?fa=view&id=16543 [accessed 6/29/2006].

55. C. Fred Bergsten, Bates Gill, Nicholas R. Lardy, and Derek Mitchell, *China: The Balance Sheet* (PublicAffairs, 2006), p. 25.

56. See, for example, Elizabeth Economy, "Don't Break the Engagement," *Foreign Affairs* 83/3, May/June 2004, pp. 96–109. For a discussion of the liberal democratic tradition in late-nineteenth-century and twentieth-century Chinese political thought, see Orville Schell, "China's Hidden Democratic Legacy," *Foreign Affairs* 83/4, July/August 2004, pp. 116–124.

57. Ross Terrill, "The Myth of the Rise of China," *The Australian*, September 19, 2005.

58. For more on the democratic-transition hypothesis, see Edward D. Mansfield and Jack Snyder, "Democratizing and the Danger of War," *International Se-*

curity, vol. 20, no. 1, Summer 1995, pp. 5–38; Edward D. Mansfield and Jack Snyder, "Democratization and War," *Foreign Affairs*, vol. 74, no. 3, May-June 1995, pp. 79–97.

59. Minxin Pei, "The Dark Side of China's Rise," *Foreign Policy*, March/April 2006.

60. David Shambaugh, "China's Military Views the World: Ambivalent Security," *International Security*, vol. 24, no. 3, Winter 1999/2000, reprinted in Michael E. Brown, ed., *The Rise of China* (MIT Press, 2000), pp. 105–134.

61. The changing role of these and other motivators of past Chinese foreign policy is assessed in Allen S. Whiting, "Foreign Policy of China," in Roy C. Macridis, ed., *Foreign Policy in World Politics*, eighth edition (Prentice-Hall, 1992) pp. 232–267; Richard Weitz, "Meeting the China Challenge: Some Insights from Scenario-Based Planning," *The Journal of Strategic Studies*, vol. 24, no. 3, March 2002, pp. 19–48.

62. Michel Oksenberg, "China: A Tortuous Path onto the World's Stage," in Robert A. Pastor, ed., *A Century's Journey: How the Great Powers Shape the World* (Basic Books, 1999), pp. 306–308.

63. Dan Blumenthal, "Fear and Loathing in Asia," *Journal of International Security Affairs*, Spring 2006, pp. 81–88; Evelyn Goh, "*Meeting the China Challenge: The U.S. in Southeast Asian Regional Security Strategies*, (East-West Center, 2005).

64. Steven R. Saunders, "Japan: Untagling the Contradictions," in William M. Carpenter and David G. Wiencek, eds., *Asian Security Handbook: Terrorism and the New Security Environment*, third edition (M. E. Sharp, 2005), p. 154.

65. Kurt M. Campbell and Tsuyoshi Sunohara, "Japan: Thinking the Unthinkable," inKurt M. Campbell, Robert Einhorn, and Mitchell Reiss, eds., *The Nuclear Tipping Point: Why States Reconsider Their Nuclear Choices* (Brookings, 2004), chapter 9.

66. Dana Dillon and John J. Tkacik Jr., "China's Quest for Asia," *Policy Review*, December 2005, available at http://www.policyreview.org/134/default.htm [accessed 6/29/2006].

CHAPTER 8

1. Biological terrorism may become as threatening in coming years, as microbiology advances and provides possible means for "superbugs" to be developed, but the nuclear threat remains much more serious today overall.

2. Some have argued that proliferation among stable nation-states is not dangerous, given that all have a strong incentive to avoid the use of nuclear weapons. In fact, in this sense proliferation could even be stabilizing. However, even leaving aside the possible connections to terrorist organizations, this argument does not hold up very well in light of the difficulties of building survivable nu-

clear-deterrent forces, operating them safely, and avoiding miscalculation and mistake. See, for example, Bruce G. Blair, *The Logic of Accidental Nuclear War* (Brookings, 1993); Scott D. Sagan, *The Limits of Safety* (Princeton University Press, 1993).

3. For classic works on the importance of a strong central power and strong alliances to reduce the dangers of proliferation, see Michael Mandelbaum, *The Nuclear Revolution* (Cambridge University Press, 1981), pp. 159–166; McGeorge Bundy, *Danger and Survival* (Vintage Books, 1988), pp. 490–505; and Lawrence Freedman, *The Evolution of Nuclear Strategy* (St. Martin's Press, 1983), pp. 283–329.

4. Great powers have certainly behaved this way before. For example, see Aaron L. Friedberg, *The Weary Titan: Britain and the Experience of Relative Decline, 1895–1905* (Princeton University Press, 1988). Even if America's weariness, and any relative economic decline, are not likely to be permanent, the world is so dynamic and dangerous that even a relative withdrawal of American assertiveness lasting five to ten years would be most worrisome.

5. Richard N. Haass, *The Reluctant Sheriff: The United States After the Cold War* (Council on Foreign Relations, 1997).

6. Joseph S. Nye Jr., *The Paradox of American Power: Why the World's Only Superpower Can't Go It Alone* (Oxford University Press, 2002), pp. 154–163.

7. Matthew Bunn and Anthony Weir, *Securing the Bomb 2005: The New Global Imperatives* (Nuclear Threat Initiative, 2005), p. vii, available at www.nti.org/cnwm [accessed 6/30/2006].

8. Bunn and Weir, *Securing the Bomb 2005*, pp. 89–121; Graham Allison, *Nuclear Terrorism: The Ultimate Preventable Catastrophe* (Henry Holt and Co., 2004), pp. 140–210.

9. See Michael A. Levi and Michael E. O'Hanlon, *The Future of Arms Control* (Brookings, 2005).

10. For a good discussion of the technology and politics through the Clinton years, see Bradley Graham, *Hit to Kill* (PublicAffairs, 2001).

11. Michael A. Levi, "Dreaming of Clean Nukes," *Nature*, 428, April 29, 2004, p. 892.

12. See Richard L. Garwin and Georges Charpak, *Megawatts and Megatons: A Turning Point in the Nuclear Age* (Alfred A. Knopf, 2001), pp. 301–310; Steve Fetter, *Toward a Comprehensive Test Ban* (Ballinger, 1988)

13. See, for example, Ashton Carter, "How to Stop the Spread of WMD," *Foreign Affairs*, vol. 83, no. 5, September/October 2004, pp. 72–85.

14. See Graham Allison, "Preventing Nuclear Terrorism," in Will Marshall, ed., *With All Our Might: A Progressive Strategy for Defeating Jihadism and Defending Liberty* (Rowman & Littlefield Publishers, Inc., 2006), p. 110.

15. See Jan Lodal, *The Price of Dominance* (Council on Foreign Relations, 2001), pp. 21–41; Harold A. Feiveson, "Nuclear Arms Control at a Crossroads," in Harold A. Feiveson, ed., *The Nuclear Turning Point* (Brookings, 1999), pp. 3–14.

16. On this latter point, see Mitchell B. Reiss, "The Nuclear Tipping Point: Prospects for a World of Many Nuclear Weapons States," in Kurt M. Campbell, Robert J. Einhorn, and Mitchell B. Reiss, eds., *The Nuclear Tipping Point: Why States Reconsider Their Nuclear Choices* (Brookings, 2004), pp. 1–17.

17. Bruce W. Jentleson and Christopher A. Whytock, "Who 'Won' Libya? The Force-Diplomacy Debate and Its Implications for Theory and Policy," *International Security*, vol. 30, no. 3, Winter 2005/06, pp. 47–79.

18. U.S. Central Intelligence Agency, "Unclassified Report to Congress on the Acquisition of Technology Relating to Weapons of Mass Destruction and Advanced Conventional Munitions," January through June 2002, available at http://www.cia.gov/cia/reports/721_reports/jan_jun2002.html#7 [accessed 6/30/2006].

19. Douglas Frantz, "Black Market Nuclear Probe Focuses on Syria," *Los Angeles Times*, June 24, 2004.

20. Michael A. Levi and Michael E. O'Hanlon, *The Future of Arms Control* (Washington, D.C.: Brookings, 2005), pp. 108–109.

21. For a related argument, see Sam Nunn, "Nuclear Pig in a Poke," *Wall Street Journal*, May 24, 2006, p. 14.

22. Robert Einhorn, "Limiting the Damage," *The National Interest*, no. 82, Winter 2005/06, pp. 112–116.

23. See, for example, Daniel Byman, *Deadly Connections: States that Sponsor Terrorism* (Cambridge University Press, 2005), pp. 79–117.

24. See Paul Pillar, *Terrorism and U.S. Foreign Policy* (Washington, D.C.: Brookings, 2001), pp. 157–196.

25. International Crisis Group, "Iran: Is There a Way Out of the Nuclear Impasse?" Middle East Report No. 51, February 2006, available at www.crisisweb.org.

26. Ivo Daalder and Philip Gordon, "We Should Strike Iran, But Not With Bombs," *Washington Post*, January 22, 2006, p. B3.

27. For more, see Michael O'Hanlon and Mike Mochizuki, *Crisis on the Korean Peninsula: How to Deal with a Nuclear North Korea* (McGraw Hill, 2003).

28. See the forthcoming Brookings book by Jack Pritchard, former U.S. negotiator with the DPRK; see also Joel S. Wit, Daniel B. Poneman, and Robert L. Gallucci, *Going Critical: The First North Korean Nuclear Crisis* (Washington, D.C.: Brookings, 2004), pp. 392–408; and Michael O'Hanlon and Mike Mochizuki, *Crisis on the Korean Peninsula: How to Deal With a Nuclear North Korea* (New York: McGraw-Hill, 2003), pp. 31–39.

29. See Michael O'Hanlon and Mike Mochizuki, *Crisis on the Korean Peninsula: How to Deal With a Nuclear North Korea* (New York: McGraw-Hill, 2003).

30. See Doug Struck, "Citing Iraq, N. Korea Signals Hard Line on Weapons Issues," *Washington Post*, March 30, 2003, p. 30; James Brooke, "North Korea Watches War and Wonders What's Next," *New York Times*, March 31, 2003.

31. For a similar view, see Gary Samore, "The Korean Nuclear Crisis," *Survival*, vol. 45, no. 1, Spring 2003, pp. 19–22.

CONCLUSION

1. For an excellent history of enduring political realignments in U.S. national elections, see James L. Sundquist, *Dynamics of the Party System: Alignment and Realignment of Political Parties in the United States*, revised edition (Brookings, 1993).

2. For an analysis of President Wilson's approach to national security, see Henry A. Kissinger, *Diplomacy* (Simon and Schuster, 1994), pp. 218–245.

3. See Richard E. Darilek, *A Loyal Opposition in Time of War: The Republican Party and the Politics of Foreign Policy from Pearl Harbor to Yalta* (Greenwood Press, 1976).

4. Sean J. Savage, *JFK, LBJ, and the Democratic Party* (State University of New York Press, 2004), pp. 328–330.

5. A useful summary of this period can be found in Raymond L. Garthoff, *Détente and Confrontation: American-Soviet Relations from Nixon to Reagan*, revised edition (Brookings, 1994), and Jay Winik, "The Neoconservative Reconstruction," *Foreign Policy*, no. 73, Winter 1988–1989, pp. 135–152.

6. For a useful discussion of the prospects for "trading places" on defense issues, see Loren B. Thompson, "Trading Places: Republicans and Democrats Rethink Defense," Lexington Institute Issue Brief, May 12, 2006.

7. Ibid.

8. See James Mann, *The Rise of the Vulcans* (Viking, 2004) for a wonderful description of those prominent Republicans, including Richard Armitage, Dick Cheney, Condoleezza Rice, and Colin Powell, who gathered around Governor George W. Bush as he began his run for president.

9. See Loren B. Thompson, "Trading Places: Republicans and Democrats Rethink Defense," Lexington Institute Issue Brief, May 12, 2006.

10. See Catherine L. Mann with Jacob Funk Kirkegaard, *Accelerating the Globalization of America* (Institute for International Economics, Washington, D.C., 2006).

11. See Markos Moulitsas, "Hillary Clinton: Too Much of a Clinton Democrat?" *Washington Post*, May 7, 2006.

12. See Mann, *The Rise of the Vulcans*.

13. Walter R. Mead, *Special Providence: American Foreign Policy and How It Changed the World* (Routledge, 2002); for a classic statement of this worldview, see Jesse Helms, *When Free Men Shall Stand* (Zondervan Books, 1977).
14. For an assessment and critique of religion's role in foreign policy, see Madeleine Albright with Bill Woodward, *The Mighty and the Almighty: Reflections on America, God, and World Affairs* (HarperCollins, 2006).
15. See Bryan Hehir et al., *Liberty and Power: A Dialogue on Religion and U.S. Foreign Policy in an Unjust World* (Brookings, 2004); Kevin Phillips, *American Theocracy: The Peril and Politics of Radical Religion, Oil, and Borrowed Money in the 21st Century* (Viking Press, 2006).
16. See Peter Waldman, "Evangelicals Give U.S. Foreign Policy an Activist Tinge," *Wall Street Journal,* May 26, 2004.
17. Private conversation with a senior Republican political consultant.

Index

Central Command (CENTCOM)
  disempowering of, 55
  early Iraq War plans of, 54
  Islamic states and, 141
  on post-Saddam planning, 54
Central Intelligence Agency
  on Syria, 221–222
  on terrorist financing, 125
Chalabi, Ahmed, 53
  assumed leadership of, 55
Chavez, Hugo, 198
Chemical industry, regulation of, 135
Cheney, Dick
  Bush's selection of, 47
  on Democrats' pre-9/11 view, 30
  torture ban opposed by, 64
China. *See* People's Republic of China
Chinese embassy bombing, Belgrade
    (1999), 188
CIA. *See* Central Intelligence Agency
Civil liberties, 123, 124
Civil War, American
  domestic policy and, 237
  foreign policy and, 237–238
  Republicans/Democrats during, 1–2,
    238
Clark, Wesley, 43, 80
Climate change. *See* Global warming
Clinton foreign policy
  Bush, G.W., administration v., 49–50
  "democratic enlargement," 3
  engagement/enlargement in,
    146–147
  hard power policy agenda and, 76
  legacy of, 49–50
  PRC in, 188
  progressives' support for, 3
Clinton, Hillary, 42, 165, 184, 240
Clinton presidency
  defense issues during, xi
Clinton, William Jefferson
  ACRI and, 92

Asian financial crisis and, 30
bin Laden, Osama, and, 77
Bosnia/Kosovo and, 3, 30
budget surplus under, 62
Bush, G.H.W., and, 30
defense budget and, 24, 27, 78, 93
defense speeches of, 95
distorted complaints about, 24–25
DoD of, xi
domestic policy focus of, 18
in election 1992, 23
on Europe, 30
financial renaissance and, 30
gays in the military and, 25–26
Korea and, 25
legalized insubordination and, 24
Lewinsky, Monica, and, 26
Mexican peso devaluation and, 30
military and, 23–32, 39, 77, 78, 80,
    85
missile defense and, 217
North Korea and, 30
Powell v., 25
Qutar speech, 2004, 155
Rwanda and, 3, 77
Somalia and, 26
special forces training mission and,
    106
successes of, 30
Taiwan and, 25, 30
weapons modernization and, 94
Coal, 173, 176
Code Pink, 19
Cohen, Eliot, 79
Cohen, William, 27
Cold War
  Central Europe after, 66
  defense budget drawdown after, 27
  defense spending averages in, 27
  democracy promotion and, 139
  Eisenhower during, 5
  end of, 22